And Forgive Us Our Sins

And Forgive Us Our Sins

Vincent Nicholas Mirabella

iUniverse, Inc.

New York Lincoln Shanghai

And Forgive Us Our Sins

iUniverse books may be ordered through booksellers or by contacting:

iUniverse
2021 Pine Lake Road, Suite 100
Lincoln, NE 68512
www.iuniverse.com
1-800-Authors (1-800-288-4677)

Because of the dynamic nature of the Internet, any Web addresses or links contained in this book may have changed since publication and may no longer be valid.

The views expressed in this work are solely those of the author and do not necessarily reflect the views of the publisher, and the publisher hereby disclaims any responsibility for them.

Everlasting and unending thanks and praise to my dear friends Roberta MacDonald and Laura Gibowski for helping me in editing this book with correct spelling and punctuation. Thank you and God bless you for your endless hours of help.

All photos throughout the book were done with the assistance of Roberta MacDonald

ISBN: 978-0-595-46976-5 (pbk)
ISBN: 978-0-595-91260-5 (ebk)

Printed in the United States of America

This book is dedicated to the memory of my paternal grandmother Paula Mirabella, my mother Maria Angelina Madonia Mirabella and all of the Mirabella family. Also, any women who have changed name through matrimony as well as any members of the family with the surname Mirabella.

Vincent and Grandmother Paula

Contents

Credits

Everlasting and unending thanks and praise to my dear friends Roberta Mac-Donald and Laura Gibowski for helping me in editing this book with correct spelling and punctuation. Thank you and God bless you for your endless hours of help.

All photos throughout the book were done with the assistance of Roberta Mac-Donald

Laura and Roberta MacDonald

Starting Out

As editor I am starting out this story about one of my very best friends, I know him as Nick. I am Roberta, and I have told Nick, I would assist him in telling you, about his life. By the time you finish reading this book, you may well have more questions, than answers and you will also have learned so much about the life of Nick. You may ask now, "Why is that important?" Read on my friends, and you will see.

In years of late, my friend has taken to using his surname, which is Vincent. So there will be times when the reader, will be reading about this individual's life as seen through the eyes of Nick, other times Vincent will come forth to tell part of the story. There will be one chapter devoted to a third character, Margo, one who played a short but important part in this man's life. This is a man who has changed in the past few years. He was diagnosed as a bi-polar, manic depressive with obsessive compulsive disorder. Nick is also a diabetic who suffers from severe diabetic neuropathy in his legs. Diabetes will affect the nervous system, and can become so bad it is difficult for the person to walk. In the year 2001, he was in and out of the hospital several times, all stemming from not taking care of his diabetes. At the beginning of 2002, he is home and recuperating, so now we will go on with the story.

First I feel that the reader must know who I am, and how Nick and I began over some thirty years ago. I met him in 1975 at the Ramada Inn in Winston Salem, North Carolina. He was the chef in charge of the kitchen, where I went in to apply for a position as a waitress. I remember his office was at the back of the kitchen. A very small room, which had such a cluttered desk you could not see the top of it, and behind the desk sat Nick. There was just barely enough room for two chairs in the front of this desk, and as small as I was, I had to squeeze by the desk in order to sit down. Nick started the interview, asking why I wanted to work there, and I explained I was a single parent with two small children to feed. We talked for a while about my past jobs, and somewhere in the discussion, I remember Nick saying to me "You can come to work, but I want you to know I am a SOB to work for." I told him I didn't care; I needed to feed my kids. He told me to be cleaned and look like a lady and be there the next morning at six o'clock sharp.

From that day, until now we have been best friends. I will admit, there have been times when we haven't talked for five or six years, do to some of the ailments listed above, but we have always remained friends.

Within the past couple of years, Nick had to retire from the one love of his life, which was teaching ballroom dancing. But we are jumping to the present without the reader knowing the past. A past Vincent hopes will let the reader sit in awe and wonderment at. Wondering how any human being could have actually lived this life and survived as long as he has.

PART I
Forward by Vincent

This is the story of a young man who as he grew older became aware of his bipolar disorder, never knowing what it meant. As a child he yelled and screamed and taunted everyone. Till his teenage years he yelled and screamed and taunted everyone he came in contact with. He continued this type of behavior throughout his adult life only he included being arrogant also. He could not understand why this took place, but he knew; he really truly knew this was not his character. Every little thing would upset him and he would yell and scream and taunt. Finally he was analyzed as bi-polar on the day he went out and spent a ton of money and got himself into a lot of trouble. The doctor told him, "You're bi-polar, which means your happy one day and your sad the next".

And when I was happy I was really happy, I mean the world could just go away and leave me alone I would love everybody, I was kind to everybody, and everything was wonderful. But when the sad phase kicked in, I was low and down. To describe it would be, you almost curl up like a snail in a corner and you just want to die. You don't want to do anything but die.

So you are reading the story of a man who as a young boy lived with this bi-polar and didn't know anything about it until the age of forty years old. This can help you understand as you read this story why he did some of the things he did. So please let it try and be a lesson while reading the book; to those of you who may need help. If you have these feelings of anger and don't understand what they are, please seek professional help. But now please enjoy the book.

PART II
Life Stories

1

Introductions to the Family

I recall as a child, not being raised by my father and mother, but by my paternal grandmother Paula, a lady I grew to know as strong and stern yet very loving. So loving, in fact, she probably destroyed the future of my life by her spoiling and coddling of me and for her having such protectiveness over me. I remember as far back as probably age three, four or maybe five and being dressed in my little sailor suit and sailor hat.

My father was obviously a man of the navy, so they dressed me like my dad. I have pictures of him, and remember him taking me to the flagpole and to the park.

Grandmother and I lived in a New York tenement house; a three-story tenement house, but we lived on the bottom floor. It was a streamlined kind of tenement. One when you walked in, you entered into the kitchen first, and if you turned left, there was my bedroom, and if you continued on down the hallway, you would come to my grandmother's bedroom and then the parlor. You could see each of these rooms as you entered, and I can remember as a child, playing in the kitchen and in the parlor as well.

Grandmother Paula was a lady at the mercy of the welfare department, but being a child, I didn't know why. I knew she had given birth too many children, and I remember her children who were still alive.

There was my Aunt Mary, a lovely sweet girl, although I knew her, I think I would like to have known my Aunt Mary better. There was Aunt Mea who I really loved, and I can remember she married into the Gandolfo family. There was the youngest son, my Uncle Nicholas whom everybody loved. He was a handsome and sweet man, who really gave me a lot of attention. And there was my godmother, my Aunt Lena who later changed her name to Maryann. She didn't like her name, so she later had her named changed and became Mary Ann. She married into the Farrow family to a man who was to be my godfather, however I never met him.

My Uncle Benedict died before I was born but he was the talk of the house. I've seen pictures of him, and he looked as if he was quite a nice man. My grandfather Vincent, whom I was named after, I never had the chance to meet, but I know he was a carpenter.

I remember my grandmother only owned two dresses. A house dress with little slippers she would wear around when in the house, and a little dress with brown shoes, she would wear when going to visit her sister, who was my great aunt Maria. Maria was afflicted with a disease I believe was St. Vitas Dance, which would cause her to jump quite often. But still she was just a sweet, kind and humble lady. Even though she was a spinster, they buried her in a wedding dress when she died. It was just the talk of the town. She was a dear, dear lady. When I would visit her, I used to sleep on two chairs from the kitchen put together, just because I didn't wanna go stay with my dad. I'd sleep on the chairs and fall off and then try to sleep in the bed with her and the poor girl would get up in the morning black and blue. I was a wild, tormented child, they say, from the minute I woke up to the minute I went to sleep.

I see myself just shining through everything even when I couldn't understand what was going on, but it was only by the grace of God I knew I had to be ahead of everything. It seems God sends to all of us tools, and the ways and means for us to come to him. I learned this from my very early childhood, God wanted me for himself only, and even until today, he still does. Yet I seem to buck him and that causes a lot of problems. I don't know why, but he chooses some of us to want with our heart, soul, mind and body. Of course, he does that for all of us, that's why he made us.

It seems when I was young, I would never go to school, even though the school was right around the corner. I was afraid to go to school, I was afraid to go outside, as I didn't mix well with other people, and at that time I didn't understand why. Of course the truant officer would come, but to no avail, as I would run and hide. One time Mrs. Heights, a big, tall German lady with a bun in her hair, who looked very "mistress-like," came. She grabbed me by the hand and walked me to the school and made me go into the class, but I turned right around and came right back home. I didn't know it at the time, being so young, but this would cause so much grief to my grandmother.

(*Vincent starts showing the first signs of obsessive-compulsive disorder*)

So I was a spoiled child, living with my grandmother on welfare. Now my grandmother always insisted to all of her children that would come to visit her, "I need five dollars for Vincent's shoes, or you take Vincent to the store, buy him a suit."

It was always, you give him this, and you give him that, and all of her children were absolutely dominated in one way or another by helping to raise this child.

Here in the present, as I put these thoughts on tape, within my apartment, I have many clocks, of different makes. Cuckoos, chimes, bells, and as I sit here in my living room, there's a clock with chimes going off. It's chiming 11:00 o'clock, but it's really 11:15, it's one which is not leveled. I hope that you won't mind if I sit here for a moment and just listen to the chimes.

Vincent as a young boy 1943

2

My Grandmother Paula

When I was very young, my father took me away from my mother, at the time I did not know why, but I became this child without a father's or a mother's love. My grandmother had all of these children of hers who were young people, career people who were trying to marry, and make ends meet. They wanted to have little children of their own, and yet it seems they still had to support me. And because of this, the animosity began to grow against me at a very, very early age. However my grandmother provided for me even though she was very poor, poor almost to the point of being penniless she still always managed to feed me. I remember liking hot dogs and all the little pasta she would make. Grandmother would spend the rest of her day after her daily chores sitting by an old coal stove, in the kitchen where she would bake a potato, a sweet potato on the stove and this would be her dinner. She would religiously sit there and read the Bible through beautiful little wire-rimmed glasses. While reading her bible She would say, "Vincent, don't do this. Vincent, behave yourself," and I must have drove the poor saint to tears, I'm sure. This recollection of her sitting by this little water boiler and this little wood stove certainly brings me great comfort while I sit here now in my older years.

She was definitely very severe with all of her children regarding me. Of course, I didn't know at the time, but I was a restless child, a hypersensitive child. A child who was absolutely ungovernable and disorderly in all sort of fashions, and because of being spoiled, I learned, without any knowledge, the phrase, "I want." I want this, I want that. Today I would probably be diagnosed as having Attention Deficit Hyperactivity Disorder (ADHD) . If I didn't get what I wanted, I would throw a tantrum, but then she'd whip my butt blue, and I'd still carry on like a fool. It's a shame at a young age we don't have the gift to adjust and to learn. She taught me to love God, to have respect and to never answer back. Boy, if I didn't, I would eat brown soap and blow bubbles, I'll tell you. *(laughter)*

I have been sitting here trying to recall all of the things you will read about, and I find this is like putting pieces together to make an incredible puzzle. Why I was the way I was. That is a puzzle by itself.

I remember there was a cellar, in which we had storage bins. Grandmother would make me go downstairs into this cellar with her, and I believe this was the most frightening part of my life, as I would have nightmares for days to come. I was so insecure and this was so traumatic that Grandmother had the statues of St. Joseph, the Virgin Mary, St. Teresa, and the angels you know the typical Italian Catholic maga maga but still very sincere. One thing the reader must understand is all these dear Italian ladies were very sincere and they all believed in God, the saints, and what have you. Every night, grandmother would light all the candles, and it would stupefy me as I sat there, they would wiggle and wave, and you'd see all the shadows, and I would just be in a terror.

So much of a terror, that I would do this as she's sleeping in her room; I'd go "Ma."

She'd say "Wha?"

I'd say, "Nothing, goodnight, love you."

A couple of minutes later, "Ma."

And she'd say "Wha?"

Again I'd say "Nothing."

"Go to sleep, Vincent or I'm gonna get up and smack ya."

Five minutes later, "Ma.", then she'd get up out of bed and just beat the boop outa me, and this went on throughout my early childhood.

As I grew older, my biggest fear was my grandmother would go to sleep and never wake up again and then my life would end. I was so attached to her and loved her so, yet I gave her so much grief.

I remember the 'feast'. Every year there was the Feast of St. Joseph and the Feast of the Virgin Mary, and these feasts are a really big event. Really, just something else, because the streets would all be closed, and then they would walk the statue, through the street, and then you pin money on the statue. There were all different foods you could buy, such as 'Sphinges' an Italian type doughnut and is really good, and the Italian sausages and then all the rides.

I recall one time I wanted a quarter to ride this silly ride that went up and down which scared the guts out of me, and Grandmother didn't have a quarter. I carried on like a darn fool, until she got me the quarter, and I got to do my ride. I was just spoiled rotten. I would always cry, "Nobody loves me. I have no mommy, and I have no daddy," and this would just break her heart. It was just awful, I was just awful. I don't know why a child behaves in this manner, but there's an instinct of cleverness and a little bit of the devil. Children find a way to prey on a person's weakness, but I do not believe that I did this intentionally. I was just love-starved, I suppose. How can I say that when I can not think of any more love one human being could give, then my Grandmother; old, very wise, and very strong. And because of me her children began to hate her because I was totally ungovernable.

As I grew a little older, my uncle Nicholas who had two little daughters, Pauline and Jeanette, they were just children. We always went to their house for Easter, and this one year, Uncle Nicholas had bought Pauline and Jeanette these enormous rabbits, and as a kid they seemed six feet tall to me. They gave me a nice little stuffed bunny, and my grandmother took that bunny and threw it at them and took the other child's big bunny and told them, "If you can't buy him the same thing you buy your children, don't buy him anything." No parent wants their mother or their wife or their lover to come up to the kid and take their presents away, this is just not done. Now because of the respect factor where you're respecting your mother for doing this, but you want to cut her heart out, I'm sure. She was totally unruly about that. I would have been perfectly happy with the little bunny until I got home. Then I would say, "Why didn't Uncle Nicky get me a bunny as big as theirs?" So the man had no money. But I don't think in any way he hurt me because see as she dies and goes on, he was my savior, he was the one I called Dad. Aunt Rosie was the one I called Mom, even until today. Boy, when I called him the other night and said, "I'm writing a book," he started laughing. My uncle always laughed and always whistled. I said, "Uncle Nick, tell the time when I was sixteen or seventeen and said I'm gonna kick your butt, I'm tired of you bossing me around." He said, "Well be my guest," and he cleared out the living room and beat the crap outta me. He just started laughing. He's got diabetes real bad now I hear. But they were very good to me. My uncle can't be five, six years older than me. So it was quite a deal. Let me tell you if anybody gets the gold medal, it's my Uncle Nick and Aunt Ro. They took me the way I was before, after, and during. Well, bless them all. I had already started to become a problem with Uncle Nick.

Then grandmother grabbed me by the ear threw me out the door, and off we went in a huff.

But you know everybody that ever got tired of me ended up leaving the country. They moved to California. I had a roommate, we lived together, he moved to Mocksville. I had another person I lived with, they moved to New Jersey. So let's not blame grandma. My heart goes out to Uncle Nick, because she wasn't doing it to be hateful to her son but her heart really went out to this little crap of a person, he ain't got nobody to love him. That's terrible.

My godmother Maryann would come and sit with me and take me to her house. She also had two daughters, Pauline & Maria, actually, Maria Angelina, and oh, she was the apple of my eye. A beautiful, blonde, attractive, young lady, sought after by all the young men. Oh, she would have some of the prettiest men come after her, the most handsome, and I used to think that they were all princes. And then there was Pauline, her sister. Pauline was, one of those tom-boy kinds of girls, a beautiful girl, but she'd fight and beat people up and she would slap me around, when I'd get in her way. And it was because of me, that she couldn't go here and go there, and it got aggravating. She was a young kid, who wanted to go out to the park and be with the boys and carry on, and she couldn't because of me, but Pauline was okay. She was the young teenager who was penalized because she had to baby-sit me.

Then there was Anthony. He was the light of my Aunt Maryann. He was a very handsome blonde-haired young man, very physically fit. He had a lot of friends and girls coming out of the supermarket where he worked. I mean he had the most gorgeous, beautiful girls, and of course, I would always want to buddy up with him and try to get in my male bonding, but he wasn't interested in any of this. They were all young and trying to make their own lives, and I, Vincent was a nuisance.

Anyway, we would go back and forth from Grandma's, to Marie's (at my Aunt Maryann's house), and Marie and Pauline would ride the bus and they would take me, and boy, oh, boy, the minute dark would come and I got in bed, I would cry and scream and carry on. They would have to get up in the middle of the night, take me on the bus and take me back to grandmother's house. I could not stay, I had this obsession that my Grandmother would die and go away or fall asleep and she would never wake up again

This shows the increasing signs of Vincent's OCD

I remember one occasion as time drew near, Grandmother had developed kidney problems, and as a child, I had no idea of what this was all about, but they came and they put her in a hospital, and I had to live with my Aunt Maryann. I went to church, the Catholic Church, and I used to hear if you pray to your Saints, or whatever, they would talk to you and help you, and I'll tell you that was an experience. I went to the statue of Saint Anthony, and I promised him if he would let my grandmother come home that I would walk barefoot during his feast and pin the money on his little case that was around him. I promised to be a perfect child and never be obnoxious or boring or hateful ever again. And, lo and behold, my Grandmother did come home, and I kept my promise. I walked in the feast on my bare foot, and something kept saying, "Do it on your knees, walk on your knees." All these old ladies, God bless them, walk on their knees, and pray and carry on, and I'm telling you it was amazing to watch. Grandmother stayed home for a while, and she did quite well.

3

Camp

When I was maybe seven, my family decided, "Let's send him to camp for two weeks, and give Grandmother a break, and it will give him a chance to identify with other children." Well, that was the horror from hell, that camp. They sent me to the Bowden's Boys' Camp. It was a welfare-type run thing, I don't know where it was, somewhere in the woods. They would take me up the mountain at night, and all the boys had to be there, and I was so afraid of the dark, and I would cry, I was just a total little sissy. At this camp was when I first heard the word "sissy." But during that stay at the camp, I observed other people. There was about ten, to fifteen boys in a bungalow, and the caretakers had their own private rooms. I remember these caretakers, or whatever they were called—camp directors—if the boys were bad, they would take them into their room, and you would hear the stick whacking them. Well, eventually I put two and two together, and I actually found out the noise was all fake. All of these caretakers were in there seducing or molesting these boys, which I didn't know what that, meant at that time, and luckily never found out personally. There was one kid, who would be in the corner of the room, and every night he'd get up and drop his pants right in front of all of us, and he would masturbate, but at that age, I didn't really understand what he was doing. He kept staring at me the whole time I was there, and then one day he stole my pillow, and I beat him up. He didn't understand that I could do this because he thought I was a true little sissy. But, he stole my pillow, and I wanted my pillow back.

Then they used to do this thing about gold rocks. They would take rocks, and put gold paint on them, and then you would hunt for them. Well, I went and painted my own rocks, and I got caught, and was punished. I became so home-sick while I was there, I wrote a letter and it said, "You must come home right away, Vincent. Your grandmother is very, very sick. She needs you. You're Aunt Mea." And I spelled Aunt "ant." That did it, they got the letter, but they still wouldn't let me go home.

I had my first experience with the theater there, when they had a play, I entered a play and got a standing ovation. The play was about me on a desert, and I had to act like I was dying, and all of a sudden, needed water, water, water. Anyway, I became the hit of the camp, even though I hated every minute of it, and I hated everybody there.

I can't even remember if I ever made a friend or not. But anyway, I promised God if he would let me go home, I'd be a good boy again, and I kissed the floor, literally got on my knees and kissed the floor and told my grandmother I would never disobey her; that I would love her and I would behave. But two days later my compulsiveness was back, and I was a monster again.

Being at that camp, that was one of the most frightening times of my life.

I also remember I was a little skinny boink, just a little skinny thing, and the family, all were afraid of me being so skinny so they got a tonic for me. Boy, oh boy, I became so fat drinking that crap. Sometimes when I sit here, these thoughts that are coming into my head don't make any sense; they all seem so out of order.

4

Cousin Marie

Now I was home with Grandmother again and during this time I would go and be with my Aunt Mary Ann or my godmother, or my cousin Marie would come and pick me up with all of her boyfriends. She really only had one or two, but she'd take me to the movies when ever they went because in those days you know the guys wanted to try and get their hand on the girl's shoulder and to get close to her.

Aunt Maryann

It's not like the kids today. I remember at a recent gathering I saw a girl literally put her hand down a boy's pants in front of people. In my younger days, this behavior was unheard of. If you even saw a girl's kneecaps, she was immoral. My cousin Marie was indeed a beautiful, proper, quite a lady. And her beau, as they say in the south, was this most magnetic, beautiful, dark complexioned Italian named Rocco. He was nice boy, and they fell in love. Marie and Rocco would come and take me to the movie theater, and I'd sit in the middle of them, and it's a wonder that Rocco never ended up hating me. But it was Marie's idea. Marie, oh the minute she would walk in the door, I would have to go with her. She would take me to the circus and the zoo, and here and there, but just staying with her was enough.

I am sitting here and listening to the playback of this tape, and I have to go back again to a thought about the church business. I remember one time I went to the wrong church. I think it was what they call a holy-roller's church; because they were all screaming and yelling and jumping, and I almost had a heart attack. But they were wonderful people, who tried to get me to come back and go see their movies, but I would walk on the other side of the street after that.

On the streets of Brooklyn, we happened to live by the city sewer department. As a child, three blocks away from where we lived on Wilson Avenue, was also a sauerkraut factory. And talk about a smell. I imagine if we put the sewer smell and the sauerkraut smell together, it might give a whiff of something pleasant, but the smells separate, it was horrible.

Cousin Marie

5

My Mother

Then there was this most beautiful auburn-haired, very lovely, beautiful, shining face of a lady that would pass by and say, "Hello, Vincent," and I would have to run from her and hide. Everyone told me she was a witch. Don't tell a little child his mother is a witch. Witches, oh! And you know for years they did this to me. My grandmother never knew about it. But it was my mother; my mother with her sister would come and see me. Her sister Santa, her real name was Santa Madonia, who later married a man named Collette and they had a daughter named Francis whom I met once as a teenager. I would love to find Francis, because she was so sweet to me. But on that side of my family, my mother's side was my grandfather Joseph who was a shoe cobbler, my grandmother, Marguerita, big, big white-haired Italian lady, who was very emotional. She kissed me to death every time I would see her. And then of course my mother and my Aunt Santa, her husband, and Francis, and that was all on the maternal side of the family.

I would run, and they were all so cruel to my mother. I have forgiven everyone now for everything they did, but the biggest mistake made was, you never take a child away from the mother. Never. The child needs its mother regardless of how ruthless a mother is a child needs its mother. My cousin Marie was the only one, now don't forget she's a child, telling the older people, you don't do this, this is his mother. Marie would take me and she got me to know my mother, so I would not be afraid of her. And then one day my mother took me, the family finally broke down and let me go with her without my father his lordship, (*Mr. Cock*) knowing. I got to spend a day with my mother, and we went to an ice cream parlor and had ice cream. I remember her telling me she was dating a guy named Dick—Richard—nice guy, and he was nice to me so I would hug him when we finally met. One day he threw me on the floor and called me a "sissy" because I hugged him. And my mother beat the pure crap outta him. As a matter of fact, she threw him down three flights of stairs and that was the end of Richard. And there goes that word "sissy" again. My mother was quite protective and a quiet lady. She never spoke any unnecessary words, and when she would talk to me, it would be only one time, and I never had any trouble obeying her. She would hug me and caress me and told me how I looked like my father. Then I remember one day, a strange experience; we were upstairs on her third floor looking out the window one Sunday afternoon, and there was this gross looking man who would go in and out of this tenement house, and boys would be going in and out, in and out. My mother said, "Vincent, that man is a queer." I didn't know what that was. Then she said, "You stay away from him, and if I ever find out that you grow up to be a queer, I will disown you." And those words just stuck with me from there on, even if I didn't understand a word she said, but I didn't go outside and play anyway. When we went to the ice cream parlor I had a big ole ice cream soda—I'll never forget it—and then all too soon it was time to come home, and we passed a window where they had all these little baby chickies. Well, don't you know, lo and behold, she bought me a dozen chickies (*baby chicks*), and we took them home and kept them by the coal stove and fed them. Well, I got restless and got tired of my chickies, and eventually they all died. Those are the memories I have with my mother as my first experience as a child. There was a separate occasion however when they let me go for a walk with her and I found her to be someone that I could not simply be outrageous with. She was a lady, very fashionable and very stately.

Vincent's Mother

I remember as I grew older, I would meet her in New York, and we'd go have lunch together, and the policeman in those days directed traffic on the busy streets of New York. They would literally stop traffic to let my mother cross the street, and they would whistle at her. In those days, if a girl was whistled at, the girl would go home perfectly happy because she was being whistled at, because it meant she was quite a girl. My mother, Maria was beautiful, absolutely wonderful. She told me one day, "I dated this man, and his name was Clark Gable, and he wanted to marry me." It didn't mean anything to me until now, because now I know who he was. My mother was a singer and sang at the Downstairs Club in New York. She took me there to hear her and boy could she sing. And after the show, she would go home, no shenanigans, no playing around. Quite a woman, she was quite a woman. Quiet. Never, ever was one for idle conversation. And when she said "no," it made no difference who she said no to, it was no, and you didn't bother her again. And all of the treacherous things they told me about my mother were lies, they were absolutely lies. I probably would be a better man today, a secure man today, if I had the opportunity to be raised by my mother. However, I didn't know her long.

6

Faith as a Child

In our faith they say if you can win back a soul to God, and he promises you if you bring another soul to him, he will help you die in his peace, and boy I'm betting on that. There is no purgatory for Vincent. It's either gonna be heaven, which is a bit bleak at the current time, or definite, positive hell, and I am not talking about heaven or hell as Catholic. I am talking about the escape of being denied the presence of our Lord.

But now let's go back to the child, Vincent. And as we go along I'll remember some incidences as a child about the neighbors and my Aunt Maria—I think that was her name—my Grandma's sister. I guess she would be my great aunt. All of the hoopla as a child. We went to church, you know, during Lent. The church would put on the passion and death of our Lord Jesus Christ, and I remember sitting on a side bleachers with my grandma, and it was during the crucifixion, and all of a sudden I heard, you know the raising of the cross, they were getting ready to crucify this man, you know it was so real to me because this man really did look like what I guess we know as Jesus. All of a sudden I went flying off the bleachers, and I was going to beat everybody up on stage so that they could not hurt my Jesus, and I guess it embarrassed my grandmother, and when we left the church, all these people carrying on. But, I was good, I would defend, I would protect, and that was quite an experience.

Another occasion, we were at St. Joseph's Church on Troutman Street. All these little old ladies God loved them all because they were all in mourning. All of their husbands died and you hadda wear black for years, and you hadda beat your breast. They would all say Hail Mary's and pray their thing and go to communion and then walk out of church and just talk about each other and cuss and swear and carry on. I don't think it takes away from their sincerity, but they were good, humble, wonderful people, and still they are very sincere. You know, I guess you can screw up and be sincere and not know any difference, but that's all in the hands of God. And once this black veil went flying around the church and out the window, and people could see it for miles, so help me. The priest told us it was the devil and blah, blah, blah. But anyway, the traumas, oh the traumas I've experienced, and now that I'm older all these things will collect themselves into a true form of life.

Once when I was a child, a little boy, a priest told me, "Vincent, as a child, you read, you see people's souls, and you must learn to leave this alone or you're going to be a very unhappy person." I'm soon going to be 52 years old, and I'm still love-starved, I'm still craving for affection, still want to share my life with someone. But, I would like to continue on with more of my childhood experiences. During the age of six or seven, was a time of knowing my grandmother, with her Bible, and I would learn about Christ and the Bible through her talking and chatting with different people who would come in and out to her home. One particular family in my mind was people who were of the Jehovah Witness faith. Grandmother would talk to anyone about anything when it came to the Bible. This little family, had a young boy about twelve, and I was probably six. They bragged about what a great preacher he was going to become and blah, blah, blah. While they were visiting, the little boy would come to the parlor and play with me, and it seemed he'd always want to play by taking off your clothes. I'd run back to the kitchen, but I never said anything, and the kid got up on the pulpit there, and he just gave us a demonstration about all he was going to talk about Jesus. Looking back, I'm telling you, how misguided we can become. But they convinced Grandma we should go to see this big ole' sermon he was going to preach. After his sermon, I got up and went on and carried on and preached the things I heard from Grandma and all these other people. It was really amazing. So I did that, too. It seems like at six years old, you want to be and do anything that's good from any male, so I was imitating these people.

So here I am walking along the streets of Brooklyn, and I ended up at the community center where something was going on. It was sorta like a talent night, and I saw people dancing and acting, and of course I ran home to Grandma and said, "Grandma, I gotta have taps on my shoes." Well, Lord in Heaven, what I didn't go through to get her to get me those taps. I had these big giant taps at the front of my shoes, the little taps at the back of my shoes, and I told her I was gonna go and be a star. So I ran to this thing because they had the tryouts going on for about three days, and I gave them my name, then I got up on a stage, and I tap danced. Well, let me tell ya, somebody asked me where did I learn how to tap dance. It was the most horrible thing they had seen, but you know I was sort of impulsive. I don't know, but I was evidently brave and did these ridiculous things as a child.

When I got a little older, I met this little fellow that lived near by, however I have forgotten his name. He really liked me and he was really nice to me. As children, we were always told by the police, "If you're a bad boy, we lock you up". And in those days there was a fear and a respect of the police department. My friend and I found this big ring filled with keys so we thought we would do the right thing and take it to the police department. When we walked in, we looked all the way up on this big, tall counter, and there was this big, obnoxious looking policeman. We gave him the keys, and then they said, "Now for your reward, we're gonna show you the jail." You know, those people locked us up behind bars, and went away and left us there in that cell. Well, I was fit to be tied, but it didn't make me lose my respect for the police. The guy was just kidding; and I guess he might have been a bit drunk, I don't know what his problem was. But when they let us go, and I went home and told my grandmother, she put on her housecoat, and then went to the police department. She made me point to the policeman that did that to me, and then she beat the pure, pure, you name it, anything with a "p", and she beat the pulp outta him. And that was the experience with the police department I would rather forget.

Growing older, I had my first experience with a black fellow. His name was Reginald—Reggie—and he hadda pass by my window. Reggie was big ole fellow. Now we never had a problem in my community with people of color. I knew he was a different color, and I was a different color, but that was something we never questioned. At least I didn't. Reggie became a nice friend to me. He'd take me to the candy store, and he'd take me to the ice cream parlor, and he'd walk with me through the fields, and he was just a good fellow. He'd tried to teach me how to play ball, you know, and there was no problem with that, because as a child it was ok if I were to mingle with blacks or whites or Puerto Ricans, Jews or Germans. They were all just children of God, and there was no malice or prejudice or none of this calling people, "nigger and guinea" (with due respect to the blacks and Italians, that's just how it was). Well, the bad people did, but back then was a lot different than it is today. There were so many blessings in those days. The innocence and the purity of people was quite different than today.

Grandmother would sit by the parlor window and look out onto the street, which had a fur store on the corner, and I would go in there, and the lady was nice to me, she would talk to me, and we became sort of friendly. To the left of our tenement was a wonderful Italian bakery that sold lemon ice and cookies and cakes, and the people that owned that were Julius La Rosa, from the Italian singer family. Anyhow, we were surrounded by those two buildings and big wide streets, and this is where kids would play, on the iron stoop. In those days, the bathroom was in the middle of the hall, and both families on the floor hadda use the one bathroom. But then we became modernized, and we ended up with our own bathroom put in our apartment. We had an old sulfur refrigerator. One night I hadda run to the bathroom, and my Uncle Nick was working and trying to fix Grandmother's refrigerator, and the sulfur escaped. Well, I was caught in that bathroom and about died. It was such a traumatic experience, I came flying outta there, I thought I was gonna die that sulfur had such a stink. So that's another experience of the trauma continuing.

I'm telling you, it was never a dull moment, and although I was a little bit adventurous, I stayed mostly to myself, playing with the girls. I always ended up playing with the girls, and so, there went the "sissy" thing again. During the summer, if you got up at 8:00 o'clock and you walked three blocks to a church, there was a day type of camp where children stayed all day, and you know they feed us lunch, and they had games and fun, so I'd get up and go. I hated every minute of it, even though there was a lot of nice activities for children of the poor, I couldn't just get anyone to identify with me and take enough time to make a little man out me, this little monster.

On Mother's Day Sundays, this was a big day, because you got to go to your mother's on Sunday, and visit with her. Anything else like not going to visit your mother on Mother's Day was unheard of. It got to the point where Grandmother's children would not come and see her on this day, and they really broke Grandma's heart. It was because of me, because of their immaturity that they would not come and see their momma anymore on Sundays or Mother's Day or Christmas or Easter, and I started to hate every one of my uncles and aunts because of that. I really did. I remember one time my Aunt Mary Ann came in, and she was the one who always stood up to her mother. However, she was a dear lady, and one day, she said something to my Grandmother, I think she told her to, "Go to hell." I came running in from the outside, and here's my Aunt Mary Ann under the kitchen table and my grandmother with a big butcher knife, and she was bound and determined she was gonna get her daughter and cut her tongue out for that disrespect. Well, thank God for Uncle Nicky, he came in and rescued my aunt. But I'm telling you, respect, respect, it made no difference, it made no difference, if you were correct or incorrect, you never ever showed disrespect to your elders. Never, ever. People were killed back then for disrespect.

In this book, there will be chapters of things that I have done for people. Still I feel that I'm not man enough to be a man because I don't go around scratching my groin and huffing and puffing and walking bow-legged and trying an act like there goes Mr. Cock Vincent. I've always been soft, gentle, and arrogant snot, and I still am. I am very arrogant, very self-protective. But I'm getting better, thanks to the group at my dance studio, they have tried to tell me when I do these things.

Before I forget it is Monday in the beginning of June, rather hot outside, I enjoy being inside with my dog, Valentino Mirabella I, a little black Tibetan terrier. At this time, I'm a dance instructor. I own the Mirabella Ballroom Dance Studio, and the students and I are preparing to go to New York in August for a contest. My life is filled with all these wonderful people, and I love teaching them the art of ballroom dancing. Now, I have to pause, as I've got to look human and go to work. I just did what I thought was a whole bunch of taping and I didn't have the tape recorder on so I'm going to have to repeat those horrible events about the butcher shop, the butcher and his children, Mrs. G's candy store, when I get back …

Here it is a Tuesday morning, 8:30 a.m. and it's going to be 94 degrees today. I've thought all night long now, and it seems like writing this book is helping me to recall a lot of my past. However, I think right now I am coming up with all of the things which probably made impressions that were of a negative nature on me.

7

Mrs. G's Candy Store

An interesting story is the one about Mrs. G's candy store. This store was directly across the street from us on Wilson Avenue. Wilson Ave was a rather busy street, and when I was learning how to cross the street, I would dart and run, and one day I got hit by a car. It knocked me down, and ran right over me, but it's amazing that all the commotion, the hoopla, and all the people running and gathering scared me more than being hit by the car. It didn't really hurt me, didn't touch me, I got up walked away, and all the maga, maga. Italians, oh, a miracle, a miracle, a miracle! Well, guess it was a miracle. On another occasion at Mrs. G.'s, candy store, in those days, we had candy stores, and candy stores were like an ice cream parlor, mixed with a tobacco shop, mixed with a newspaper stand outside. People would come, put down their pennies and take their paper. Basically mostly everyone was honest and trustworthy, and Mrs. G. had bins of such things as tootsie rolls, and Mary Jane candy, the little peanut butter bars, and what have you, and then there was a big counter that faced the tobacco shelf. As you continued to walk again, streamline room to the rear were all these little ice cream parlor chairs and tables and the kids would have their ice cream sodas. You know for a nickel you could buy anything. There was one day when I just decided I would like to have a handful of Mary Jane's, and I just took a handful and walked out of the store. Lo and behold, before I could cross the street, here comes Mrs. G.; and we go get my grandmother. My Uncle Nick was there too and he came. I don't know where the priest appeared from, but there he was, and everybody in the world was there, and all I could see and hear was "bad, boy, bad boy," pointing fingers at me, then grandmother whooped my ass. She whooped my butt blue, there were occasions when she whipped it red, but this time it was blue. Let me tell ya this, perhaps that was one of the greatest things that could have happen to me at that young impressionable age, for I never stole as much as a peanut from anyone ever again, not even a rubber band from work. So that cured that. So

Mrs. G., every time she would see me would guard her little Mary Jane's, and I haven't eaten a Mary Jane candy from that day on.

The people were really nice Jewish people living in an Italian community. We're going to have to see that as I began to grow the Italian community becomes a Jewish community, and the Jewish community a black and Irish community. That comes a little later with all the gangs and whatnots.

8

The Butcher Shop

Directly across the street from us, maybe two stores down from Mrs. G.'s was our butcher shop. In those days that's exactly what they were, a meat-selling shop, and they'd cut and grind your meat and have sales. Religiously every week, I'd have to sit on this big ole' bench, and watch all the old women just go on, oh, this hurts and that hurts, and did you hear about this, and did you hear about that, and blah, blah, blah. I'd sit and play with the sawdust that was all over the floor. There was big ole fat butcher with his little mustache, and he seemed very nice. Every time I'd go, he'd give me a hunk of baloney, and of course grandma just couldn't be grateful enough. Somehow, he must have told her that I could come and sweep the sawdust off the floor, and earn some pennies or something. Anyway she sent me at four o'clock. She said, "Oh Vinzie, its quatro, quatro, you go and you sweep the floor for the butcher and he'll pay you." So I went, apprehensively, because I really didn't want to go. He had two sons, one boy was, you know, the big shot with the muscles, the kind all the girls would come around and faint. And then he had the other son who, well, he just had to be there to help his dad. He didn't like it, but he was a good kid and did what he was supposed to. He always said hello to me and talked to me but then he would go about his business. Well, I walked into the butcher shop, and all of a sudden the butcher locks the front door and turns the sign in the door to "closed." Then he says, "Now, you come here, Vincent," but I started to sweep. All of a sudden I looked into the back room, and here is this slob sitting down on a wooden chair, totally naked, his pants pulled down, and he was just sitting there with his genitals flopping over the front of the chair. He tells me that if I didn't come and play with him, he would put me in the freezer, lock the door and nobody would ever find me again that he would chop me up and sell me like a pig. Being scared, I started to approach him, because see, he had me where I couldn't move, but all of a sudden, I took my foot and kicked him in the groin, now when I look back, I think it's really funny. The old man fell three times, got his underwear caught in the chair; and then he couldn't get off the chair, he was on the floor, and lo and behold, his son walks in the back door. Now to save face, the attraction was simply this, that he had lured me with a big ole' bag of hot dogs and a big ole' bag of kidneys. In those days, Italians could do wondrous things with things like kidneys and lungs and brains and ooh, chicken feet, chicken heads, it's amazing. Anyway his son came in the back door, saw his father just buck-ass, just a howling. I remember him just a cussin' me, and I looked at the son, Mr. Macho, then I just walked out. On my way out, I just said, "Well, those are my hot dogs and my kidneys," and I took both bags of hot dogs and kidneys and ran home to Grandma, and boy the smile on her face. Oh, we're gonna feed this child for a week. But I never said a word about what happened. The following week, Grandmother takes me by the hand and I go sit at the butchers, and the man gave me my piece of baloney and talked nice to me and never again would we ever talk of what happened. I guess they were starting to understand this little child was no pushover after all.

9

Shopping Having Fun as a Child

There were occasions when Grandma would take me by the hand, and we'd walk to Knickerbocker Avenue. This is an avenue just filled with all kinds of grocery stores, and vegetable stores and clothing stores and it was a little bit like Mott Street in New York City for the Italians. We could get things like snails and dried cod fish and this, that and the other. But I knew when we'd go to Knickerbocker Avenue; I was going to get some new clothes. Another interesting thing was about four blocks north of us was the Star Theater.

I would like to take some time and talk a little bit about things children did for fun in those days. Because we were so terribly poor, we of course had the Dodger Stadium and Yankee Stadium right there is Brooklyn. But, nobody ever thought to take me to a ball game. However there was the movie theater, and every Saturday morning at ten o'clock, for 25 cents, you could go to the Star Theater and see what seemed like a thousand cartoons, and movies, you know, Abbott and Costello and the Three Stooges, and Frankenstein, kid's movies. One time they played horror movies, and even though I didn't want to go to the horror movies, I went anyway. Here I was sitting in this theater with my big bag of popcorn and bag of Wise potato chips and a root beer. Remember, this is for a quarter you get into the movie, but they gave you a pass so you could get back into the movie for free, and then you would buy all you could to eat, and you just sat and giggled and laughed. And there were always stage shows that went along with the movies. There were some occasions when a lot of the great stars who were young children then performed at the Star Theater, the Fox Theater, and the Roxie Theater. On one occasion, all of a sudden I turn around, and there was Frankenstein coming down the aisle. Well, let me tell you, I peed in my pants, and ran out of the theater, just hysterical. This is what I would say was another trauma in my life.

We had to pass this pool hall on our way to the Star Theater, and in there were all these gross fat and skinny Italian men, with their little guinea stinkers. They were actually called pirogues, and they would be playing bocce ball. The young boys would be shooting pool, and they would holler at me "Hey, Kid, how ya doin', Kid. Where ya goin', Kid? You're Paula M's kid." Ya know, they were just good guys. Young kids weren't allowed in the pool hall, but one day I walked in and found out why young kids weren't allowed in there. There all over the wall were all these naked pictures of Marilyn Monroe and Rita Hayworth and so on, I can still see all that now. I don't think I ever got to do anything in the pool hall, you know like play pool, but I do remember the posters. So these were the way Saturday's were spent at the Star Theater during the summer.

Other things we would do is play games like stick ball. Every mother in town hated this game, and would cover and harbor and even lock up their brooms. This was because the boys would take the broomsticks and a Spaulding bat, and they'd play stick ball right there in the street. We also played games called cork-cork allevio, the game hide and seek, and there was a game called Step on the Devil's Cracks and Break his Back. I became obsessed with that game. Grandmother couldn't take me for a walk down four city streets without me stepping on every blessed crack. I really wanted to think I could break the devil's back. It was silly, but I really believed it would break his back, so there I was running around all over the place stepping on cracks on the sidewalks. *More signs of Obsessive Compulsive Disorder being shown*

Girls would play with their little dollies, but they also played hopscotch and pottsie. The guys would play tag and hide and seek and just simple games. But one of the bigger game events was roller skates, and it seemed like all the kids had roller skates. Everybody had roller skates, but of course, I didn't have any. I would sit and watch everybody zooming by me with their roller skates. When they were tired of roller skating, the boys would then go around to all of the supermarkets and they would sit and wait for the orange crates to be thrown away. You see, in those days, oranges were packed in crates of wood, and when the boys got the crates they would take them home. Then they would get a piece of two by four and put the skate wheels onto the two by four and nail the crate to the two by four. When they put a little handle bar on it off they'd scoot with a scooter, and it seemed like they had scooters all over the place. And those who where more fortunate, and without scooters had bicycles. And so this is what they would do with the scooters and had a great time....

I can hear that clock again, so I move into another room with another clock, but this one has a little better tone, and there it goes hitting 9 o'clock. Now there goes the cuckoo clock. This apartment I live in is just full of clocks. I never thought I'd ... here goes another one ... so anyhow this is my company, my clocks, and my dog. I have three televisions and I have them all playing at one time. Sometimes it just sounds like we're having a big old party here. But still it is lonely.

10

A Scandal

There was this one guy at church who would take the young boys and let them watch him and they learned how to play with girls. Sexually, I suppose. It was in little cove in this big courtyard. And one day when it was dark with just a little light shining onto that door, I sat right there watching everything he was doing. They didn't even see me because they were so involved, but all of a sudden she screamed and there I was sitting, and then the boy chased me all around. He said he was going to make me do these naughty things to the girl. You know. I couldn't jump but you know for a little boy that they called "sissy" I ended up climbing over a six-foot fence. The guy that was chasing me went crashing into it and cut his nose on a piece of barbed wire. Let me tell you, that boy chased me around for four days, and said he was going to kill me, but I managed to outrun him. Somehow the whole neighborhood heard about it, and one by one they'd come up and say "Hey, Vinnie, good boy!"

11

Tenant Neighbors and Friends

I'm going to pause for just a bit and see what else I can conjure up in my memory here. It's so funny how you think of these strange, weird things that happened so many years ago. I can tell you a little bit about some of the little girls in the neighborhood. I remember two that made a lasting impression. One young lady, a rather big girl, she was wheelchair ridden, and whenever I was around. she really frightened me simply because she had an affliction. This affliction left her with no control of her body movements, and as a little boy I didn't understand why that was. This girl was rather triangular in looks and I remember it absolutely traumatized me every time I'd see her. She would scare the pure potato soup outta me by riding by me and going, "Boo." Well I would just fall to pieces. I'd feel what they called the fringe coming over my body, and I would run and cry and hide. That girl caused me a lifetime of nightmares, and she would do this on many, many occasions. Grandma would never explain to me what the problem with her was. Her mother would scold her for scaring me and then she'd laugh, bless her heart. It seemed as though she got a big kick out of just terrorizing me, she really did. You gotta remember on warm nights, all the old gals would gather around this or that person's house steps, or they'd walk across the street and go sit at another person's house or sit on the fire escapes and the stoops. Well anyway, this one day, I was kinda forced to sit within maybe a tables length away, outside with this young lady who was talking to this girl and working with her. You know, they'd get along real nice, and they'd play and she'd smile and she'd laugh but then she'd go "boo" and I'd jump right out of my pants again. But then for some reason I just hadda find out why this girl was like this, and so I very bravely sat there in front of her, and I peered into her eyes, and I would stare at her. Oh I think this probably went on for twenty maybe thirty minutes, it seemed like it was forever, but I was bound and determined to try and not pee in my pants and be afraid of her. And as I gazed into this child's countenance, I saw such a hunger and such a yearning for her to break out of this evil affliction that she had, that she really comforted me by seeing there was so much pain, and then I could forgive her for scaring me. Then I did something that was really crazy. I got up off the step, and I went to her face, and I went, "Boo," and she started to laugh, she just about jumped outta her chair, and it scared the hell outta me. As a matter of fact, it caused me to pee in my pants. It seems I did a lot of peeing in my pants as a boy. But then I just hugged her and gave her a kiss and ran away, and that was the end of that. After that, I never was frightened of her again, but I still stood far away from her and I would wave, you know, and she'd kinda smile. It just broke my heart that she just couldn't come out of this possessive, evil thing that had a hold on her. I don't know if she had cerebral palsy or she was remedial, but anyway she had a lot of heartaches, and my heart still goes out to her even now.

Then over the fur store, lived a girl named-Tina, she was a very fashionable little girl, a little bit older than me, and I noticed that of all the girls. Well, she'd come out, and she had these breasts, I would always be staring at her breasts cause she was the only girl who had something coming outta her chest. Nothing was coming outta my chest. Tina was rather pretty with long black hair that her mother would fix. She'd come out and wheel her little baby carriage, and she'd flirt with me, you know. But I didn't know what that meant back then, but she'd smile at me and then she would say "come on and play with me" and so we would played together. There was this other game that the children invented—talk about a nightmare, I sometimes still have that nightmare, and I feel so guilty. The game was called "God, I Am Only Kidding". We kids would get together, and we'd wish something evil on someone, and then say, "God, I'm Only Kidding". Now if you said, "God I'm Only Kidding," the game was okay, but if you didn't say, "God, I'm only Kidding," then people started to get nervous. I know now that it was a stupid little game, and I have no idea who started it. Anyhow, Tina said something about my grandmother, and then she said, "God I'm Only Kidding," so figured, well, if the shoe fits wear it, but I did not like her grandmother. She lived diagonally across and to the right of us in a nicer kind of tenement house. It had a spiral staircase you know a winding staircase. Her grandmother would always yell at me even from far away across the street, she'd yell at me. You know it seems I spent my whole childhood being yelled at, being pushed, being slapped, go away kid, even was kicked and left out and I'd have to sit and wait and look and see if I could get involved, and they wouldn't let me involve myself in any of the things some of the people would do. So I had to fight back and evidently I was bound and determined nobody was going to push me down. So anyhow, turned around to Tina and said, "I hope your grandmother falls down the stairs tonight and breaks her neck and dies." And I never said another word after that. After a long silence, she looked at me with a tear in her eye. Oh, that got me, and I said, "God I'm Only Kidding." Well, I guess I got her good; she was always so evil about my grandmother. And I really was only kidding. But that night, well, Holy Moses, it was 11:30 at night, I know it was 11:30 at night because the church bell rang—you know, it used to ring one time on the half hour and used to ring once for every hour on the hour; and this mess went on day and night, but we got used to the church bells, but anyway all of a sudden there was all this commotion and ambulance and noises. Well, lo and behold, the poor old lady fell down the winding stairs and banged her head against the cement part of the floor, and it killed her instantly. So I want to tell you from that day forward, it really freaked me out. I had nightmares that this lady would come get me outta the bed, I'd wake up, and be scared half to death. Well needless to say, there went that game we certainly never thought to play that game again.

12

Public School: PS-53

Now I'm going to talk about me being just a little bit older. You remember, how I told you earlier that I used to run out of school. Well, eventually I did go to school, even though I can't remember a whole lot about my school PS-53. I do know I would run from the stairs of the school that were awesome to deal with, all the way to the stairway of my tenement house. It had the little stoop stairs, and then you would walk in through the door and there were the mailboxes. Then you walked in through another door and you proceeded down the hallway. Being a three-floor tenement house, the stairs I was taking were to the left, they were the first flight of stairs going to the middle floor. That's where this big guy 'A', fat butt would hear me coming in the door and he would come down and hide in the little cove that separated the staircase from the bottom floor and the doorway which went down into the cellar. This little shit would hide there and then come out and scare the hell out of me.

Well one day, grandmother come out and beat the pure crap out of him, she knocked his head against the staircase, and then went up stairs and cussed his mother out for him scaring me, and then that boy would never talk to me again. But I remember that when he would go to school, he'd wear this big white strap that went from his waist to his shoulder, then down his back and around his waist. This strap hadda big silver shiny badge on it. I didn't know what he was, and then later I found out that he was a school monitor. So I said to him, "You're a monitor and you direct traffic," He said, "Yeah." Just being a real creep. Well, one day when he came home, I don't know how I acquired his big old white shiny strap with his badge, but I put it on, and then I went to school. And in the big room of the school, we would always have to line up according to class we were in. So this day I just stood right in front of my group with the monitor and badge thing and made them all stand at attention and follow me out of the school and then I told them to go home, because they had no school today. Then I would stand on the corner and tell the little children, "Give me your hand," and

I'd walk them across the street. Well, I eventually got caught, and boy, did I get a butt whooping. There were about forty kids that went home that day, and had a free day. You would think this should have made me popular; everybody should have liked me by then. But no, there were still a lot that didn't. I hadda tell ya that story, as it just hit me, and I thought it's quite interesting. So you see I did a lot of crazy things.

There was this kid named Frankie that I wound up meeting, he was a dark-eyed sort of ruffian, with black-hair. He lived on Sydam Street, which was all the way over to the left of Wilson Street. Frankie would take me home to his house and make me a peanut butter sandwich and then we would play with his dog for a while and then I hada go home. His mother had to work and when she'd come home, he'd get rid of me. We'd read comic books and oh, you know in those days comic books were a really big deal.

If I had all those comic books that I had then, I'd probably be a millionaire today. But I remember my cousin Marie took all of them and she never returned them to me. We also would collect baseball cards, you know, I had every Babe Ruth I could think of. I'd kill now to have just one. Anyway, one day Frankie took me over to his house, and I'd really started to like him. He did a lot of weird, stupid, strange things, and I'd just sit and watch. But then this one day, (*I got stuck with all the true butt-holes excuse my expression*), he pulled down his pants, and he had this little cocker spaniel puppy and he would let this little puppy lick him. He got up abruptly and came over and pulled down my pants, and I just fell on the floor. When I got up, I kicked him in the face, and then walked out the door. I guess he thought he was going to let the puppy lick me too. I went home and I told Grandma, but you know there were a lot of times I wouldn't tell Grandma. I think the reason I told her this time was cause he embarrassed me, anyway, I remember late that evening when we were walking and I said to myself, uh-oh, we're going to the left, here we go to Sedam Street. Frankie came running and he run back into his bedroom and Grandma just sat there, and I heard her saying in Italian a couple of real hard-core cuss words to the mother, and the mother was just fit to be tied, and all I can remember was looking through the hallway, and she had Frankie by the hair. She probably whooped his butt, I'm not sure, but I never saw or heard from Frankie again. And so there goes that friend.

It seems I was the one always running off friends. In trying to identify, it made no difference, I would emulate, imitate anyone, whether it was a girl or boy.

In school, I remember meeting this tall blonde-headed, "buxom" beautifully painted faced lady, our new teacher. Her name was Mrs. P., and she told the children in the class if they got an "A" on their homework, she would go to the candy store and buy them coloring books. Now in those days coloring books were these big, giant enormous, books. For the girls, they had Anne Blythe and Doris Day coloring books, for the boys there was Batman and the guy who used to stretch himself like a spider; Spiderman coloring books. Mrs. P. would buy the big old box of Crayola crayons. So one day after school, I just automatically found a way to be walking next to Mrs. P., and she said to me, "Vincent, you weren't a very good boy today in school, but maybe you'll do better tomorrow." I said, "Oh, I will, I promise." And she held my hand. Well, when she touched my hand, I turned as red as a beet, and then I felt a tingling in my body, and I said, "You're going to the candy store, aren't you?" and she said, "Yes, and I'll take you with me," and she bought eight coloring books and eight boxes of crayons. I looked at her and said, "I want that one," She said to me, "Well Vincent, this is only for the good children who did their homework, and got an "A." I said, "Well, I'm a good boy." She said, "Yes you are a good boy, but you don't get a coloring book and crayons. If you go home and do your homework …" It was ABC's, and one plus one, and I was just a mess with math. Mathematics still, thank God for the calculator and whoever invented the calculator, I am even told at the bank I am to the penny, once again, thank God for the calculator. However I never did get the coloring book or the crayons, but one day, I guess this was probably a Friday, which was the day when everybody got their awards, their rewards, and their little ego things. Mrs. P. said, "Vincent, I'm gonna take you for a walk," and she took me over to Mrs. Greens right across from Grandma's. I went and asked Grandma if she could take me, and she bought me the biggest hot fudge chocolate sundae that money could buy. That was my memory of Mrs. P., who was just the most beau-ti-ful, soft spoken, kind and delightful teacher. So anyway, there we are with Mrs. P. and my little elementary school, PS-53.

(You know as I'm going through listening to these tapes, and I have a lot of run on thoughts. I'm taking a break, and we will continue with the trauma and tragedy of this child real soon)

13

Vincent and Jesus

I've taken considerable amounts of time off reflecting on this age business between the ages of 6 to 12, and I just find it was all a matter of growing, impressions, and survival. Of running up and down Knickerbocker Avenue and attending church and learning about God and learning about man and about Brooklyn. I reflect now I was just learning about people and their "evilness" and their hatefulness, and about being pushed here and there. I was always trying to be a step ahead of everything and everyone and trying to outsmart them. Not in a way to be clever or vindictive, but in just a way to survive from these people. Between the years of seven to ten and then ten to twelve were some interesting stories. Those were the years when I had all the experiences with a lot of church functions and the CB's and patrols.

Keeping in mind the most impressionable thing is I was learning about God, and Jesus Christ his Son, the Holy Spirit, and the angels and all the saints. Why we were created and here, all put to me as a little child. 'Reading' all these boys and girls, at that very early age, however no one was anything like the little boy Jesus. So Jesus became an imaginary friend needless to say, but let me tell you why. This relationship with two children, Jesus and Vincent was a lot more than imagination, because he was sort of my hero. How blessed could anybody be as a child to have Jesus as his hero and his friend. So it was through that innocence and "unknowingness", that Jesus and I were buddies. I would talk and argue with him, and I would ask him why is this person doing that, or that one doing this. I would ask him to go with me to the store, and you know, I think if anyone had seen those kinds of thoughts in my head, they would have really put me away. It seems they tried so many different ways to put me away, but this one would have done it. Keep in mind that ninety percent of my childhood; I spent with this young fellow Jesus. To this day on my mantel, I have something, invented by man, a picture of Jesus when he was a child. He became anything I wanted him to be and he always was my buddy. I didn't know he could be God. I just knew he was an excellent, perfect, perfect child, and a perfect man. Can you imagine, someone dying to save your soul, and I knew him as a boy. Golly, if only I could have understood then, maybe I would die a saint now, but anyway. I feel like 'm a derelict, a pervert, but not really, you know, just at heart. I am very human, with many, many shortcomings.

(there goes those clocks again; it's that time of day).

Anyway, I need to make it clear, this relationship with me and this Jesus. It's quite holy and quite sacred and quite respectable. I'm so glad I'm doing this book because I'm looking back and seeing the holiness and the joy of being a child even through all of the slapping and beating. Even the kicking and "sissy" this and "sissy" that, go away, kid. The times they'd lock me in dark rooms, and oh, everybody had a heyday with me, but I would immediately think of my buddy, and with due respect, dear Lord Jesus, it seems I and he'd come right through brick walls sometimes. I'm so glad I got to think of this part this morning, and we needed to really expound on this relationship.

14

Born Italian

So now we will continue to put these things in perspective, and attempt to continue this story, but the writers are going to have their hands full. We're going to begin with my Baptism Certificate.

It says:
Certificate of Baptism,
Church of Our Lady of the Rosary of Pompeii
225 Segal Street, Brooklyn, New York.
This is to certify that Vincent Mirabella, child of Anthony and Maria Madonia Mirabella, born in Brooklyn, New York, on the 11th day of September, 1941 baptized on the 9th day of November, 1941, according to the rite of the Roman Catholic Church by the Reverend A. Caso, the sponsors being Vito and Mary Ann Ferro, as appears from the baptismal register of the church.
Date: November 9, 1941, Reverend Angel Caso _____ Pastor.

Have you ever noticed when people write documents and certificates, the writing is so sloppy and so mixed up that one can't know one movement from another?
I don't remember from when I was born on September the 11th, 1941 or any time as an infant, while in the care of my mother. Although there are photographs of her holding me as a baby, and possibly of my baptism. But from the very inkling of remembrance, it was always my grandmother Paula, whom I lived with and was raised.
We're going to have to clarify the fact that even though the innuendo states this child was wretched and spoiled, it was really not so. I think what took place was because my grandmother, had raised, oh, I'd say 12 to 14 children, most of them now deceased, and in the above we read about were her child survivors, all married. They were young 20 year old young adults who married and started to make babies and begin their own families. I suppose every man, has a pride and dignity,

and sometimes when offenses or transgressions are committed against one to another, I guess that may have been the purpose of me being removed from my father. Perhaps the offense the mother of this child, through her weakness, probably had an affair with another man. Probably because of Italian heritage, and the "un-forgiven" sin it couldn't be forgiven. But nothing was said of the father while he was in the service and doing his thing. Later as I did get to know my dad, he did not communicate with me. He spent his whole life resenting the fact that I was his child. There was never any affidavit of him playing around, you know all of his foreign countries he went to fight in the war, but the story was told in many folds.

But I spoke with my mother as we grew older, and I still think that for a man to play God is probably the most vicious of all transgressions no only to himself, to his God, but to his family. He destroyed this young lady's life; by denying her to even know her child. Though she died loving him; she also died with the comfort that she did get to know her child for a short time. Not only did the father destroy his life, his mother's life (the grandmother), but also the life of the woman he married and of the child that was bore.

But we don't blame anyone, for these were the times. This was Italian attitude and culture, and I think it could be well said it's okay that this happened if at the time, the father did not reject the child, but took him, his first born, his little boy man.

Vincent with his father

He could have really turned Vincent into quite a man with his influence. But instead, his influence was that of rejection as this Vincent, *(there you go, cuckoo)* grew older, his father just made it very clear to him, "I am not your father, I never had sexual intercourse with your mother."

And I told him, "Well, you poor soul, God couldn't have made a more ugly person to look like you than me." Same crooked fingers, and the whole business, but anyhow that is neither here nor there. But it is the fact that this man who was in the navy, left this child with his mother and she had to raise him. I don't know that he ever contributed to any support of the household. But I do know that this grandmother cared, nurtured, and raised. She put the fear of God and man, along with having to teach this child how to love, respect, to be fair, and understand that life is not a bowl of cherries. All of it was on her. Well, I'm sure she did an excellent job with all her other children; because every one of them were basically God fearing and married. When you married a woman in the Italian heritage, there's no divorce; no divorce.

But for some reason, if a man felt dishonored, they'd take the child away. What nerve. No man has a right to do that. If fathers would have been that of pure soul and a man who loved God, then this never would have happened. When I look back at pictures, this Anthony was certainly quite a lady's man, one with women flocking around him, below him, above him. There are pictures where you can't find another man in the picture. He had many, many beautiful ladies. He was a soft-spoken and very well-liked person. We will talk about my relationship with my father later in the book. But due to the fact this child had to be raised by this older lady. It wasn't that this child was raised to disobey his grandmother or not to love his grandmother, but it was due to the fact that she had so many other children who were required to baby-sit Vincent. They had to take Vincent and find some interest in Vincent. And as their children grew, these cousins and first cousins resented the fact that Vincent was always demanding. You couldn't do anything bad in the family without Vincent telling Grandma. You see, when the uncles and aunts and cousins would tease me to the point that they would frighten me with nightmares it would cause me insecurities, and I just couldn't handle it. So I would tell Grandmother, and then she'd whoop everybody in town. Grandmother had been very well loved by all her children, more or less; and by her friends. It seems there was always someone at the house, and it always thrilled me to death to see Grandmother there with company. And then the children would come, and Sundays were always a great event. On the holidays, they would all cook, and we'd take down two doors, you know, just doors, entrance doors, and put them on saw horses. After all, these guys were carpenters, at least most of them were following in the footsteps of their honorable fathers, and it provided them a great trade, and a great living. An uncle, the one that we talk about, Nicholas, who, at my confirmation; I chose his name. He didn't choose to be at my confirmation for me to pay him this tribute, but this guy was the carpenter. Well they would put up some saw horses and tie the tables to them, and we'd have a table from the kitchen all the way down to Vinnie's bedroom. It would fit twenty to forty people, and first we'd start with soup, and then we'd eat the roast chicken, and pastas and lasagnas.

And it is something that today we see all of these exotic foods, ones that we ate as children due to poverty. Such as snails, today they're escargot, and quite expensive. We would eat lamb's head. Can you imagine eating the head of a lamb? It was the most delicious, wonderful thing you could eat if you could only get past the eyes. And they'd roast the lamb's head with garlic. Everything was garlic in our family, you know. But this lamb's head, boy it was delicious even if it sounds gross. And then there were fried lungs and brains and eggs. All of these seem to be disgusting things we ate as poverty-stricken people, but today are quite gourmet and quite expensive and elaborate. So I guess there's a little thing from the mouths of innocence. You know because we were so poor we had to eat this, and now today people pay though the nostrils for just a taste of a snail or escargot.

The food was all incredible, the homemade breads, and homemade pastries. Oh, my uncle Morris, my Aunt Mary's husband, and boy he'd get out the meat grinder and they'd grind their own meat and they'd get the casing and make the most marvelous Italian sausages and drazoles. Oh, let me tell ya, that for poor people we ate like kings and queens, and praise God for that.

They would feast, eat and party and everything was respect. You couldn't tell Grandmother anything negative or what have you. So the youngsters in the family tried to sit and tell this lady, "You can not spoil and coddle this child; he has to go out and get his ears clipped." You know at six, seven years old, and I was already going out and getting my ears clipped, but they didn't know that. They were all too busy avoiding, doing the superficial things for me to appease grandmother. Actually Grandmother should have told them, "Just back off, and I'll handle him." But what happened was because she demanded this and that and the other with help to raise Vincent? Obviously this tells me the father never did a thing.

I remember as I grew a little older, she would tell her son (my father), "You need to take this child, and make him a part of your life and raise him." But he wasn't having any of those bananas. I still didn't don't know what the guy's problem was; but even today, I try so vigorously, and in so many ways, to make the guy proud of me, you know. However, now it's not important, and I could give a pot piss and a shit (excuse the vulgarity) about who's proud of me, or who isn't. They can kiss my fat Italian butt, because I don't really care. I am proud of what have done, and some things have done I am not so proud of, and I know that I try to walk in the eyes of God. I don't want to paint a picture here to anyone that I'm Mr. Holy, oh no, I'm Mr. Misfortunate [sic], due to the fact that I know the rules and the laws, and some I don't keep. Woe to you who know the rules and don't keep them. I don't make excuses about what my rules from God are. You know, I hear all these good-hearted people tell me, "Well I didn't ask to be this way, and I didn't…." Oh, bull! You're that way because you choose to be that way regardless of what your problems are. So I have come to a point in my life where I know who I am, I know what I am, I know what I do, I know where to go, and I know what I choose. My values are a bit different from most of the average person's values; therefore I'm still having a hard time you know, with people.

But I could give a hoot; I always say if I had won that 10 million dollars, it wouldn't be anything extravagant. I would move to a mountain, live by myself, get a lion and a tiger and a panther and dare anyone to bother me. I would l-o-v-e to live by myself away from everything and everyone. It doesn't mean I don't like people, I love people, I just want to be alone and I'm not. The people who are around me in my environment, which is neighbors and you, know the fair-weather friends are wonderful. I love them all. Everyone I come in contact with I love. (*Here we go with the bells; that's the nice clock, you know*)

I don't want to get too far off into the present, but I want you to know as a child, I understood everything that went on, even though everyone talked in the Italian language, that was the first language I understood. It was also the first language I could speak. Unfortunately, we are Italian of Sicilian stature, it is not unfortunate that we were Sicilian but unfortunate we were not the lettered Castilian Italian. We spoke sort of broken English, you know. We would never say gabanetta for a bathroom, it was always bacarazo. Well, who ever heard of a bacarazo, but that was our Italian, and was the respect and the honor. You always kissed your elders. You know here they were calling me a "sissy," and here were all these men, kissing each other, boo, boo, boo. Respect, respect.

The biggest story excuse me, for being so vulgar this morning, but I think it's the only way to make it understandable. These men walked around scratching their groin and spitting and saying "Here, here, look at my muscles," yet they were the biggest pussies you'd ever want to come across. There was nothing manly about half the men I knew. I think I was more of a man than any of them will ever be. It was all superficial, fake and insecure. But a man couldn't cry a man couldn't show any emotion. Whoever it was told them that or put that in their heads destroyed a lot of lives.

Because I wanted to be accepted here I'm going with all these boys and girls of my family, and I was just was a nuisance. I wanted all of them to like me. I did have one cousin from my Aunt Mamie and Uncle Sal, they had three boys and a girl, and one of their boys, Vincent (*another Vinnie*) he was a good cousin to me. He'd come and get me. In fact, I'll talk about him being there for me when my grandmother died. He would play with me, and we'd spend the night together at their home, and sometimes he'd even let me sleep in his bed. He just loved me, and his brothers would make fun of him because he loved me. I would love to see my cousin Vincent. I think he resides in California, and he is a married man with a family I understand. Just a fine fellow. He was a good male cousin. Then there was my Aunt Mary's son; John and her daughter Rosalie, who married a man named Hanson, an Irishman. The first broken Italian heritage and it was a hopp-dala for the poor girl. And there was my cousin Pauline, her sister, Pauline R., who married Ignatius R. A wonderful man and he was definitely all man, a father image, a family image, a macho man. Ignatius didn't act like a macho man he was a gentleman and a man of God. He would have loved for me to come live with him, but he couldn't. A lot of these blessed people couldn't, they had their own families. They couldn't afford this little bastard child, as they tried to call me. But there was no bastard child about it. Just a sorry father who wouldn't accept his responsibilities, said with no offense to my father. I love him, you know. I love him as much as the Bible says to love and honor thy parents. But what the Bible fails to tell you, is we all, you and I must, dear reader, if I am to love, like and accept you, you must earn my respect as well as I must earn yours. This is regardless of who you are and what you do.

I have an assortment of friends, and so help me, if you knew half the kind of people I hang around with, you would faint. The good, the bad, the evil. I have friends that will come over and pull your teeth out of your face one by one for me but they all respect me. And if you're doing something wrong, I'm gonna tell you. I don't care if you kill people for a living, I'm gonna tell you "You're out of turn," and they have respected me for that.

So now that I've lost my track; let me back up and see what I'm blabbering about …

Disclaimer

Again, we're going on with the run-on business, but I want to make it very clear, **THE INTENTION OF THIS BOOK IS NOT TO BRING SHAME OR TO GET EVEN VINDICTIVELY TO ANY MEMBERS OF MY FAMILY.** Especially my father who really is a good and wonderful human being. I found this out in later years. It is simply what happened to one little child, who grew up to be as I am, one which grew up with believing what I believe. A child who did grow up, and that is why I am so adamant to let you, dear reader.... think I wanna name this book, <u>And Forgive Us Our Sins</u> because when some of you read this, you will identify with it.

It wasn't just poor, pitiful me, that is not what we're trying to write about. I just want to let you know when I die alone and am buried before sundown without any hoopla, I hope a priest will be summoned and give me my last rites, and then put my butt in the ground and leave me alone and let me go to my God in peace. I don't want flowers; I don't want any hoopla, (we're getting off again). However, if you're gonna love me, I ask you to do it now. Come and tell me, "Vincent, I love you," and hug me, and don't give me any of this baloney that you have to play wits with me. Give me my flowers and buy me my little presents now; come and see me now. I have lived in this apartment for the last 10 years, and the only people that come and see me are people who are looking for something. And, you know, I throw 'em out and say, "Go away, leave me alone, I've got a headache, don't bother me, I don't want to be bothered". *(There we go with the pretty chimes now. Thank God for these little bells. Well, let's listen, here we go, that's a quarter till ten.)*

Again let me impress upon you, dear reader, it is not my intention to do dishonor or to embarrass and hurt my father's or my uncles' and aunts' feelings or anyone in the family, but I feel I have to tell you what happened to me, and I say to the family, if the shoe fits then wear it. I'm not here to hurt, but we've got to find out why what was so, was not so, and what was so. Oh, boy, this is the one, I really think that every one of you dear people who will read this book may sit down and write your own life story. But, now you have to be terribly honest, and it can be frightening perhaps, but write your own story. You don't need a psychiatrist; it'll all come back to you, and it will help you see where your pain comes from, and why you do stupid things. I think up to this point I should be the most hate-oriented person, the most beastly kind of revengeful soul. However there is no hate or hurt or heartbreak in my heart now, so I write a book.

I haven't watched television in five days. I used to sit and watch every darn thing on TV and bore myself to death, especially in this day and age with all these stupid things in the daytime. They're absolutely ridiculous, people piteously trying to find a way out of their problems and always blaming it on the other guy. You know you make life what it is and you do what you do. No one else makes you do things, not unless you're at gunpoint, and then they make you do something and then you do it. But no one has made me do anything but me, or anyone else I know do anything but themselves. I'm sure I had a lot of influences so we gotta talk about that.

So let's understand the facts. This has helped me you know, it has helped tremendously just to know myself a little better, and I gotta know myself completely. I wanna to die as a whole person, and this is the beginning. We have been dealing with age's 6-7, and now we're going to continue with 8, 9, 10, 11(, and then the tragedy of my grandmother's death was when I was 12 years old.

It seems now that as I'm trying to write this book, it's in my brain day and night, 24 hours a day. The next section will bring us up to when my life changed completely with the death of my grandmother.

15

Religion

As I got older, the family put me in the "Sea-Bees". Oh, I hada be like my dad, and they were going to make me a sailor, only I couldn't swim. I still can't swim, and I'm terrified of water. I won't even sit in a tub of water because I'm afraid I will drown. It is an incredible fear. In the past few years I have gotten to the point where I will walk around in water occasionally. Anyway, them putting me in the Sea-bees didn't work, because I could not get my laces sewed up right, those darn things had a million holes. So I was thrown out of the Sea-Bees, and that took care of the sailor business.

So now we're going to go into eight, nine, ten and eleven. I was a little fat butt. I got pictures of me in my sailor suit, just a little ole' chubby thing.

Vincent in Sea-Bees suit with Grandma Paula

Grandma, you and your tonic, God love ya. Anyhow, I spent my time, I remember Grandma calling, "Vinzie!" and everybody in the neighborhood, and the next block would yell, "Vinnie, your grandmother's calling you. Go home." So you see I was out all over the city, all over the town, gettin' involved in this, and involved in that, just becoming a boy who stood one step ahead of everybody. I knew who the bad kids were, and I knew the good kids, and the wimpy kids. I knew all kinds of kids. And you know, it's funny, reader, if we can just simplify this whole garbage bag load here about this story. If you will just be nice to the people around you and do the things you do, as long as you don't offend anyone around you. We need to let each other in to each other's life, accept each other regardless of race, creed, color, and all that bunk, and just let live and let be without hurting one another. It is so important for all of us to be accepted, I don't know why. It was an obsession with me. Now, however you could kiss my fat Italian butt, I could care less, but it still hurts. Love one another, be kind to one another, don't be so judgmental and be so down on everyone with, "I am better than you." You know, when you tell people or you put someone down or make fun of them, you're telling the whole world, "I'm better than him." I think the simple answer is find out who your God is, learn about him, love him first, and then from there, love your neighbor as yourself. Boy, that's an order, huh? We all say, God's rules are simple, they are, but they are deep. And if you're going to love your neighbor as yourself, you know, there's no merit in doing nice things for the people we like. I mean, what kind of merit are we gonna get from that. We have to do things for the people we do not like, people who threaten us, people who frighten us, and the people who we are intimidated by.

I'm going to tell you a story about a woman, here at my older age (yrs?), who spent twelve years intimidating me, just like another woman, when I was a child intimidated me, and then one day I decided, "You're history, Bitch." There goes that vulgarity, I am not sure why it happens, but it is part of my story, I guess it's a feeling.

So, we're going to go on to tell you about that part of my life when I was just seeking and following and doing all of these crazy things. I do know that I spent a lot of time around St. Joseph's Church learning about the Saints and God.

Now I have to explain to you people about the Italian Catholic older generation of people. First of all, we were all raised to love, adore, and worship God, in the person of God the Father, God the Son, and God the Holy Spirit. This is a gift, and we're not going to sit here and become too theologically involved. It is a gift, and I am grateful for that gift. Many say, "You worship the Virgin Mary because you have a little reminder, with the statue of the Virgin Mary," and, "Oh, you Catholics talk to the Saints and pray and worship the Saints because you have statues and pictures." Well, I say these people are ignorant, not to hurt anybody's feelings. We pray through the Saints, and through the Holy Mother of God.

I do not believe there is anyone out here, in reader's land, currently reading this book, that didn't go through their mother to get to their father or vice versa or even used one of your friends to help try and influence your parents to let you go here or go there and do this and do that. So, any of you that say we go straight to God, God bless you, so do those of the catholic faith, we just have other little tools we use. We have experienced holy people who have died and become canonized Saints we are told that we can pray through them. Let me tell you, I've done it, it has worked. I don't know that if I didn't go straight to God, the same thing wouldn't have happened. He is the one that allows this to take place regardless of whom you go through. But I think that what God really wants is the innocence of soul, of mind and sincerity towards him, so it makes no difference who you go through as far as I'm concerned, we get it done. And sometimes because of our sins, we are a little ashamed to go to God. I think that is healthy, to love God that much.

So I gotta make it clear these Italian ladies throwing kisses to pictures of the Virgins and the Saints, praying through them and asking them to talk to God were all holy and sincere. You know, it's rather comical, and not to make fun of it, but oh, mercy Jesus, these ladies become so emotional, and it's quite a thing to watch. These old gals just, "Lord this, Lord that, and Lord the other". And the feasts were not just a big party; there was a church service; honoring the Saint that protects the parish and the people of the parish. Walking the statue in the street had really nothing to do with money, or with maga maga. It was just simply our expression of faith and loyalty and allegiance to the stepfather of Jesus or to the Virgin Mother, of Jesus or to one the Saints who have weathered their love for God. It was all holy and sincere, and still is. That's the way we want to let you understand that these feasts even though they were fun-filled and had lots parties and firecrackers and these little pinwheels you would hold in your hand and you'd blow on it and it would spin in a little circle, you know. Just all the little, material things. However, the relationship with one soul with one God, with one soul with his God, is for God to judge, not you or I. And in no way do I want this book to portray to you that I am opinionated. I make comments because things were because it was at that time and because of what I think has taken place to destroy or hinder a person's growth.

You're gonna find it was the greatest form of ammunition, and the greatest strength that I had. The fact I was rejected or felt no love by my father, and now you know you find out that the only person you really wanted to love you is God. When you want everybody else and their grandmother's love and you put God before them, and that's heavy. Some of you will find that to be foolish, but I hate to tell you, reader, that is the way it is.

I'm going to take pause now and hold off for a while. I have gotta get something substantial, and I'm really avoiding hitting twelve years old. This is what I'm doing; I've been trying to avoid that part of my life. The one I'm going to have to face directly. (Listen to the pretty clock. Now you're gonna hear it.) Talking about the chimes as we spoke about earlier, I always knew what time it was because of the church bells. (There goes the other clock.)

Let me tell you all day long on the hour, the bells would ring ten o'clock, ten times, eleven o'clock eleven times, twelve o'clock, twelve times … but after 10:00 p.m. at night, you got one for the hour and two for the half hour. It seems strange. Like it should be two for the hour, but the bells went on continuously, and it became a form of life.

The smell of sauerkraut, the church bells ringing, and then we had these air-raid drills, talk about nightmares, now, I'm recalling. Occasionally the air-raid sirens would go off, you know, loud as it could be, and everybody would go flying in the house, and they'd start saying their rosaries. They'd get on their knees and oh, man, the traumas, but they all worked out.

(Let's pause for a few minutes more here)

Okay, let's talk about ten, eleven and twelve years old. Let's just say, because I don't remember exact dates, that during the age of ten and eleven I was a pretty big boy for my age. I would spend time with my Aunt Mary Ann and all the girls were teenagers, some of them were married and having babies and what have you. I remember we'd get on the bus to go further down Wilson Avenue to visit with Aunt Mary and her family and Aunt Mary Ann. Italians ate a lot of fish as well, you know, squid, octopus, all those disgusting things that everybody peers at now, (and I have a freezer full of octopus). I called Marie to ask her how to cook it, because I had forgotten what to do so it's still in there with the squid. But anyhow, Aunt Mary made oyster stew from heaven. Everybody couldn't wait to come home Friday night and eat Aunt Mary's oyster stew. So I remember her making oyster stew and taking me through the house and playing with me and she would say, "I want you to be a good boy, Vincent, we love you so much." Oh, she was certainly a saint, indeed. I never heard Aunt Mary say a bad word or talk bad about anyone or what have you.

Now, we're going to come up to about eleven years old, and I understand that my Aunt Mary, *(cuckoo, cuckoo clock, oh, tell you, think I'm going to have to pause all these interruptions, but I don't know how we're going to come up in this book [with] the tone of the cuckoo clock, and all these watches and stuff; we'll get somebody to do that.)*

lived on Wilson Avenue and of course we lived on the other end of Wilson Avenue, but it was a considerable walk so we would ride the trolley car actually. Oh, those trolley cars! As kids we'd get on the back of the trolley car and pull the electricity thing off, and then the trolley car would stop and we'd run and just about get hit by cars, and oh, boy. Actually, I did it once and that was enough, but it was adventurous to stop the trolley car. Bad kids we were. Anyway, we would ride the trolley car from our house on Wilson Avenue to Aunt Mary's house at the other end of Wilson Avenue. They had moved into a better environment, a bigger home. Aunt Mary used to live on Star Street which was right around the corner from me, but I was told that I don't actually remember it.

16

Death and Despair

Unfortunately in March of 1953, my aunt Mary passed on with leukemia, and I had related to my cousin Rosalie that I did not recall this funeral. She told me that Marie my cousin Marie took care of all the children, and so that was certainly a sad day. And in November of that same year, actually in August of that same year, 1953, my cousin Rosalie lost her two twin children, and then in November, my grandmother Paula was placed in the hospital. I thought it was a brain tumor, but my cousin Rosalie seems to think it was blood in her kidneys. She had kidney problems, and of course I recall when we talked about going to St. Anthony. She came home and was at the funeral and she had lost her daughter, you know how devastating that had to be. The older children recall her saying to our Lord as all mothers do, "Why not me, Lord, why my child?" You know to see a mother lose her child has to be one of the most incredible pains. It doesn't take too much calculating to know the pain it causes a mother. Christ right there on the cross, his mother saw him die, probably even worse. And that is what we are spared; we know not when the lion will come, but the Virgin Mary knew exactly when Jesus was to die for our sins, and that's just a reflection. But anyway, in August my cousin Rosalie lost her two first born children, and at the same time in November, her sister Pauline, at this time Pauline, had lost her baby just as grandmother was placed back in the hospital. Of course then my grandmother passed away. You see in September I became twelve years old and in November my grandmother passed away. I'll try to tell you what I can remember about when grandmother passed away. I had to ride the bus or the trolley car (they had both) down from PS-53 which was around the vicinity of 106 Wilson Avenue, way past 415 Wilson Avenue almost all the way to Cornelia Street. I would get off the bus and then I'd turn right and then the street to the left was where we were.

The third or fourth house was my godmother Aunt Mary Ann's at that time. Mary Ann and I came in after school, and for some reason, I had the giggles and

I saw all these people walking around, and then I saw the man from the Funeral Parlor. I knew that man, because I used to see him all the time. I didn't want to think of anything, so I went in the living room and put on the cartoons and I was giggling and carrying on. And then my very tasteful and tactful, Pauline, Marie's sister, just walks in (what a shit, she was, and she still is a shit), but I love her, but she turned around and said, "Well you're not going to be laughing after I tell you Grandma just died."

Well, it didn't hit me. I was still giggling like a fool. And then wham, it hit me and I fell apart, my whole world ... I could just see this gloom of doom, and I couldn't find Marie. My godmother was crying and carrying on; they were making the funeral arrangements. To see that tiny, white-haired sweet lady lying there in the coffin devastated me.

(The only other time in my life that I've suffered such pain and sorrow was only recently when this little animal, Shamus, my little dog of 13 years—14 years—passed away. That got me. We'll talk about that later)

Anyhow, I wanted to throw myself in the ground when I saw the coffin going down and all I could say was, "Grandma, Grandma come back and forgive me, I'll be good". All that silly stuff and the people, it was just a great loss. And then I was yelling at my father, blaming him. At this time, he had a new wife and I hated my father, so I blamed him. I said, "You didn't love your mother, you didn't respect her, you didn't provide." And the poor man about beat the hell out of me and almost killed me. My father was very good at beating me. He'd slap me and pull me and say, "You're a sissy," and "You're just worthless," and "Why do you always get in trouble?" He was just horrible but God love him. I was so terrified of my father.

Next we will get on with my life and me growing ever older....

17

After Grandmother

Anyway, Grandmother was now buried. Some of her children had already gone to her tenement house and wiped the place out. My dad took me by the hand to her house and I remember he wanted to know where this and that and the other were. I didn't know what he was talking about back then, but I recall when Grandmother would take me to her bedroom she would open this tin box and tell me, "When I go to God and when you grow up, there are enough funds …". And she had these beautiful rings, you know, a beautiful purple amethyst, and this was supposed to be mine. Well, it seems everything disappeared, and then one day a little later on, my Aunt May's daughter, Francis, had that ring on and then I understood. It seemed to happen, treachery of that kind in my family. Before the blood was drained from your body, your children were at your home and they would rip you off. It's who comes first gets it all, so when my father arrived, he couldn't find anything. We saw one of my aunts coming out of the window. I guess they all had an argument, and then they left. But there they left me, with my father, and in his frustration he called me sorry and started to beat the hades outa me, so I took a kitchen chair and busted it over his head and ran. Well, you know, you don't start anything you can't finish. He finally got me, and continued to beat me. All of a sudden I found myself living with this uncle or this aunt, all over the place. I went to live with Seia Maria, because my father and his new wife put me with this old lady who had Saint Vitas' dance, and couldn't see straight. That hada be the most selfish, cruel thing for them to do. While I was there, I'd have to go down into the cellar of her house and bring up coal buckets full of coal, and then there were the nightmares about this darkened cellar. I don't know why. They'd throw me in the cellar, you know, to shut me up. I wanted to live with my godmother my Aunt Mary Ann, who was the toughest member of our family. A very matter-of-fact and this is what you do type of woman, and oh, I loved her with my heart and soul. She would protect, love and coddle me, but yet want me to go out and get some experience under my butt you know and act and carry on the right way. I know for a fact she took my father to court for support, and of course what ended up happening was we rode the bus home and she came away from the court with no support. My Aunt Mary Ann was crying and saying, "I really don't want to put this child in this orphanage ...," but that was what had to happen.

Finally my father's hand was called, and they made me go live with him on Green Street. Let me tell you, I spent my life in the parlor, and slept on the floor. I wasn't allowed to come home right after school, instead, after school I went to the movie theater close to Green Street. Then I would walk seven long frightening city blocks to get home, and it would be between 11:00—11:30 at night.

It didn't matter rain, snow, wind or hail and then when I'd get to the house, she'd let me in and throw me back to the living room. If I was wet, she'd beat the hell outa me because I was wet. But she did feed me well. She'd bring me my food and I'd eat it there on this little round coffee table on the floor. When I was done, she'd pick it up make me go pee and wash my face and then she sent me to bed on the floor. And this went on for quite a period of time. I remember my half-brother he was a little red-headed kid. He was not allowed to talk to me, and when I was lying in the living room on the floor which was cold ... oh I remember the cold ... I could see this child in his comfortable bed. Even though he wasn't suppose to talk to me, he'd get up and come and hug me and say he loved me and then go back to bed and go to sleep. One night he wanted me to sneak in and get into the bed with him so I'd have something comfortable. Imagine a little boy feeling these things. But I wouldn't think of it. I said "that ... lady will kill you".

This type of treatment went on for a long, long, time. You know, I never saw my father the whole time I lived with him. However I recall one night I hada pee, I hada go to the bathroom really bad, and so I got up and said, "May I have permission to pass your room?" Remember the streamline of those houses; so I had to pass their room to go to the bathroom. They said, "No, wait a minute." Well, I waited for more than a minute and then couldn't wait a minute longer. So I went through the bedroom, and there they were, having their little time in the bed. I went and used the bathroom and then got out. When I came out, she grabbed me and beat the pure poop outa me.

Then on Saturdays I remember they couldn't get rid of me—she couldn't get rid of me—and I'd have to be there. One day I took a shower on a Saturday, even though my father was supposed to come and bathe me and all of that, but I did it. Afterward, I made the comment that most Italians do when they feel refreshed, "veviel audrta," it just makes my heart feel good. I really felt good, I was clean.

My stepmother's, mother, lived in the house with her husband, Frank and Grandma Ma Inposstatto, was their name I don't remember this grandma's first name. But I remember she severely reprimanded her daughter and told her it was the work of the devil. Her beating on me like that, how could she beat an innocent, small child? One time her daughter beat me until I was bleeding. Her mother had to bathe me in oils and love me and ah, what a sainted lady. I had the opportunity not long ago to visit with her, and for some reason my half-sister got angry with me for some stupid reason. But I can also recall there on Wheelfield Street, actually just two doors down from my Aunt Mae and Uncle Sal I lived with my father only two doors away. I don't quite know how we moved from Green Street to Wheelfield Street, but I do remember I was still living with them. I remember my father was on an outside screened porch drawing one day, you see, my father was a wonderful artist, he drew some beautiful things, but he never shared any of that with me. My stepmother was there pulling his hair out of his head with both of her hands, and it was then and there I began to get the impression my father wasn't very much of a man with women. I know this woman abused him because of me. Now I want to let you know why I believe my stepmother was like she was. I believe it was because I was a product of his first marriage, with one of the most beautiful and stately women in the whole city of Brooklyn actually. I know this caused a hate and resentment because of what had taken place, and back then things like this was always taken out on the child. She couldn't beat up my mother, he couldn't beat up my mother and they couldn't beat up each other, so they would beat the hell out of me, almost brutally and almost to the point of death. But on this day he was the one getting abused and getting his hair pulled.

One day I remember he hit me so bad I was black and blue and it felt as if he almost knocked me cross-eyed, because my eye was swollen shut. I ran from Wheelfieid Street and got on the bus which ended up at Knickerbocker Park where I would go and play. It couldn't have been four blocks away from Wiloby Street off of Wilson Avenue where my uncle Nick and his bride my godmother, Aunt Rosie lived.

Aunt Rosie, Vinnie and Uncle Nick

Their two children, her sister and her mother all lived in this tenement house which occupied the whole entire house. There were times when I would run to the park and there would be my Aunt Rosie, and I would just fly to that park bench and hug her and cry. She would look at me and say, "Who did this to you?" When I told her, she immediately got her baby carriage, and her children, and we went off up two streets to Wiloby Avenue. At Aunt Rosie's house she took care of my wounds and then called my Aunt Mary Ann and they came over. I was so afraid of my father that if the doorbell would ring, I would fall apart. If I heard footsteps I would think they were his, and I'd run and hide in the cellar. Funny with my fear, the cellar became my refuge.

When I went down there into the cellar, I would run and hide between the walls where even my own aunts and uncles couldn't find me. And only when they could assure me it was not my father, would I come out. But it seems I always had the fear that this man was gonna appear.

18

Running to Refuge

I think what we're going to do now is to go with each of the uncles and aunts I've spent some time with; an trying to recall my life with them and the experiences with them, and it's really interesting. Shamus hears this tape playing back and he looks at the tape, and he looks at me and he can't understand what's going on. So this little fellow is sitting right here on the couch next to his daddy, and we're going to start. First we gotta get into the home because the experiences with the uncles and aunts; were after and a couple before, so we're going to figure who was before, who was during, and who was after, but we're gonna talk about the children's home and adjusting.

So there we were I had run away from all the misery at home, to my Aunt Rosie's who would let me stay there a few days. And of course there was no room; literally, there was no room so I would go to my aunt Mary Ann's. Then Cousin Marie would come and take me and I would live with her in the apartment upstairs, it had two rooms. I started to heal, and feel all this love from my cousin Marie and from my godmother, Maryann. Those are the recollections I have at the age of twelve of experiences I had with my father. It seemed as though he couldn't find anywhere to put me, where I could stay and behave, because I just wanted to stay with Marie. Soon though with welfare she hada get a court order for me to stay. I remember he came storming into my Aunt Mary Ann's house. I mean he came flying through her front door to come get me, to kill me if he could. She said, "if you lay one hand on him, you will die. Here is a court order...." Which once again, I didn't know what all this meant. She told him, "You cannot touch this child, you cannot come near this child, and if you do, you're gonna be hung from a hook." Well, after this my father was full of a lot of animosity and a lot of violence and something happened to him. I'm sure if you are the first born in your family, you will know as the first born of the family, you have to grow up to be the man. This means you take out the garbage, and do all the other stuff because you have to set the example for the other siblings. Oh, hogwash. Anyway, I don't know what happened with my father, it seems he just couldn't stand me. You know, one day I asked him, "Why don't you just shoot me, blow my brains out, then you don't gotta worry about it", and you know me saying that didn't phase him one bit. I think if he'd had a gun, he probably would have taken me up on the offer. But as I was coming into my own this was what was taking place. All of my uncles and aunts had the good heart to try and make me a part of their lives. I know they struggled to feed their children, buy their clothes, but they were good to me. My Aunt Rose let me tell ya, my Aunt Rosie, she became like my mom, you know, and I loved her dearly. She was a lady, the whole time I knew her. She never owned any living room furniture because she always budgeted the money. She raised her children and was good and took care of me, and my uncle Nick was just the apple of my eye, you know. He tried so hard to be like a dad that he became dad to me. One day I asked him for permission to call him dad, because I never had any problem calling him dad and hugging him.

Now we're at the point, in my life where I lived with my aunt Mary Ann, and for a little time with my Aunt Mamie and some other times with my uncle Nick and Aunt Rose. But I mostly remember I stayed with my Aunt Mary Ann

My cousin Marie I remember worked as a secretary or maybe it was a stenographer in a doctor's office there on Euclid Avenue. Another big deal street because every day I'd run there and she'd take me to lunch, then I'd come back and meet her when she would get off work. Once a week she got a paycheck, and you know, after she separated all her money to support the house and this and that, she'd say, "Come on, Vinnie, we're gonna go shopping." She'd buy me coloring books, planes, guns and all sorts of toys, then we'd go to the movies, go out to eat and then we would come home. When her date would come, she'd take me with them. Let me tell ya, my cousin Maria was something, what a girl. She's still alive, and she's still a character, I love her. As a child, I loved her more so; than anyone could ever know.

In the house there was Anthony and Pauline and well Pauline, she was just mean. "That damn Vinnie," It seems I was more trouble to her. I remember when they used to smoke it was a big deal back then. You know you just didn't smoke, but Pauline would throw powder all over the house before my godmother would come home. My godmother would act oblivious like she didn't know it, but I know she did. Oh and Pauline was so slack, she wouldn't wash windows she wouldn't do anything. She was a real little bitch. Pauline was just like her mother in attitude, daring, defying, going out with boys, and you know, just kicking ass. All of the girls were jealous of her she was and still is a beautiful girl, just a tough butt. I think that if only she would have "buddied" up with me a little bit, some of it would have rubbed off, you know. But anyhow, that was Pauline and I hated her, hated her, hated her, and she probably hated me. I can remember her scratching me with her fingernails and her slapping, but she would probably say, "No such thing," but you know, a child remembers. So now comes one of the times when my godmother was working as a sewer on a machine all day. She would come home and then work for a company called the Fuller Brush Company, going door to door, just so she could make ends meet and raise these kids and provide for Vincent.

Nick & Cousin Pauline

19

Off to St. John's in Rockaway

Well, I hear them talking in Italian, and she could, no longer physically support everyone. Little did any of these people know that all they hada do was give me a place to sleep and a few crumbs of bread, and I'd a gone on with the rest of it.

You see during all of this time in my personal self, I was making friends with every kid in the neighborhood, every gangster, they all loved me. All the kids loved me, and after a while I went from "sissy" to "Vinnie" and then I became respected. As a matter of fact until this day and probably until I die, the people closest to my soul and my heart have always been the strangers, the non-blood, the person in the street, across the street, the neighbor, you know, the stranger.

Now as they say, we're coming to the moment of doom. When they took me to the St. John's Home for Boys in Rockaway Park, New York. We were on the bus and my Aunt Maryann was just crying, with my little box of clothing and possessions, and they took me to Rockaway Park, New York. From St John's Home you could hear the roar of the ocean, it was a wonderful establishment, run by Marionist priests and brothers, and the sons of Mary this order was called and they dealt with educating poor children. You came through this little gate in the picket fence, and then walked down the aisle and into the bungalow. There was Brother August Kemmon a big gentleman who reminded me of Alfred Hitchcock. But what a simple, wonderful soul he was, but a strong taskmaster.

Then I was taken to my dormitory. Well, I cried and I cried and I cried, and Brother August said to me, "Vincent, don't cry, you're gonna love it here. It'll take a few days for you to adjust. If you cry, the boys are gonna call you 'sissy.' And I think I remember saying to him, "Well, what's new?"

Again I have to clarify, as I'm rehearing all of my blabs here. I need to talk about my aunt Mary Ann, in her home on Cornelia Street, which was a beautiful home, the bottom floor was a big living room and a big dining room and the big kitchen and a bathroom off of the kitchen. Then at one time they added on, so Anthony could have his own quarters. When you went up the stairway there was an apartment that she rented to this lady named Agnes who was quite a nice girl, and then my cousin Marie also lived upstairs, it was two rooms, a bedroom and a guest room or a living room, or whatever, but everybody slept everywhere. There was this little pretty Pomeranian named Tiny. And Tiny and the big ole cat would come and be my friends. So I guess in clarifying, Maryann was my god-mother but she was also my Aunt, and in her home were her three children, Maria, Pauline and Anthony. Of course Anthony worked at the grocery store and saved himself enough money to buy him a new car, you know being a typical male, he was a handsome fellow, and always had all the girls. I mean he had some gorgeous women. (*Excuse me, the telephone.*) Anyhow, Anthony was a typical 19-year old to 21-year old who was in the service. In those days because of the First World War and the Second World War, which my Grandmother Paula had been raised through both of these wars, I guess the sirens would freak out the older people. My father was in the war, along with my uncle Nicholas, and my cousin Anthony, who went into the army as a paratrooper. He was in the great big para-trooper battalion I think it was the 23rd or 93rd platoon. I mean this guy was truly a man's man. You know he parachuted and all, but I recall that cousin Anthony was gone for along period of time, and you could see the sorrow. It was, "I didn't get a letter from my son," or "I got a letter from my son." One day my godmother came home from work and Cousin Anthony was there and everyone said, "if you say a word we will cut your tongue out, you're not gonna blow this for us."

Aunt Maryann was in the kitchen and here comes dumb butt Anthony, like an idiot, she didn't even know he was home, he laid on the floor in the living room to surprise her, but how stupid can you be to scare your mother like that, and as she came out of the kitchen, there was this ass on the floor in his uniform. But landsakes, the party we had, like the prodigal son coming home. Let me tell you this lady partied for a month, she loved her son Anthony. My cousin Marie gave me a lot of attention and affection, because Marie was such a good-hearted girl. The other, Anthony and Pauline, I didn't get along with them, so they kind of gave Marie a bad time. But now Marie I think was the oldest and you didn't pull no crap with her. She'd slap the crap outta both her brother and sister. She didn't wanna hear no crap. So anyway, all these kids now we're going to see what a sad thing that our family is one of evil, vindictiveness, hate and treachery. How sad, how sad that God could bless a group of people as a family and they grow apart with the hate.

You know maybe I'm really glad that perhaps I didn't have to go through all this stuff. For a long time, I wanted to know why my father didn't love me, why I didn't get to keep my mom and my dad you know and then I found out, and you're gonna be surprised at that. But please be patient as I'm jumping around a bit.

20

A Pause in Time

Unfortunately when you're writing a book, things start coming into your head. And you know some other things they won't come to me until I'm talking for some strange reason. So to those of you I am sharing this privilege with to listen to my babbling, just be patient. However I'm gonna stop for now as it's about 12 o'clock, on Monday, Shamus is in the back resting, and I've got to pay him some attention. I gotta get ready to go teach the cha-cha and the rumba and the mambo, and all those other dances. When I get back I will continue with the Children's' Home, St. John's for Boys, Rockaway Park, Vincent, that's a wonderful experience. Anyway I gotta think about it and remember what took place. I have several things outstanding right now in my mind, and I'll share them with you when I rerun this tape again and see what other corrections need to made.

Those of you in the carpentry business know the work horses are made of wood and have nothing to do with the animal. Correction number two: I'm living here in this apartment (there goes Shamus) going on 13 years, (oh, hush). I'm going to have to take this thing around with me it looks like all day because everything I recalled, I have now forgotten, so I'm gonna have to recall it all again.

21

The Brothers

They just threw me in line with all the other kids and they all looked at me up and down, and in and out, and over and under. Some would come and pinch ya in the butt and some hit ya in the head just to see what you could take. But I remember several characters, a Brother Norbet, a Brother Richard Duffey, a Brother Ed Carey, a Brother Charles Luttenburger—that man is a saint—and a Brother Matthew Betts who won my soul to God. So we're going to talk about these gentlemen, who were my teachers, my counselors, my house parents. And then the nuns from Germany and the little lady that worked in the laundry room (*cuckoos, I'm telling you what, one day I'm gonna pull a plug on all these cuckoos*).

You know the cuckoo clock stems back from my very beginning when Grandma had her cuckoo clock in her kitchen and I remember she said it was going to be mine, and then it got in the hands of my godmother, Maryann. It seems all of my child possessions, they disappeared, too. I didn't have pictures of anything or anyone and I hada go beg and borrow them, and then nobody gave me what I wanted anyway. Eventually I had to hijack some of the pictures that you will see throughout this book, from my cousin Marie, so to her I say 'thanks cuz'. And so that's the kind of lifestyle it was, you know.

So the cuckoo clock disappeared, but I went and bought one and it just cuckoos itself to death, it seems I've had this thing forever. So I go in and out with these thoughts. I'm going to have to work on my enunciation and my pronunciation and my diction and speak rather correctly, so that those who are editing my book will not have such a hard time. I'm learning so many things about myself speaking to a pocket recorder. Anyhow, we're going to go have our dinner and we're fortunate tonight to eat a steak. Shamus is going to eat his biscuits. I don't give him people food and it breaks my heart, but he's going to live to be old, I hope.

Let me take a little pause, collect my thoughts, and I'll come right back.

I wanted to add that Father Joseph, God rest his soul, was a gentleman priest who boxed my ears, and managed to get me straight then told me things. Sometimes I think these holy men of God know the future. In fact, I know Father Joseph was the main influence at the Children's Home. Where I became confirmed as a Catholic however not too good of one in my confirmation. I'm not currently living my practice of Catholicism. However, that's my problem, I suppose, and God's. While at the Children's Home I also want to talk about boys like Kelly and William, who even though we shared the same last name, he was not related to me. And then there was J. P., we used to call him Elvis, and Freddie and Mark. Mark, he was the bully of bullies, and Kenneth, and a little boy named Pepper, (*boy everything's just pouring in. I don't guess I'm gonna pause. But these were people who made striking impressions on me as a child*). Then there was Arthur and his brother. Mr. Lacarta who would come and feed all the kids every Saturday, God bless him also and Sister DePaul, who was a beautiful, beautiful Sister, and Father LaFazzio. Actually, he was Brother LaFazzio. (*Bloody blessed, what a pretty clock sound that is.*) Okay, and there was Brother Samuel. All of these people who were major influences on molding this young but rather wild boy. But I have to admit, when I got into the home, I was rather calm, compared to some of these youngsters. Let me tell ya, these brothers knew how to train boys and make them into men. There was Brother Frank who was in the theater part of school, and didn't like me very much, and I didn't like him either, you know.

22

My Musical Side

I remember of a group of boys called the "Four Peanuts" who were a barbershop quartet. I played in the band, and we used to do the summer shows outside, so now we will talk about the band, me and my clarinet. Can you believe that? And then I learned, thanks to Brother Charles, who taught me the piano. The only problem is, I wouldn't get off the John Thompson book, Grade A, one and two, a and b, all numbers, and land sakes when one finger hada cross to another number, I was in trouble. So there I was a cheater, but I could play my numbers real well. I'll never forget that, and a clarinet. Can you believe `ole Mirabell' playing a clarinet, and I was pretty good, pretty good at the clarinet. *I think I had taken my clarinet out of the closet one-day recently; I couldn't even blow through it. I can't even breathe, let alone blow on a clarinet.* And it was the St. John's Home for Boys Band, Rockaway Park, New York, and we went all over. The St. Patrick's Day Parade we played in, and almost every parade there was. There we were in our red jackets, and our gold bands and our high hats and let me tell you what, I would play the clarinet and squeak. (*Laughter and we're coughing way too many cigarettes.*) We were treated quite well at St. John's . You know, we all acted like poor little orphans, but let me tell ya, those children who are orphaned get more than any child with a family in any environment. Or at least it seemed we had everything. There were so many charities who donated toys and education equipment. And we would go on this trip and that trip and let me tell you, talk about being spoiled rotten. However you know God gives back what man takes away, double fold, and still deep down inside you didn't have your mother and father and someone to cling to and love you and build a life and a relationship with. So what does God do? He gives you many brothers and sisters and uncles and aunts and cousins and you know the song, "Cousins By The Dozens," and so as a child although it was treacherous, now I begin to form some sort of intelligence. (*Laughter*) Now scholastically the intelligence sucks. Brother Matthew S.M. used to spend each summer, two, three hours in the morning taking his time to try and teach me mathematics. Well, let me tell you, one day he said, "Vincent, I have become a failure. You don't understand mathematics, and you probably never will." So I was good at history, and a little bit better at English. But actually, I have copies of my report cards, and I usually tease my dance students and tell them they get a red "F." *Boy, my report cards were "F, F, F, F, and F minus."* *(Laughter)* Can you believe it, "F minus," I mean I was a mess, and then when it came to conduct that was a "U", so I guess I was probably something to deal with.

I know I was restless in the Home, and the kids you know carry on and beat you up. I was always getting beat up, but I always got back at them, you know. Let me tell you about this one occasion after I had been there for a while and about Mark, who was the big time bully. Every Friday, we would all get a quarter, and after dinner, all the boys would go into the recreation room and Brother Duffey or Brother Ed would go to the library and bring back two big reels of movies. I mean we'd have movies from 7:30 to 11:30 pm you know, full-feature theater movies. Then we'd all take our quarter and march down to the canteen. Now for a quarter, you could buy anything and everything so the kids would go in and double up on ice cream, popcorn, potato chips and soda pops and then off we'd go to the recreation room, and watch the movie. Generally speaking, I never would go to see the movies. There I was again, being alone but not totally, because Brother Charles would take me down to the band room and teach me how to play the piano, which I really enjoyed. And he would try to talk with me, you know, he was just a wonderful fine, fine man. Eventually he trusted me to go into the band room and play the piano on my own. But to make this story a little shorter, one Friday they played a movie called, "The Day the Earth Stood Still," and it was the first movie I remember I had seen with my cousin Maria and my cousin Roco in the movie theater. I remember jumping up and yelling, "Say the word, say the word!" and Marie just sank in her seat. Well, when I heard about this movie now at the Children's Home, I wanted to see it. I knew it was going to bring back memories of my cousin Marie and my cousin Roco, so I took my little quarter, and then here is Mark. Now, let me tell ya, you didn't say 'no' to this boy, he said, "I want your quarter, Mary." (Now they were calling me Mary), and I said, "No, you're not gonna get my quarter. "Well, everybody else in the canteen just fell out, and you could of heard a pin drop, it got so quiet. "Is this Vincent crazy, he's telling Mark, 'no.'" And I said, "No." Then he tried to take the quarter out of my hand, and he started hitting on me and I said, "Ouch, don't hit me, don't hit me," and I was getting all meek. Well, anyway, he slapped the pure pee outta me, and knocked me down on the floor.

You know sometimes in a fraction of a second, you see the light it seems and as I looked up, I saw blood all over my face, and something said to me, "No, no, no, and no!" Let me tell you, I jumped at Mark like a rat on a cat, and I beat the pure potatoes outta him. I cracked three of his ribs, busted his nose and gave him a black eye. I beat him so bad, they hada take him to the infirmary, first the hospital and recuperation in the infirmary. There he was with a broken leg, a broken arm, three broken ribs, and a busted nose, no fabrication intended. It seems I saw green and then green turned to red, and well, I just destroyed him. Well, I said to myself, "Yeah, Vinnie!" Now I was even nice. How nice was I? Well, I didn't wanna hurt no one, I didn't even wanna fight, I didn't want that. So, I went to the infirmary, and here's this kid in traction, and I come up to apologize and to be a gentleman about it, and what do you thin he says to me, "I'm gonna get you when I get outta here." So I then walked over to the other side of the infirmary and brought him a mirror, and said, "Look at yourself in this mirror, and tell me how can you be so stupid as to tell me when you get out, you're going to get me?" I said, "Now look at yourself." Then I said, "I'll tell ya what, how about I just kill ya now." And then, oh, he started crying, "No, no, no!" So I said to him, "Well then don't act like a dumb butt." And he said to me, "Well you humiliated me." So I told him, "I'm gonna kick your butt every time you walk down the street and pass my face when you get better." After that I never had another problem with Mark, even though he terrorized every one of those boys in that children's home. I just wasn't gonna have any of it. So from "sissy" to "Mary" to "kickbutt", is what happened on that occasion. Now, as I lived at the Children's Home, they had a lot of activities for the young fellows. I recall every summer we were allowed to go and walk on the boardwalk and we were allowed to go swim in the ocean and mix and mingle with the other kids. The Home was on 111 Th Street, and Rockaway Park Playland was on 116th Street. The church would have a raffle you know, where you buy chances for a quarter, and you could win a car. And the boys who would sell the most books at the end of the summer got a prize. Well let me tell ya, I would sell an sell. I'll tell you what, that's how I learned to communicate with people and I used to talk people into buying from a quarter's worth to a whole book of tickets which a whole book was $5.00. But then I would go to Rockaway Playland, and ride the rides and spend all the money. So, it never did work, and then I hada go beggin' and borrowing to replace that $5.00. I only did that the one time.

The brothers were teaching us responsibility, and I'll tell you, it was a lot of work and a lot of fun. Brother Edward, when we got to his dormitory at night, would make us run on the beach all the way to Rockaway Playland and sometimes they would open up Playland for just the Children's Home kids and we'd go on all the rides and all of us would have hot-dogs, you know. So in a way, we were very blessed youngsters.

The boys at the Home always seemed to have the best equipment for sports. I mean St. John's Home for Boys was big time. The Rockaway boys had the best ball team, best football team, best basketball team, and the best band. They were just big, big hard kids to beat. Boy every day it seemed somebody would get a package with goodies and cookies and candies. I never got any packages, but that's okay. I also remember that school was rather strict, but also that they were good people, and they turned out a lot of champions. A lot of men today who are retired, who were educated quite well at St. John's Home for Boys.

Now, we're gonna pause because something is trying to tell me what I wanna say, and I got to stop and listen, so let me play this again. It's a Tuesday morning, it's rather cool, today is April 15th, and Uncle Sam took all my money, and so did the state. Quarterly taxes. I have a wonderful accountant. She is just wonderful.

I just recalled we all were required to play sports. So, when we had our little team matches there at the home, of course, nobody would pick me in baseball. I was the world's worst player. Strike one, strike two, strike three, and then they'd say, "Let's give him another chance." Strike four. (*Laughter*) I was the pits at hitting the ball, however I could run, I remember they would put me in center field, because, maybe I couldn't hit a ball, but sure could catch it. But therein lies another problem, because once I caught it, I couldn't' throw it.

There is my neighbor, Gloria, and I'll tell you what, even when she whispers, the whole world can hear her. God bless her, she's got a pair of lungs. And her daughter, she'll screech and the whole world ... we could make her an alarm system. Anyway, they're good neighbors, good friends.

So, where were we, oh yes, I couldn't throw the ball but there was this one boy, one of the Four Peanuts now remember this is one of the four singers, a little pudgy thing. And this was another kid who would torment the heck outta me. He'd dart in and out of places and hit me, then run, call me "Mary," and this that, and the other. And he would aggravate the pure bananas outta me. Well, it was my turn and I hada get up to bat and I was bound and determined to hit a home run, and there was this one boy named William. He was an older boy and I wanted him to be like a brother so bad, I could taste it because we both had the same last name. Well, he would avoid me like the plague. I remember him being a very big and masculine older boy, one who also had a lot of pretty girlfriends. It seemed like all these guys had girlfriends, and they would go off the property. But I digress, I was up to bat and it was Mark who was such a good ball player. He was pitching to me, and he'd say, "Come on, Mary, and hit the ball." I hollered back, "I'm gonna hit ya in the face", but you know, that was just anger. However this time when I hit the ball, it streamlined right through and into his face, knocking out his teeth, but I made my home run. (*Laughter*)

When I think back, it looks like everything I hada do in my life I did because someone would put me against the corner; as they say. From that day on, when I was younger, you didn't tell me I couldn't do something, especially when I knew I was capable of doing it. Evidently I started to see that I was working real good whenever I was under pressure. Unfortunately as the years went on it was a shame, because there was no pleasure in anything I did. To this day there still isn't, as all I did and still do seems to be out of fear or survival, you understand.

Next, when they tried to put me into basketball, I don't remember a lot, but I did learn how to dribble pretty good before it was the end of basketball. So they required all these sports, which I loathed and detested, and I didn't want to go and do, but I went because I had no choice. You see back then you went when you were told. The one nice thing about St. John's Home was every Sunday morning we would all get dressed up and then go to the chapel and have mass first, then we would all go to church.

Three times a week you would get marched into the showers, where you would have to brush your teeth, and take a shower, and the Brothers would make sure you were cleaning all the right areas and learning your hygiene. I remember that Saturday nights, was one of the three nights so we could be nice and clean for mass and church in the morning. And life was as such, that we really wanted for nothing.

The Four Peanuts were four little fellows who used to sing barbershop quartet, and once I remember they were on television on a show called 'Name That Tune' and boy I'm telling you it was a thrill and delight to see them on television. Of course the band was in the audience and the Four Peanuts were on stage and they were going for the $25,000 prize. It was good for the children's home that they were on television. But let me tell you about this little quartet. These four boys went to states all over the country, and they certainly did sing some wonderful harmony and they were great little singers. And this was the story about the Four Peanuts, who it seemed went on forever and ever and made lots of money for their education and their future, and all they were; was basically good boys.

Then there was Jo Anne, I don't think I will ever forget her. She was from Wounded Knee, South Dakota, from a very poor Indian tribe. She was a princess in the tribe, and that made me so impressed with her, I just wanted to touch her. But there was this little old overweight boy, who would never let me get near her and talk to her, so one day I made my way through to her.

Somewhere along the way I became rather attached to Brother Charles, and I really admired Brother Carey; I remember I couldn't wait to get to his dormitory. When I think back, we all had dormitories which were broken down into the first, second, third and fourth divisions. You were a man when you reached the fourth division, and then you started to receive privileges. You could go here and there and everywhere.

Anyway the fourth division was run by Brother Norbet. Now let me tell you he was the sourest human being I think I ever had met. I don't know how he ever thought he had a calling to serve our Lord, but of course I'm being rude. It seems every time I saw this man he would give me a knuckle sandwich. One day he caught me up in the infirmary when I didn't have permission to go to the infirmary. You see, the infirmary was in another building, and directly across from the infirmary was where the sisters lived. There was a sister, Sister DePaul a young sister, who was very pretty. I used to think she was Sister Teresa, you know. And I would ring the doorbell where the sisters lived and they would let me come in. They had their little chapel, and sitting room and they were all very, very devoted holy ladies.

Now when I look back, I think Sister DePaul was a novice or coming out of the novitale and taking her simple vows, perhaps, and I would just sit and talk to Sister DePaul, and the other sisters would say, "You have to go back." One day Brother Norbet caught me coming out of the sister's quarters, and he just beat the 'he double hockey sticks' out of me until I was seeing stars. There was this flight of stairs and I couldn't get away from him, and he fell down the flight of stairs, but now when I think back, maybe I may have tripped him. Why? Because while Brother Norbet was beating on me, it was like I saw my father beating on me, and it was absolutely uncalled for; for this man to go around beating children, although it seems there is one in every crowd, and in every environment.

Anyway, that was the end of old Norbet, oh how I hated him and everybody else did, too I thought. I just don't know what his problem was; he was, and probably still is a very devoted, holy man of God, even today. You know as a child you don't understand why people do the things they do, you just remember what they did, and the impressions put onto a child are quite magnificent. He would walk down one side of the hall, and I'd walk down the other side of the hall all just to avoid this man.

I promise I'm gonna try not to cuss for the rest of my story, as I need to control that foolishness. You can't profess you love God, and then turn around and cuss like a scutbutt. I'm hearing a noise out here; let's hold on here and go check this noise out.

I'm sitting in my living room, and I have the windows open and the door open, and its 8:30 in the morning, and I've been talking since about 8:00, and it's all the little noises in and out. I very seldom sit in my living room, and it's rather comfortable. It's really nice, and I'm leaning over the coffee table talking into this machine however it seems I can't get comfortable, but the living room is a nice little room surrounded with beautiful things.

Due to the fact I had to go to mass, I started to learn the priests would talk about God and the rules of the Catholic faith and the commandments. I had heard a lot of this before, but I would go and talk to this one priest, was he something. He would call me a "dommy bogenstrow," whatever that meant. (*Laughter*)

The Four Peanuts

23

An Altar Boy

Before I go into telling you about how I became an altar boy, I need to tell you about my first encounter with Father Joseph. God love him, because of him it was for me to become confirmed in the Catholic faith. To go through my confirmation; I had to study and memorize so many things, and then the day came for me to be confirmed. I chose the name Nicholas at my confirmation. A lot of people later in my life called me Nick or Nicholas because I chose the name Nicholas to honor the uncle that I really loved, my Uncle Nicholas. So I chose the name Nicholas, and we had our confirmation. There was a Dr. Walsh who was the stand-in for all the boys whose godfathers or sponsors would not or could not appear. Big old Dr. Walsh was quite a holy man; he was involved with all the boys. He really spent a lot of time with all us kids. Anyway on my day of confirmation, he stood in for my Uncle Nicholas who did not come; it seems he didn't want to be bothered. As a matter of fact, the whole time I was in the Children's Home, my godmother, my cousin Pauline, and Maria came to see me only a couple of times maybe and take me out on the boardwalk, and they would go out and swim.

So now that I've interrupted the story, let's go back. I made my confirmation; and now I'm becoming an altar boy. I decided I wanted to be an altar boy. Oh, Lord, here comes Vincent, an altar boy. So, Father got John P and myself and one other boy, I think—*(cuckoo, there's the clock)* and we would have to go into the library room and learn the Latin responses to the mass. I remember, Father Joseph; used to call me a doomcoff three times a class; because I couldn't say anything right. Well, lo and behold, anyway after an awful long, long time of study, I finally got it and here came the day I learned my Latin responses to the Latin prayers of the sacred holy sacrifice of the mass.

(Laughter) You know I keep laughing because, I'll tell you why, it's because when you write your own book, you're gonna look back on your life, and things are going to

make you laugh. If as yourself, when you're reviewing your life, could have done so many things that would make you laugh, it's a wonder how you survived these things.)

Like I said, I got the script right, I was learning to understand what the responses were so they would make some meaning, even though I didn't always comprehend it, I could blabber my Latin. So we would get to the altar and then the priest would teach us about ringing the bells and how we were to come up with the cruet for the washing of hands (*laughter I can't help but laugh when I think about this*). Anyhow, the whole boy's home came out on this one Sunday and I had a serve mass. The first time I served mass, I remember I did everything so wrong, that the priest came down the stairs and boxed my ears, and threw me out of the chapel. Good Lord in Heaven I was mortified; I had screwed everything up so bad, it's a wonder the Lord didn't … but I think the Lord was very generous about it. I was so nervous, and did everything wrong and I couldn't say the answers in mass and the ones that I did say, it seems I gave the wrong answers. "The Lord be with you," and I'd say, "Have Mercy on your soul," or something. Anyway, we finally got it right, and it really was a prize to be an altar boy because you got all the benefits.
The only one thing I didn't like about being an altar boy was that you had to get up early. We had Sunday masses at the Home and right across then across the street from us was the convent. I think it was called St. Joseph's Convent, and it was a very exclusive girls' school, which was run by nuns. We would go over there to serve mass, and let me tell you, if you went there to serve mass on a Sunday morning, after the mass Sister Rachel, (who was such a grump, but nice at the same time), would cook us the biggest breakfast. Bacon, eggs, pancakes and sausages and then cocoa, and cakes. We couldn't wait to serve mass at St. Joseph's so now you see how we were as humans. You would think about the privilege of being there in the very presence of God to witness the acts of the conversion of this bread and wine into the actual sacraments. You know, as devout Catholic's, we really believe (there's that gift of faith) this wine, (*there we go with the bell, pretty, it's a quarter till 9:00*) and this unleavened piece of bread, or the host, when the priest said those words, they actually become the body, blood, soul and divinity of our God, Jesus Christ, so anyone who receives Holy Communion in our faith definitely has God in their body. The greatest privilege as an altar boy, and as a reward, was the nuns fussed over you. I remember meeting a Sister Maureen, a big tall beautiful sister, and every time she had her vacation at St. Joseph's across the street, she would call for me, and I would go ring her doorbell; we would go and sit in the little tearoom.

24

Regarding Catholics

Everybody talks about the Catholic religious subjects as alcoholics and perverts and pedophiles and lesbians. Well, I'm going to tell you folks, maybe so this is possible in any lifestyle, that there's the good and the bad. But from the time as a child that I witnessed and experienced these holy men and women of God, that is what they were. Holy men and women of God, people who took off the old life and put on a new life, learning how to sacrifice, how to pray, do penance, and just become the children of God. Father Joseph, the priest, well this guy was so holy, he could swear and I think he'd walk on air, and holiness has nothing to do with being morbid or self-righteous or walking around. You know those people who run around, verse this, chapter that, Matthew this and Mark that—well, maybe they're sincere, but it's all bullcrap. You don't carry on about God; you act God. You get up, and you do your daily blessing, and you tell God, "Let me reflect you this day the best I can," and then you go about your business, and it's no maga maga, and it's no, "Look at me, I'm holy, look at me I'm fasting."

Anyway, this is my opinion, later I will elaborate on this further. But as far as I'm concerned, and I'm pretty slick, you know, about knowing the ins and outs of people's bull. These people were definitely all dedicated to the service of our Lord, to becoming holy and to pleasing God and dealing with the human animal, the children of God, and I'm going to be very adamant about this because it's so. So now, for all the alcoholics and all the pedophiles and all that bull crap I'm sure there was some you know, however misfortunate, but even those people love God. However, it does exist, it did exist, it will probably exist to the end of time. We're all human, and this is it, but that's no reason to not see through and to the holy men of God, and let me tell you, I have met some holy men and women of God.

Now I am off the soapbox, and back to the relationship with Father Joseph. I knew I could come and ring his doorbell every night and get an orange or an apple; but I hated oranges and apples, I still do, but this was a way to get into his little room. He had just a little room, and he had all these beautiful porcelain statues of angels that he collected. In fact it was Father Joseph who told me how very real angels are and the different denominations of angels. The archangels, the seraphim's, the cheraphim's, and Michael the archangel and about the whole story of angels. And if the story of angels is believed, and I can't see how anyone wouldn't believe the story of angels. But I guess you only believe in angels if you have the gift of faith. Let me tell you, that the greatest prize possession a man could be offered by God is the gift of faith. So here I was getting into angels and I found my nightmares started turning into sweet dreams. (I think there was a song called, "Sweet, Sweet, Sweet Dreams.") And Father Joseph was the apple of my eye you see, because if I didn't want to do something with the community, I'd find a way to get Father Joseph to let me do something for him. If I didn't want to get into any of these other things the kids did, I could run to Brother Charles. I don't know if I traded in fun for sorrow or sorrow for fun, but anyway Father Joseph would find a way to sit and talk with me. I wanted to know all about the Blessed Virgin Mary. She was my mother, she still is my mother and your mother too, whether you accept her or not. Jesus gave her to all of us.

And I saw my mother through the Virgin Mother.

(I'm always saved by the bell. It's 9 o'clock here in the living room with this nice chime. I need someone to come in here and get all my clocks right so they all go off at the same time. Anyway, here we go with nine ... I think the reason why I have all these chiming things around is when I was a little boy, I walked into somebody's house, and they had a million clocks, tick-tock, tick-tock, tick-tock, and it used to spook me, and dripping water used to really get on my nerves. I had to train myself to be able to accept dripping water and now the water could drip forever. I conditioned myself, and all these tick, tick, tick ... after awhile you don't hear anything, but when you have company which is very rare, they go, "What are all these clocks. I could never sleep in this house." Well that's maybe one reason why I got all those clocks. I even got rid of my guest bedroom.)

Anyway, back to Father Joseph, and us talking about the Virgin Mother. He used to say, "Vincent, you know you're always getting in trouble, you're always being written up, and you're always being put into the corner. It seems I spent more time in the corner with a dunce cap on, (they did that in those days you know) than anybody I could ever remember.

Anyway, again, we're going to come to a second time in my life when a priest said to me, this priest, a holy man of God, sat me down one day in his room and he made me eat this banana (*I didn't like fruit, but now I like bananas*). I was eating this banana like a little chipmunk, cheeks all full, like little pig. He said to me, he says, "Vincent, Vincent, Vincent ...," three times. Then he said something in Latin and then he said to me, "You must learn to understand what I'm going to tell you. The reason you get in so much trouble with people ...", now remember this is a totally different human being, far removed from me as a little child. I think I was around twelve years old now, and this priest, he says to me, "Vincent, you have the gift to read a man's soul," verbatim those words were repeated to me, "and you must learn to not see too far, or you will grow to be an old, lonely man." He was trying to tell me I probably have the ability to look into your face and then tell you, before you would do it, what you're about to do and what your makeup is. You know all my life I've been telling people the things they didn't want to hear, and it would automatically make me a creep. But any of those people who went home and would reflect on what I would tell them would come back, there were very few I think three in the whole lifetime, and say "You were right, Vincent, what do I do to make it better?" Those were really noble people. The rest they walk around talking about you behind your back cause you hurt their feelings and you insulted them and you just hear their poor little heart palpitations, and they're just wrecked because you read their souls. So here again, this priest tries to impress upon me, "You do not do this, learn how to use this."

25

The Nuns Funeral

This next story I remembered had to do with a funeral for one of the poor old nuns who died, and they had a solemn High Mass. Now for those of you reading, and who don't know what a High Mass is, it goes on forever as far as a child is concerned. A lot of pomp and circumstance, but everything we do in our faith has a liturgical meaning. I had the incense, what I mean is I was to carry the incense and pick up the little top and the priest would light the charcoal and put the incense in. Now let me tell you, Father Joseph was insane with incense; he would just flabbergast everyone with the scent. Well, here I come with the incense, and then I see this body in the coffin and I kind of klutzed and my hip went into the corner part of the coffin. Let me tell you, (*lots of laughter*) the casket just rolled and wiggled and jiggled and that little old dead nun was just a rockin' and a rollin' in that coffin. I had nightmares for what seemed an eternity after that. Father Joseph grabbed me by the ear and said, "You doomcoff," slapped me up side of the head with the thing you bless people with, you know, the aspurgus, and then I caused (*laughter*) a scene you would not believe. I had learned to control peeing in my pants, but let me tell you I felt that gush, and I had to control it. I finally managed to get everything in order and everybody calmed down. God bless the poor nun—she needs to pray for me. Well we finally got the ritual done, you know, and took the casket to go to the cemetery, and he said, "You're not going anywhere, get out of here," and kicked me in the butt and off I went, so at least he spared me that. But it was just something even though it was an accident, you know. Actually, I was always so scared, and it seems Father Joseph, because I did everything wrong, made sure he did his thing and made sure I was out there to do mine, and he would nudge and poke me. God love him. If it wasn't for Father Joseph, I don't think I would have any faith.

I don't think I'd know anything about my God and I don't think I'd know anything about church liturgy. Boy, oh, boy, I was the biggest and most clumsy, miserable kid. I was a klutz from the beginning of the day, till the end, from day one.

I remember when I tried to learn to ride a bicycle, I rode it backwards. Everybody used to go down the slide, and there's nothing to a slide except the kids would go in face first, but when I would go face first, I didn't have sense enough to stop myself, and I fell and busted my face and I ran around with a space in my tooth all my life.

26

Reese Park

Another experience at the Children's Home was when the kids were sent to Reese Park which was a very wealthy Jewish and Catholic retired community, and you had to take a bus all the way to Reese Park. One day Brother August said, "Vincent, I have this lady, and you're to go to her house. She's going to pay you ten dollars and your going to clean her house" now ten dollars was a lot of money. Well, all around the Children's Home I would be cleaning, and I'd go with the nuns and wipe their dishes, and I'd go into the little old lady in laundry room and help her learning how to fold clothes, however I didn't stay around there a lot, because it was always real hot. So off I went to Reese Park to this lady's house. Now this lady had to be the meanest, nastiest creature, she was hell, she was a terror. When she had me in the kitchen, I had to scrub something, and I was on my hands and knees scrubbing, and she came back after about 20 minutes and said, "Boy, you haven't done a darn thing. You get into that cabinet and use some elbow grease. Ten minutes later she came back and said, "Land sakes, what in hell are you doing?" and I said, "I'm looking for the elbow grease." I had no idea what she said actually meant to put it to the metal. Anyway, I got up, threw her bucket of water all over the floor, and I told her to go to hell, and I snatched her money from the kitchen table. It was seven dollars; the hussy wasn't going to give me ten. I took the money and slammed the door, and when I did this urn fell off the wall. She was just a real witch, she was, and off I went. I missed the bus, and I had to walk all the way back to the Children's Home. It seemed like it was forever, and I got there just in time for supper. Brother Ed said to me, "Where you been?" And I said, "Oh, I had a horrible day." Well, anyway, Brother August had already heard about it, and he was there waiting. I was just a cryin', I was so upset, and he comforted me, and he said," Tell me what happened?" I said, "I couldn't find the elbow grease, and she came in there, yelled at me, all she did was yell at me." then I told him, "Now, Brother August, it wasn't right. I didn't know how to do what I was doing. She was so hateful" And I then I went on and on. He said, "Go have

your supper and I'll write you an excuse, however she said you stole her money."
I said, "I didn't steal her money. She was supposed to give me ten dollars and she
only had seven." So bless his heart, what a nice man he was, he went into the little
kitty, and he opened it up, and he gave me the other three dollars, and then he
gave me another quarter. He said, "Here, here's your tip," he says, "I'll take care
of it. So that's the way it was with me, I wanted to do everything right, but it
seems I always did it all wrong. If you said up, I went down.

You know, in those days you didn't admit a kid was right, but when our kids
were right, the people at St. John's would give you a fair shake. So it was the end
of the witch. Now there, I'm saying w-i-t-c-h, I'm not saying the 'b' word.

*I guess I'm on a roll now; all these things are coming in my mind, and again they're
all pieces and bits, and I really think we ought to write the book just the way we're
doing it—pieces and bits. I don't think it would be interesting any other way. Anyway
we'll leave that up to the writers—whoever they are. I really have no idea how we're
going to put this on paper and make any sense, and when I ask for information and
guidance, people just babble, but they're not telling me a thing. They're telling me,
"Now you gotta put it on paper." No kidding. I know that already.*

27

Boys just being boys

Now, I started to get in with Kelly and some of the other bad boys. Well, they weren't really bad boys, but they were, you know, just boys. And I remember how in the winter, there were all these little bungalows where people would come for the summer; and then in the winter, they'd close them up and off they'd go back to their permanent ones.

I didn't really get in with the bad boys, but I followed them, and they would go on Saturday; when we were allowed off the property from one until five with a permission slip. But let me tell you, five didn't mean a minute after; it meant 5 o'clock. So I would follow these boys, and they'd go to the train trestles and they'd take down all the board that were on the windows and break in to the little train booth stop. And we'd get in, and they would sit there and smoke cigarettes and talk about girls and just act like boys acted, you know, real mysterious and adventurous. Then one day a lot of the kids got caught breaking into people's bungalows, and theses kids would just party. Some of them were rather destructive and they'd eat the food left behind, and play their record players acting like they were the people who lived there, you know. And the Children's Home started getting a reputation for everything that went wrong in that community. If something went wrong in Rockaway Park which was a rough community, they blamed the kids at the Children's Home. Well, it turned out, that in this one case they were right; some of our bad boys were breaking into these bungalows and being destructive.

I followed these kids once and we went into one of the bungalows. It was a nice one, having three bedrooms and all this good stuff. The guys were just being guys, and all of a sudden here comes the girls. Oh, oh. So these boys, the older boys that made friends with the community girls, and they'd rock and roll. Well I snuck out and went back to the Children's Home. And then here comes Kelly, and he says to me, "if you tell" and I said, "Don't you tell me, 'if I tell,' I don't tell anything on anybody. Now you get outta my face." You see I started getting brave, and holding my own. I wasn't going to have anybody wimp on me, this Mary, Mary crap and this sissy, sissy. They started to find out; "You're messin' where you shouldn't be a messin'." I think there's a song about that, too. So then he backed off. I remembered about these kids breaking into the bungalows, and they put a stop to it, and the Children's Home won back their reputation. Afterward, everybody who would come to the beach were allowed into the gate, into our play area, you know, where all the five baseball fields, that is how big our campus was, and then basketball or stick ball, and then we had an arena where they taught the guys how to box and how to wrestle. There wasn't anything a boy couldn't do to become masculine and physical. Weight lifting and exercising. Well, I don't know, I was just having never attracted to any of these physical things. Maybe I could handle mental, but I couldn't pick anything up. But I started realizing I was I think I was between fat and limpid, so I did do some weight lifting. In fact I got pretty good, started building up my body, had some muscles, and then I would get brave, and in those days, we would wear T-shirts with sleeves, you know, and then you take the sleeve of one of your T-shirts and you put your pack of cigarettes in it. Well, here I was, Mr. Macho, you know, when you had your pack of cigarettes in your shirt sleeve. Now let's talk about the hairstyles for the kids back then, it was all crew cut, flat tops, or you had the DA (short for 'ducks ass) haircut, were all your hair from both sides ends up in back, like in the tail of a duck, and greasy. Boy, we couldn't have anything greasier, in fact the greasier the better. You know high pompadour in front. Land sakes, let me tell you, with my big nose and a pompadour (*laughter*) I really was something else.

I was just a big shot with a pack of cigarettes rolled up in my shirt sleeve, you know and my blue jeans, and the little penny loafer with the penny in it and white socks. I hate white socks; I still hate white socks to this day, I think they're gross; on any man I think white socks are horrible. And the clothing in those days were what we called pegged pants and pistol pocket pants, and I had me a pair of purple-stitched pegged pants, with pistol pockets.

It was so cool you know when I'd get all dressed up, with my hair all up in a pompadour and my duck's tail and the grease just oozing out of my brain. That was cool; everybody was cool then. And the cigarettes the kids smoked in those days were Marlboros, Lucky Strikes, Pall Mall, and Chesterfield. Lucky Strike cigarettes were the thing back then; you were a man if you smoked Luckies. So anyhow, I would start puffing and choking and croaking, but I hada be like the boys. (*Laughter*) Now let me tell you, I have not stopped since, and I'm dying of lung cancer and emphysema and everything that goes with it. Once you start smoking, that's one monkey you can't get off your back so it's a sad thing. But back then, we all thought it was a big shot thing. Off we'd go to Rockaway Playland and Reese Park and everywhere a boy could go to try to get in trouble.

I guess I was getting a little older now ending up in the third and fourth dormitory and got to be good friends with some of the Brothers. Brother Charles, of course. I only met him recently, several years ago, what a man. I mean it takes a special grace from God to deal with young children, especially today. Oh, I went back to see the Children's Home and it's all closed down and boarded up, and they have built another building. It's not the personal attention and regimentation and the absolute care today that it was at my time so God was kind to me. He put me in a place where it was for real, and it was solid, and they catered to you from the minute you woke up till the minute you went to sleep, and while you were not asleep, there was always one Brother in that dormitory to see to your needs. They were quite holy wonderful men, and a really good group of boys.

Being there, I really started coming into my own, making friends with all the boys, but yet most couldn't understand why I wouldn't do things they would do and why I wouldn't go places they would go. So I guess as a child I was restless and you hada put out too much to be a friend to someone, or so I thought. I thought to be somebody's friend, I had to be just like them and every move they made I hada make it, and everything they liked, I had to like, and I found out it was not so.

28

Black Mariah

I think it's perfectly clear the picture, the scenario. When we're growing up, we're emulating, imitating and doing all these little daring things. But as a kid you always know there is an end to a fine line, and on most occasions people will not cross a fine line. However, it seems I just hada find out what happened if you did cross the line, and of course, I would always find the consequences were quite severe. Let me tell you any time a boy got in trouble, especially in public, we had the 'Black Mariah', and every night before we would go to bed, we'd have to pay our dues. It would either be one whap on the butt or two or three or four. I'll never forget this handsome little fellow, Michael; he was just full of mischief, but everybody liked him. He was a good-looking kid, really a good boy, tough guy, but quiet. He'd get the 'Black Mariah' ten times every night. Let me tell you, this stick was solid, and when you got your butt whipped you'd lay over the bed, and they'd put a rag in your mouth, you held on to the bars, and you'd take your licks, right there, buck ass, pam, pam, pam. And the brothers didn't spoil the child; they did not spare the rod. Today it's called abuse. Baloney. I think every kid should get his butt whipped every time he snots off and misbehaves. I firmly believe it was the salvation of every boy at the Children's Home. And the Brother would lay it on you, and he would do it until you cried, and you would say, "I will not do this again, it's too painful." And let me tell you, we'd straighten up. (*laughter*), I don't remember now what it was I did, but you hada really be bad to get the 'Black Mariah'. What killed you is the Brother, Brother Ed, had to give us the 'black Mariah', this is that big fat thick oak stick, painted black, and this guy was so good-hearted, it just killed him to whip our butts, but he had to do it. Anyway, I hada get three licks. Oh boy, oh boy, oh boy, everybody got up on their beds and gathered round for me to get mine. And down came my pants and BAM! Boy that thing, if I had false teeth back then, they would have just come right out of my mouth. That was one, and I went, "Ha, ha, ha, you didn't hurt me." And BAM! Two. Let me tell you, the tears were coming out of my eyes, but

I wasn't gonna cry. This time my body took over and cried for me. And BAM! Three. Then all of us guys would go sit in a bucket of ice water to cool our butts off and then off to bed we'd go. I'll tell you what, we straightened out after that. I didn't break the rules again. Cussing was the imperial sin. (*Laughter*) So anyway, I guess I don't stand a chance. I remember those three whacks, but I never got another one in the whole history of living at St. John's Home for Boys. We became friends with our whippers—you know what they say "to the hostage you be true" well, "to the captor you be true". This straightened us out. It wasn't physical, it wasn't done maliciously, and it was the law, you learned. They didn't beat us up except Brother Norbet; he was snot. (I hate him, but not really, as I have learned to love him.) I don't know what his problem was it was between him and God, but he was really outrageously cruel. This was done with taste and dignity, and it turned these little butts into men so there we were learning. We had the freedom to do anything we wanted just as long as we kept the rules. And right then and there you started to learn, when you come to a red light, you stop. If you don't stop at the red light, the man gets you. There are rules; every day we are ruled by rules, and if you break the rules if you wanna do the crime, then you have to pay the time. So we were taught at a young age a man has to take his punches, and the Brothers would go through the whole day and if you see a Brother writing on his pad, you're doing something bad. So about 4 o'clock in the afternoon, I would walk up to the Brother in charge and say, "Can see what I did bad?" and he says, "Oh, my God, Vincent, you got an hour?" And I would have all kinds of stuff: cussing, yelling, being outrageous, defiant. I was so defiant it's a wonder nobody hung me like a chicken and choked me, and talk about testy. Now I'm learning I'm testy. There's a word in a man's language, was typical ball-buster. Excuse the expression, ladies. I mean to tell you, if anybody could move you to anger, it was certainly was me. I found as a child I was this way only with people whose favor I wanted to win. There were in my life then, as there are today certain people, I would want them to be my friend. I would choose them to be a part of my life, and if they can see my offerings to them, you get the moon, the stars, the sun, the shine, the whole world, everything. I'm always right there, and maybe it's fortunate, because the people I reveal myself to and say, "I want you to be my friend. I will give you everything I can give you because I want your friendship," but if they rejected me, well as a kid, I'd go to all these selected people. What attracted me to them, I don't know, but there was a goodness in them, however I would bust their chops. I'd pick on them, aggravate them, get them mad at me. One boy, he just whipped up on me one day. And then as he was whipping me, he said, "Vincent, what in the world is wrong with you, you're gonna cause somebody to kill you." Here I am on the floor, and he's sitting on top of me, slapping me, he wasn't really hurting me, but he was whipping me.

Excuse me, the phone…. that was Glenda, one of my dance students, just a lovely delightful friend. She's sick, she was sick yesterday, she's sick today so she can't come for her lesson.

Anyway, here's this kid beating me and telling me, "What's wrong with you, child." And I said to him, "All I want you to do is be my best friend. I just want to go where you go, wanna learn everything you do, and I want you to love me and be my friend." And so he did; he buddied up with me. He took me here and took me there, and he did this and that and I would do this and that and well, you know, I knew that there was something good inside him, and I got it out of him, and then I imitated his goodness. Well, lo and behold, it's time for him to leave, and off he goes, and I never saw him again, and it was the end of the relationship, but I will never forget that boy.

I am still this way today. Of course now today I have a hard time selecting, I see so much but there's one or two who would just absolutely rock my cradle—(laughter) I would absolutely, I would keep them and support them—has nothing to do with any bullshit; it's just the way I am, and they just look down their nose at me. I have found I'm not odd and I'm not different. I guess I'm something most people don't understand and it's honest. I'm going to tell it to you like it is whether it hurts me or you or anybody else. There's just no time for foolishness. I used to play all these games, you know, and I found out they were rather expensive, even as a child. So I cut the mustard, and I do away with the ends of the bread and all the foolishness. I get right down to it, and of course people just sit there and they look at me and they say, "Who is this person, and where did he come from?" Well, I wonder sometimes myself the same question. I'm the same way with my God, you know, I just want to get right to it. (Laughter) I guess that's good. This impetuosity sometimes is good, but we have to learn, and we are still learning, you go slow, you go easy. So I have found dealing with the human animal is such a hassle. You can't please anyone. You think I would have learned this a long time ago, so what do I do now? I please myself. I'm probably the poorest person you'll ever meet, but to look at my environment, you'd think I was the richest person. People don't understand everything I have I have worked for, I paid for, and I struggled for it, and I haven't gone to a movie in ten years. I haven't gone to a social in years. I don't go anywhere. I stay right here because I don't have the money, and I'm not gonna tell people, "I don't have the money," but to look at me you would think I was Mr. Millionaire, so the cover of the book sometimes is prettier than the inside. I'm fortunate, the Lord has blessed me, and helps make my ends meet. I'll never be a wealthy man, but at least I can pay my bills, and I eat well. And then sometimes I eat a lot of peanut butter. Some things people don't know, and I don't want them to know, but I guess they will know it now. So everybody says let's go here, let's go there, let's go do this. I've yet to have somebody come up with something to really knock my eyes out and say, "I'm gonna pack and get in the car and go." And it's just not so, so we live here alone.

Anyway, there goes my friend, and I never see or hear from him again. And life went on at the Children's Home, you know, you're in with these boys and those boys and this and that one, and I'm still teasing and hurting feelings because I like people, and it didn't get me anywhere with anybody, and I was absolutely cruel. I didn't know then, that sooner or later, you learn.

29

Momma

One day, I was told to go to the bungalow, the office, I had a visitor, and it was my mother, they said, "Vincent, your mother is here." And I was in all these rotty, rungy clothes and the Brother made me go upstairs and put on my permission clothes, the nicer clothes. Well, I fell all over myself, I stumbled all the way, I had one shoe on wrong and the other shoe was a different kind. Anyway, I couldn't wait to go see my mother. Here I was flying down the back stairs, you know. We had several entrances, but the side of the entrances you would go through at one time would lead to the yard, the basketball court, the cement, the gate, you had to go through the gate, and you're right on the boardwalk, right down to the beach, right into the water. And then the other entrance was the street off the boardwalk going into the solid area, not the sand area, not the ocean area. So here I go flying through the back door, and in the hallway there was an outdoor hallway between two buildings, and there was this grotto with the Virgin Mary. Well, John P and I would spend our life in that grotto putting flowers and saying our little rosaries and the whole bit. Anyway, here I was flying and I kneel at the Virgin Mary, and I was sporadic (*laughter*) and there she was.

(*Ten o'clock, we gotta put up with ten of these—it's worth waiting for, guess—oh, hurry up. I'm gonna talk over it, okay?*)

And there I went knocking myself over, and there was my momma, Maria Anelina Madonia Mirabella, the most beautiful sight you could ever want to see, and just as stately and; I went flying to her and hugged her. Then she hugged me and kissed me and said "Oh, my son, you're so handsome." She ran her fingers through my hair, if anybody could make me feel good, it was my mother. I really don't remember what all we did that day, but just spending it with my mother, you know was the best.

93

I remember seeing her beautiful hairdo, and she wore the most beautiful suit, it was a summer suit. I remember seeing her talking to Brother John who was going to become a priest. I didn't like him because he thought he was Mr. Pretty. I do know he was never nice to me, and I don't know what his story was, but he would always be talking to pretty Sister Vincent, and I would always see him around the girls. Now here is a man who is gonna dedicate his life to God; but now don't let me judge, there is that ability certain people have said Vincent has. I just saw something in him and it just wouldn't want to see any further, because I was afraid I would see the evil. This day he spent a long time talking to my mother, and as he came through the hall he said, "I met your mother, she's very beautiful, and I talked to her for a long time, Vincent. You have a very lovely mother." Well, I resented him saying this. My mother was apparently there for a conference, and I am not sure how Brother John ended up getting involved. He had nothing to do with me at all, but anyway when I spoke with her before she left, she told me how she thought he was a nice handsome man and that he was gonna be a priest and he was watching over me. I told her, "No, Mother, he does not watch over me and I don't want you to like him." To this day I can't believe I said that to my mother: "I don't want you to like him." But she kind of smiled at me and she said, "Vincent, I don't like anybody, I just love you." (*Laughter*) I guess she knew what I was up to. I had the feeling a girl as beautiful as she and girls as beautiful as my cousins, Pauline R., Pauline F., and my cousin Marie I am sure these girls had a lot of proposals. So I felt better, God forgive me, but I just didn't like Brother John. I figured it was because I never liked anyone who wouldn't give me any attention (*laughter*), even when I went to all these assorted avenues of destruction and mayhem; well not really mayhem, but close to it; to get attention from certain people, they weren't having any of it. And the smarter people in those days knew the way to get rid of me was to ignore me which was most difficult.

So I didn't like Brother John, and shame on me, he's probably a holy priest of God now and a wonderful person. But then I didn't like Brother Norbet either. But for Brother Norbet, I had a reason not to like him, but God bless him, too. I gotta think if we were to research on these two guys, we'd find they're no longer with the order.

(So they're outside with the buzzers, and they're vacuum cleaning, I mean lawn mowing.)

I loved my mother so, and she was so sweet, but soon she hugged me, and then she hada leave. She promised to come and visit me again, and after she left, I cried and I was sick for a week. But I got to see my mother.

You know, I still don't understand even after all these years, why the court, the welfare department or the Children's Home, why none of these people would not let me go live with my mother. I guess I never questioned my mother why I couldn't go live with her. Maybe, if I would have asked her, she would have put me in her car and taken me away. But now I will never know till the day I die why I couldn't live with my mother, the only person who came to see me at the Children's Home after the one or two times my godmother, with her gangster boyfriend, came to see me. Uncle Nick and Aunt Mamie never came to see me; my father never, ever, ever came to see me. My mother however did come to see me on several occasions.

Well, it takes awhile, but you get depressed and then all those boys, the ones who were my friends, they'd come and hug me. The camaraderie, of man to man will be a unification of men. There are things men do together which are manly and soft, masculine and affectionate and loving but they are still men. These men that I was getting to know where some people with feelings, you know. They'd even cry with me, some of these guys. And all of us kids were suffering the same things. We came from broken homes. I guess the most devastating reason to be there would be because your mother died and your dad couldn't take care of you. Or that your dad had died and your mother couldn't take care of you or they were both ill. Lots of sadness, but again I'm gonna tell you God takes care of his children, he sure does, especially little children who are innocent.

(Tino's here on the couch in his little corner and I'm talking to you on this tape, but I'd better stop because we're gonna get that interference. The buzzing has stopped, so now we're going to continue.)

30

Sister Maureen

Remember Sister Richard Maureen from across the street at the academy. Well, to the right of the boardwalk and in the next building, on their boardwalk, were all the sisters, and all the sisters would sit on the little porch of the boardwalk and fan and drink ice tea. Well one day, here comes Sister Maureen, and she met my mother, boy was I in heaven that day. I remember I kind of giggled at Sister Richard, and said, "Oh, Sister Maureen, you look like a balloon." You see, these ladies were allowed to go swimming, but of course they would be all covered in black with these big balloony type bathing suits and this big old black, what I guess you would call it a shower cap, anyway, they were just so plain, and everybody knew those were the nuns. So here goes my mother with the blanket and then somebody came out and put one of those little umbrellas, and we sat, and we ate, and we had a good time. And my mother said, "Vincent, show me how you can swim." And, oh gee, I said, "Momma, I don't know how to swim. I don't go in the water." Well, she took me by the hand and all of a sudden and I was fearless. I think I coulda fought a shark, you know, and we went to the water. You could hear the waves rippling in, and it was low tide so we got to walk out quite far into the water. And she swam; oh she could swim like Ester Williams. For those of you who do not know who Ester Williams was, she was a famous movie star who did swimming movies. My mother would swim and Sister Maureen would be swimming, and we were all a giggling and having fun. Sister Maureen used to giggle because, you know, God had blessed these women and they had to stay covered, and they couldn't allow anybody to get excited over them. They also had to protect their virginity and holiness, even though most had the prettiest face God ever made. Now the two of them, my mother and Sister Maureen were talking together and I could tell they were talking about me, by the way they would look at me but I couldn't hear what they were saying. Anyway, when we got back to the beach blanket, momma went back to where Brother August had given her a guest room. She got all dressed up, and then they told me to hurry up and go upstairs and change into my clothes, that momma was going to take me out. Well, here I come out in this little brown outfit, with a little hat and my shoes and all the boys were saying, "Oh, Vinnie's gonna see his momma," and they'd all run out to the gate and see my momma and wave at my momma, and then she'd come in and hug all of them. Eventually we would be off down the boardwalk, and we would go and eat hot dogs. I mean to tell you, in those days we had hot dogs from hell. They were a foot-long, piled high with sauerkraut and onions, and I would eat three of those hot dogs. My momma said, "God bless you, son, you're a growing boy".

I had my hot dogs and then here comes the ice cream sundae, and the soda with all the chocolate. I wanted the chocolate ice cream, chocolate syrup, chocolate fudge; you see anything white, I wouldn't eat it. So then we would go buffaloing down the boardwalk, and we would end up at Rockaway Playland. My mother would take pictures of me, and it was just a wonderful peace for me, like a little break from all the sorrow, suffering and pain. At that moment I was my mothers hero, I was her little man and there was nothing I could not do which wasn't masculine or manly around my mother. I wasn't a sissy or a Mary or anything, I was Vincent and momma would say "my son, Vincent." This time when she was leaving wasn't as bad as the first time, but to me it was still sad. She went on back to her life, wherever she had to go.

We never talked about where she lived or what she did while I was in the Home. However, that was the second experience I remember in this period of my life with my mother, and Sister Maureen. It was just wonderful time, having Momma meet Brother Charles, Brother Matthew and Father Joseph. I was coming into my little manhood.

(Now I am in the den or the library room, with the clock. I just gotta get Mr. Cox to come and fix this clock.).

Another story about Sister Maureen was when I lived on the third floor (we were surrounded by windows) where you could look out of one of the windows on the back end and you could see the beach and hear the roar of the ocean. Then to the right I didn't know what was out there, and to the left were all of the little bedrooms of the sisters. And the other boys and I always wondered (as I'm sure every child who lived in that period of time has always wondered) what did those sister wear underneath that big old veil. So we used to take bets that they had no hair. We figured they were all bald-headed and that's why they wore them. We knew they were supposed to cut their hair. One night for some reason I happened to look out my window and one of the sisters was taking off her habit and there went the headpiece. I was brave enough to watch that and I saw she had long beautiful hair, and from the back I could have sworn it was Sister Maureen. I think I saw the lady make the sign of the cross and then she turned to the window and pulled down the shade. Thank God for her doing that, otherwise I think I would have been absolutely scandalized, cause when you think of nuns, you weren't suppose to think of them as if they were women. You were supposed to think of them as holy ladies, not just plain old girls when in fact, they were. So that day I feel I received a privilege to see one of these young ladies, and that they did in fact get to keep their hair. Today they have these poor nuns running around with lipstick and high heels and dresses and oh, I think it is awful. I think a woman should be a lady, and absolutely a nun should always be a nun and they should wear the habits and not try to act like a part of the world. Nuns give up the world so they need to be and should be singled out.

31

The Church

Now today, everything it seems in our church is modern, they took away all the statues which I think is bunk. I am kind of glad they have converted the language of the mass to English, however so that we ignorant Catholics could understand and at least hear it in English, because somewhere along the line, it's going to ring a bell to someone. But there are times when I do miss the Latin liturgy, and I most definitely miss my statues, you know, and I have a house full of them. You ought to see my bedroom; it's like grandma's bedroom use to be. I do ceramics and so I made a statue of the Virgin Mary and one of the sacred heart of Jesus and another of the statue of St. Joseph with the baby Jesus. I had a friend of mine come to the house one day, and he walked into my bedroom and he said, "Boy, could never have sex in this place, it's too much like a church." And I said to him, "Well, that's the idea, suppose." But what a heck of a thing to say. But I have the crucifix, and then I have a really sad picture of Jesus with the crown of thorns. I look around at all these statues, and it helps me mind my P's and Q's. Until I block them out, and then I'm a real terror. So isn't it interesting to see that as a child I was terrified of all these statues with their candles and now as an older person I just had to conquer my fears. So now, I'm old, fat, and tired, I have my little candles, my little vigil lights, and when I'm inspired to say my prayers, I'll light my little lights, and all these statues and things are waving, but I'm not afraid anymore, you see. So it's quite a thing as I look back you know, I think am totally becoming obsessed. I'm going to take a month off, and I hope somebody offers me a chalet somewhere, and they just leave me alone and let me just gabble, gabble, gabble, gabble. Sometimes I feel writing this book is going to cost me my life, I think. I'm already on tape three, and I only have four tapes, so I guess there goes another fortune in tapes. I better buy a box of them, huh? (*Laughter*) So anyway, this is what's happening at this point in my live, and I love every minute of it. It's really preoccupying me and it's the best therapy I've ever had. Well its

1993 and I'm going to be 52, if I'm lucky to live that long, and I am learning to see this and leave it and go away from it. It has taken a long time.

32

Jerry, Danny & Friends

Well, that was the telephone, and a long-awaited call. One of my very dear friends and students, Mrs. Jerry Feldman, called and said, "We're home." Of course I'm sure they have got jet lag, you know, after all they went to China. She was kind enough to give me her itinerary, and it was like I was in China with her every day, and we kind of left it in the Mother's hands—the dear blessed Virgin. I'm always telling her, "Please, I need Jerry, send her back." She's suffering with a horrible cancer, and oh, God is so sweet and so kind, and she's just a character, I'll tell you what. We're going to get a chapter, probably two, on this wonderful lady, Eva Geraldine Hicks Feldman. Bless us, oh, Lord, what a blessing. Anyway, she's back, she's home, and I told her this madness I'm going through right now, and as soon as she gets rid of her jet lag, asked her to come and spend the day, and we'll just make bacon and eggs, and if the poor girl can sit here and listen to all this mess. But I definitely need her input. So, Jerri's back, thank you Lord, and on with it. I'm going to take a little break now, and we'll get back to Mirabella.

Believe it or not, it has been exactly a little more than a year—it will be a year on July 11 that I went through some surgery and a new birth—a rebirth in my life as you would say. This little tape recorder has been silent that long and many things have been happening that I feel the need to rectify and catch up with.

Today is April 19, 1994, and it just seems like I keep talking about God, and I'm not that holy or that Catholic or that religious, but I sat in my chair yesterday—I have one of those lazy boy recliners, you know—and I have a crucifix in probably every room, and I just happened to look at the crucifix and said, "Lord, we gotta find Danny M, can't stand this any longer. I've looked for him for 35 years, help me find him." So, lo and behold, I got on the telephone and I figured the only way I would find him was if they were still on Long Island, but I would call the Brady's—a family that was part of our friends. Of course wouldn't you know they have an unlisted number, so I cried on the poor operator's shoulder and told her my little ailment and said, "Can we try one more time, Regent Avenue, 1—Regent Avenue, a Daniel and Eva M? Now you're probably going to tell me it's not listed because I've tried for 10 years to find this phone number and every time the operator tells me 'no such person lives there'. And all of a sudden I hear the operator say, "Vincent, we have a number for you at that address." I called John four times or was it three, and he finally ended up finding Daniel, and funny enough, he's right here in Raleigh, North Carolina. So I called him and he said, "Talk about a voice from the past." I don't know if he was glad to hear from me or not, and I don't know if his family's gonna think he hung around with some kind of weirdo, or some fool, but I'll tell you this, if I was ever to give my life for any man, it certainly would be for Danny. That boy took care of me as a little fellow. I had a terrible home life, had a horrible life.

Now I'm not going to tell you he was the school bully, but I'm gonna tell you one thing, nobody messed with Danny or any of the those kids. I was a little boy across the street and said to him, "I want you to be my friend; you gotta take care of me." Ain't nobody ever called me a sissy, ain't nobody ever called me a name, ain't nobody even turned a stone—when I was with Danny, he was my hero. And I was just a kid looking for love, looking for kindness, looking for masculine and Danny was every bit a man you would ever want to think of being. Today, the 12th of April, 1994, I called Danny's sister and I talked to his brother, John. I don't have Tommy's phone number, but I'm going to talk to him. I even managed to find Jeannie G. I am waiting for her to call me back. So it's just like a big celebration, and I want to tell you, folks, it seems as if I have done nothing but cry for the last two days. These are such important people from in my life and they sort of disappeared. Danny always said I was off-the-wall, so I want to find out from him exactly what kind of kid I was, and we'll put it in the book. So I pray to God that I'm going to hear from him soon. I will go into more detail about Danny and Jeannie and the rest of them in one of the following chapters.

33

The Time of Depression

We're going to back up and tell you the events of the last year. I'm sorry for the silence. That's how depressed I've been. I'm going to tell you all about the operation, and I'm going to tell you all about another miracle. And let me tell you what, folks, I may be alone with a dog and have nothing, but our dear Lord takes care of me. He doesn't give me everything I ask for all the time and I probably wear him out but he gives me what's important, and he's one heck of a friend to have, guys. His name is Jesus Christ, the second person of the blessed trinity, our God. For you kids, he's cool, or 'bad', isn't that what you call it these days? Anyway, I have to stop now cause I gotta dry my eyes, but I promise I'm gonna talk some more. Ok, you got me going. I'm back, folks, so the story will continue. It may not make sense at times, but you have to hear it.

I had this friendship with Jeannie G at the time when she was just Jeannie B, and her sister Audrey was my dearest friends. Back then at that time in my life I didn't know anything about love, I didn't know anything about what most intelligent or most ordinary people knew, I didn't know anything about anything, I just knew I was surviving. I wanted dearly for someone to accept me and make me feel important, and back then it seemed like everybody's parents but mine liked to take care of me. Danny, the boy from across the street, his momma loved me and would always say, "What are we gonna do with you?" She said once, "You really love my son, don't you?" and I answered "Yes, I do." You couldn't get me away from that boy's house. I talked to Angelina today and she says, "I remember a blonde-headed boy that did nothing but smoke one cigarette after another." Good, Lord in heaven that far back and I was smoking like a freight train. Once again, I am jumping around, but I will try to put it all in perspective.

Jeannie used to teach (*there's that clock again, Folks, still have the clocks*) now then, and Jeannie married Andrew Guyer, he was a city fellow who courted Jeannie. They were the nicest looking couple. Jeannie went to Queens College, and when she would come home, Audrey and I would be literally sitting up waiting on her to learn the latest dance steps. I'll tell you, if it wasn't for Jeannie, I wouldn't be the successful dance instructor that I am today. So I owe that to Jeannie and Audrey, and I have been trying to find both Jeannie and Audrey to tell them so. I actually found Jeannie this morning; it seems she's at school teaching physical education. God, if and when we get together again, she's gonna die when she sees my belly. I don't know where Audrey is yet; I am going to keep trying to find her though. I found Danny and gave him a call and left a message on his machine, I'm praying he'll call back.

I'm going to be 53 years old this September (1994), and even though according to Angelina, Danny's sister, I'm older than Danny. Their family lived across the field. I would make Danny come and meet me at night in the dark to help me get across the field, and if he wouldn't meet me half way, I'd call and raise the biggest stink. (*Laughter*) But he would always come because I was scared of the dark.

I was the biggest sissy from Hades, I know, but I don't really care. All I know is that Johnny M and his brother Danny and those wonderful people, always made me feel like I had some kind of sanctuary. Now folks let me tell you a little about Danny M, I found out he's married to a beautiful young lady, but I haven't met her as of yet. I also heard God has blessed them with two beautiful children, a boy and a girl, and I think they're now 21 and 27. I hope if they ever meet me that they'll know their dad had a good friend. God has blessed all these people with wonderful wives and families, and me, well I have my dog (*tearful laughter*), and that's the way it goes.

I think I am going to stop now cause I'm getting emotional and I am going to have to come back and put this into perspective and act like and try to act like an intelligent person later. It's 11:35 a.m., Tuesday morning, and it's beautiful outside, I have all the windows open in the apartment, and Tino is sitting outside in the shade, and of course the two televisions are going, talk about being desperate for company.

I feel like I have the need to get into something bigger than this apartment, folks cause I'm hoping I'm going to have some company and overnight guests. But I better go easy, because being a hermit, it's kinda hard to get used to being around people again. It's now Friday night and the end of a work week.

Actually, I got up at 7:00 this morning, and Mrs. Rogers took me for my checkup and it looks like the cancer is under control and the legs are just a flowing with blood, and I'm doing real good, and I promise I will tell all about this operation in one of the upcoming chapters. Now it's about 8 o'clock, I took a long walk and then went in and took a nap. You know those of us, who are independently wealthy, we get up at 7 o'clock in the morning very rarely. (*Laughter*) There's a dance party tomorrow night so tonight I'm off and everybody says, "What do you do when you're home Friday, Saturday, and Sunday. You don't do anything, that's why you're always depressed." Well, actually, I work on their dance lessons and their dance steps and choreography and etc.

Jeannie Guyer and I are going to have our get-together in Melville so I pray Dear Lord, let's get all these students to go to this contest. They're all at the point of saying, "Well, maybe I will and maybe I won't." But I know I am gonna buy my ticket, and I'm going to go anyway. And if no one else comes, we'll just have us a reunion, me and Jeannie. God bless her. And so now I'm gonna be depressed (*laughter*), but I gotta record this because as you get older, you get senile. (*The phone is ringing.*)

Today is Friday, the 22nd of April 1994.

That was another one of my x-world-champion-to-be's, Mr. Moe. God bless him, he's got to go in the hospital Monday, and he was inquiring about my leg operation. He's having knee problems, circulation in the legs. So there you go, you want to be a world champion dancer and when you hit 50, you pay the bills. But he was a basketball coach and all yeah, you all know Moe; those of you that don't know Moe, I'll tell you all about Moe. I think we got about a page on Mr. Moser. He's all right though, good man, with a lovely just lovely bride, and he's just about as unique as probably anybody can be. He's a fine man, who is also very smart.

My dog, Tino, I hear him screaming outside, so I gotta bring him in. I have to apologize to my readers, for in the next few paragraphs, you will see I have put down my tapes, and have had quite a difficult time picking this story back up again.

November 8, 1994, and I have to make some corrections. The first is about my cousin, Pauline. I was sitting here telling you what a horror she was in my youth, but as we have grown a little older and I am in my 50's, Pauline has had several telephone conversations with me and has proven to be really a dear sweet cousin, and so I now want to apologize for the feeling I had for her as a youngster. That is the feeling I had, and so that is the way I have portrayed that feeling, and after all, it is what this book is about—the how come and why, you know. So now I am going to have to try and continue.

34

More on Growing up

To continue my story, uncle Nick evidently decided they would take me on after all, and so I went to live with my Uncle Nick and Aunt Rose and their family of two beautiful young ladies, Pauline and Jeanette, Nicholas Benedict Junior, and then there was Terry and then came Bobby and Rosemary. That was a lot of kids. Being a wetback—not living in a family environment but more of a dormitory environment—this was going to be rather hair-pulling and hair-raising event for my poor uncle and aunt. Anyway, during this time, I went to Brentwood High School, and like all of the other normal kids, we all had to go to the bus stop and get on the bus to go to school, and it all repeated in the afternoon to come home, blah, blah, blah, blah.

I made friends with a boy across the field from me named T.C.M., and Johnny, his older brother, and Paul, his younger brother, and Angelina—there goes another Angelina in my life and Eva—that was his momma. Oh, she loved me, and I loved her; she was always so nice to me. And his dad was always really nice to me. They were such a beautiful family and of course, I became very, very attached to T.C.M. He was a good boy and would never let anybody hurt me. He wouldn't let anybody make fun of me and he wouldn't let anybody start any of that 'Mary' crap or 'sissy' business. I couldn't wait to wake up to go be with him in fact, I think I bored him to death.

During this riding the bus back tote school business and T.C.M. being my buddy and then the Brady's being my buddies and Carol being my friend and this little group of kids really did accept me, and we were a nice group of kids. I had an adventure with each one of these kids. Riding the school bus—one time right after school, there was this guy who would just annoy me, like my dear friend in the Home. "Look at that sissy." Cause I was into the art thing and I was into plays and I was into dancing. You know there's always one num-nut that's going to call you a sissy or a fairy or a Mary and finally you know T.C.M. went and talked to the guy and said, "Chill out," (in today's language) and said, "Leave the guy alone, he's my friend, he's cool."

The guy was a real ball buster so I just turned around and whipped the crap outta him in front of God and everybody. I mean I beat him to a pizza, bleeding all over the place and I said to myself, "My, God, what have I done to this guy?" So I got down on the floor and looked in his face, and I said, "Now I'm calling the doctor, but are you going to call me names anymore or am I going to kick your face in your teeth?" He didn't say anything. Of course the kid walked around on a crutch for a week or two and I really felt bad. I felt bad, but you know you get to the point where you are tired of people getting on your stuff. Today, you know we just go and cut your legs off (*laughter*), only kidding. But when you mess with an Italian, I tell you what, he ain't gonna take none of your crap. You don't put people down; you just do not put people down. I learned that the hard way, because I used to make fun of my friends and try to make them change, I found out quickly you don't do that. God does that. You accept people for what and who they are, and how they are or you just don't bother. (*Phone*)

Enough of that foolishness, let's me reflect back once more on Jeannie, when she would teach me and Audrey those dance steps. You should have seen the likes of us, we were like pumpkins no, take that back, I wasn't like a pumpkin. In fact, I was tall and had a 36" waist with long blonde hair down to my buttocks, and all the kids said I was pretty cool. I smoked cigarettes, one after the other (which now I know was most certainly not cool), and I don't understand how Uncle Nick never smelled the smell of me smoking cigarettes. But he was going to give me permission to smoke at sixteen anyway. Let's stop right there once more and continue with Audrey and I and Jeannie. So once Jeannie would teach us the dance steps Audrey and I would learn the dance steps. And of course Audrey had to teach me all over again, I was a num-nut again. But anyhow, we would dance, and anytime all of us kids would get together, we'd dance.

They'd look at Audrey and me and I'd say to all of them, "Get up and dance." We'd try to make our friends get up and dance. All of the boys would try and make a pact with me by saying, "We'll do whatever your want, Vinnie, as long as you don't embarrass me and make me get up and dance." (*Laughter*) One of those boys was Joey Brady. But he would get up and dance slow with Carol. All of these kids were just really good kids. I remember Jimmy Rhyman. He looked like Rick, Ricky; the boy Ricky Nelson Joey married his high school sweetheart. Wouldn't it be nice if I could see them again and they'd still be married? Oh, well. So Audrey and I danced, and danced, and we always went to all the dances at the school. One time we went to the cotillion and we danced and we did a cha-

cha and won first prize. Oh look out, don't you know that gave me a head bigger than my butt; well, my head was always bigger than my butt. We won this little telephone directory book where you push it and it pops up and if you take along the side and push your little pointer to whatever part of the alphabet, it would go to the names under that letter, it was a rip-off gift, but we had won a gift, and we both went back home with bloated egos.

The very next day, I called the Arthur Murray Dance Studio in Bay Shore, New York. They asked "How old are you, kid?" I said, "I'm fourteen." "Well, we'll call you, don't call us". For a year I persisted in trying to get hold of these people to teach me dancing. Thank God for Audrey and Jeannie because of them I have become a ballroom dance teacher. (*Noise and distractions*).

But anyway, T.C.M. was always a good friend. I remember he introduced me to a sweet, sweet young lady Audrey. She's a descendent of Tony Bennett. Her father, Nicholas, and her mother, Margie, and her sister, Jeannie. Jeannie would commute back and forth to college. Funny thing, folks, the Benedettos didn't live too far from me when lived in Brooklyn, but I it seems I never met them, never knew them. In fact the dad owned a grocery story named Benedetto's. And I'm quite sure in our passing; I had to have passed by Audrey.

Audrey was a very matter-of-fact kind of girl, a little bit like my cousin Pauline. You didn't mess around, you know. So the Benedettos moved to Long Island in the vicinity of Oakdale Street. Now Bay Shore, Long Island was evidently brand new, Brentwood, all of these communities were coming into their own. My Uncle Nick was a building contractor who built a lot of the Henley Homes and many, many of the other builder's names and also did some work on some of the Robert Moser Causeway, which today is a big avenue to take you to the beach. Uncle Nicholas did quite well for himself, God love him, and he let Vincent come and stay. And let me tell you some of the things I remember doing during that period like meeting after dinner so you make sure you were real good every day so when you say, "Dad, can I go out?" he'd say yes, but I had to live in fear for every time he would want to say no. I don't really think I was a bad kid, I just feared my uncle, yet I loved him very much, and he really never did hit me, never. Except there was one time when I thought I was going to beat him up, and he said, "Come on." And he cleared out the living room, and he beat the pulp outta me. I was getting big now and thinking and acting like I was the cock of the roost. But he still put up with me, he still loved me, he was really a good man.

My Aunt Rosie would coddle me and I know she love me and she would say, "Vincent, Vincent, what are we going to do with you. You're stuck between the devil and the deep blue sea." I still don't remember what that means, but that I remember her saying it.

So, one occasion I remember, was Audrey's prom night. We all went and got our tuxedos. I just didn't know if he would let me go or not. So when he did let me go, he said, "Be home at 9 o'clock." Well, Audrey let him have it. She says, "Give me a break, Mirabella. Nine o'clock. It's 8 o'clock now." But that is the way my uncle Nick did things. This was just one incident, but I'm trying to recall some of the good whammy things I did. Like the time I came home from band practice, oh yeah, there I was, "clarineting" again. I think I had made it to second clarinetist, but you know, folks, I can not recall even one time I played with the band. I had met a Spanish boy in the band, and it ended up being that there were six Spanish brothers. I don't know if they were Puerto Ricans boys or if they were Mexican, but every one of them had a talent, and they were all musically inclined, and best of all, they liked Vinnie, so yahoo. I think it was the time when there was a war brewing between the whites and the ethnics; the Italian ethnic, and the blacks or the browns or whatever; it was just stupid, a little more dangerous than it was in the story of Borem Place. Anyway, I didn't come straight home instead of going to practice that day, I just went to Danny's and my Aunt Rosie came and found me and she said, "Vincent, I've been calling the school, having heart attacks, where have you been?" I said, "Well, Aunt Ro, I didn't want to go to band practice today, and I thought I'd come and watch Danny 'home' the birds." You see they had pigeons, but then tell me an Italian that didn't have pigeons. And it was fascinating to see Danny or Johnny out there getting the birds out and getting them to fly. Well, Aunt Ro took me home and gave me a bunch of chores to do, and I did them. I always listened to my Aunt Rose. And she would say, "Vincent, I'm going to have to tell your uncle." And I would plead with her saying, "Please don't tell my uncle, he'll punish me for a year." Anyway when he came home, it seems she never would tell him.

My aunt Rose always seemed to protect me a lot and she kept me from getting in any kind of trouble after stating I was between the devil and the deep blue sea. I called her recently where they live in California. I asked her "Aunt Rose, tell me the truth, what kind of a kid was I?" She said, "You really want me to tell you?" (*Laughter*) I said, "Really, yeah, be honest." She said, "Vincent, you were a wonderful, sweet, charming, warm and loving child." I loved all those adjectives. "But let me tell you what, if we didn't do something just your way, well then it just wouldn't get done." She said, "You were such a party-pooper, you would ruin so many fun things we wanted to do." You know what, dear reader; I had no idea that that's how I was.

Here I am now, and I think maybe I ought to name this book "That's How I Was." I had no idea that I was such a little dipstick. But Aunt Ro did save my life. I guess now I'm getting around sixteen, seventeen, and I thought I'd try my hand at a job, at working.

35

St. Vincent's

I have to turn back the hands of time once more, and go back to St. Vincent's Home, 66 Borem Place, Brooklyn, New York. I graduated St. John's, Rockaway Park, with F's, D's, C's, B's and one A+ in religion, so instead of going to Erasmus Hall for more than a year, went there one day, the only Italian boy in a school with a bunch of Jewish girls. And that's the school that her highness, Barbara Streisand, goes to, but I never saw her. So now they send me to Boy's High School. This is your blackboard jungle school that you see on TV.

Now, understand, after St. John's Home, cause I'm getting away with it, we boys transferred to Borem Place, 66 Borem Place, St. Vincent Home For Boys. What a great, wonderful, Irish priest was the man who ran St Vincent's. Now it was a case of you're on your own; in other words, nobody holds your hand. You get up in the morning; you go down and have your breakfast; you find whatever bus or train it is to take you where it is you want to go and then you come home. You take your shower, do your homework, play basketball, whatever else you have to do, go to chapel, eat supper and then you go on from there. So I kind of liked Brooklyn because it was busy like New York City. You could just get lost doing any and everything. Ever since I've been a little kid, I used to walk the neighborhood; so here I am walking this neighborhood, and let me tell you what a scary neighborhood it was. (I'll give you an example)
What happens is if you go six blocks one direction, you're in an Italian neighborhood; and if you go six blocks beyond that, then you're in a Spanish neighborhood; and another four blocks is the Puerto Rican neighborhood; four more blocks and your in a Mexican neighborhood; another four blocks puts you into the Irish neighborhood; then it's the black neighborhood and back to the Italian neighborhood. In order for me to go to school, I had to walk 54 blocks or something like that, and as I walked these blocks, I made sure I found the head hon-

cho in each of the groups and made friends with him. So now they send me to Boy's High School. This is your blackboard jungle school the one you see on TV.

Now here's the thing, if I wasn't supposed to go past the Puerto Rican's six blocks, Mineo would come up to me and say to me, "Now Vincent, I can't guarantee your safety these six block, we're getting ready to have a knock down, drag out." and I said, "It's really important for me to get there,"—it was not—"can't you just protect me enough to get past."

He says, "Well, all right I'll get the word out that when Vinnie comes past these six blocks, they gotta let you go, and if anybody messes with you, you let me know. Okay?"

I says, "Okay." And I'd walk, and he'd tell them the next day, and the guys would look at me and if they got near me I said, "Don't you mess with me; I'll tell Mineo and he'll rub your face in the dirt, boy." So a couple of them thought they were smart and he would come an' slap the hell out of them. So I made friends with Mineo. The hardest ones were the Irish; cause they didn't like anybody, bless their hearts. But I got a hold of what's-his-face (my memory is going folks) and we became good friends. So I was friends with everybody in a gang and people couldn't believe this shit, this Mirabella, this Vinnie, can walk right past everything. So because of that I'd always show off, of course! But when they would have a gang war, I would certainly stay home.

(*Laughter*) And did they have some gang wars. If any of the youngsters today sees that movie West Side Story, it was sort of like it, but today, the wars are really frightening. Kids seem today to think everybody should respect them. And I guess we should just as they must respect us. They forget that.

As a kid I didn't care how many parents or how many of my elders would hit me for disrespect cause I would always tell them … They'd tell me, "You're disrespectful." I had one, smart uncle, who said to me, "Why in the hell are you so damn disrespectful?" and I said, "Because you're disrespectful. You slap me up side of the head and then tell me to go to my room. What kind of damn dog do you think I am?" That wasn't my Uncle Nicky, he was nice to me and that was Borem Place.

There was all kind of things going on inside that school in the back stairways. But everybody left me alone, but it was still scary. When I decided I was too afraid to keep going to that school after a few years, they sent me to Manual Training High School, a vocational school.

Now I don't know a pipe from a hole in the wall, and I just couldn't learn anything, I still can't change a flat. What a pity.

St. Vincent's Home was a home, a home/school where you lived in and went to school there. There were welfare offices in that building along with a church, and there was sleeping quarters. It had a big refractory—place to eat, good food. You know, you're warm in the winter and cool in the summer, but we went out to go to school from there. Now I didn't walk to school all the time, it took too long. It usually took about an hour to walk to school. I only walked to school when I wanted to see what's up with the gangs an' see if they still liked me and respected me. We rode a train mostly and sometimes a bus. The thing at that time I think I most wanted to hear is that Vinnie is okay; he really is a good guy. And one of the things I'd tell these gang boys, like Chico, I'd say, "I know your Madre."

"Yeah, how da ya know my muther?"

"I know yer muther."

"Wha' da ya mean, ya know my muther?"

"I know your mother, so don't rock around me. Stand still when ya talk to me." I've done that all my life. You're gonna hear that about this one that came the other day, Brian.

"Hey, man." I said, "What the fuck you think I am a monkey? Hey, man. What da ya, hey, man?" Oops! Scratch! (*Laughter*) became a comedian for a little time, had people off their rockers.

Now my life starts to take place with me leaving St. Vincent's Home and going to live with my Uncle Nicholas and my Aunt Rose and their family. I was maybe sixteen, so I've done a lot in my little, young life.

36

Going to Work

I quit high school, and my uncle said, "If your gonna quit school, you're gonna get a job." Wow. So I went and got me a job. The first job I ever had was at Hill's Supermarket, I was going to become a butcher, yes I was. (*Laughter*) I'll never forget Benny and Frank; Frank he was a saint. He was one of the nicest men. (*Shouting at someone*) Anyway, I worked there and they put me in the butcher department, and you know what, ladies and gentlemen, it's sad because I had so many wonderful opportunities to make a really wonderful living for myself. It was just that I was so darn immature and still trying to learn, I was always walking around with my eyes on my butt. It seems I just could not see the light as they say. Anyway, one day they were teaching me how to bone a piece of meat, and I've got a scar on my wrist to recollect from that day of my becoming a butcher. Now to the greatest of all sins, for which I have embarrassed and humiliated my whole entire family. You see we all love lobster. Well one day they had a sale on lobster at the butcher shop, and I called my aunt, and I said, "Aunt Ro, come here today, I'm gonna give you some lobster." See, I wanted to be important to my Uncle Nick. I wanted him and my Aunt Ro to be proud of me. Little did I know they already did love me and were proud of me. So what did I do? I lowered the price on the lobsters, and God knows I bagged four or five or six bags of lobsters. You know, I really couldn't have been too stupid to do the things I have done. It had to take some sort of intelligence to do such 'stupid' things.

But then, this silly little girl, (some of you girls are so full of crap), I don't even know why some of you take jobs. Anyway, this little girl was all over herself because a claw was coming out of the plastic bag, and then who walks into the front line just come home from lunch? It was Mr. Frank, and he saw it, and he was going to help her, and then he looked at the price and he says, "Hey, there's something wrong here. Let's take these lobsters to the back." Then he said, "Did you bag these lobsters"?

I said, "Yes, I did." And he said, "Do you know this lady?" I said, "Yes, I do." He said "Well, who is she?" I said, "Well, she's my mom, but she's really not my mom, she's my aunt mom." And then Aunt Rose said, "What has happened"? You see, she didn't know I had lowered the price so we could have all those lobsters. She was not aware of this and it embarrassed and humiliated her. But now let me tell you about this man, Mr. Frank. May God bless him through eternity because he could have destroyed me and my aunt right then and there. But, he believed me that she didn't know anything about it. So he let her go, and she in turn paid full price for the lobsters. Oh, I just knew I was gonna get killed for that when I got home.

Then Mr. Frank took me in the back room, and he sat me down and he said, "You know, I am supposed to fire you." But he counseled me, and talked to me, and then he hugged me, and I cried, and I never did that again. So I didn't really steal the lobster like I did with the Mary Janes, but what else would you call it? Anyway, God in his kindness had sent along quite an advocate in Mr. Frank. I'd love to see him again, and I'm going to remember his last name forever. So that's the story about the lobster. Mr. Frank was just the nicest man, as were the women who worked in that department and then there was Benny, the Italian, the cutie-patootie of the group. All the women fainted over Benny.

Now we move on, however I'm still working for Hill's Supermarket, and I was doing real good. I became the front-end man, wheeling in the carriages and parking the carriages and loading up the groceries in people's cars. And you know you always get stuck with some lady who acts like what you call a female dog. Some of these women can be this way from the word 'go.' I'm going to have to refrain what I just said so we don't hurt anybody. Some of these 'women' would come up and try to make you do everything; just so, and take up to 20 minutes and then they don't even say, "Thank you," or tip you, and in those days, you worked for tips. So there was this one particular woman who always came when I worked and I said to her, "Why don't you ever smile, and why don't you ever give me a tip, and why are you so creepy looking all the time? Forgive me, but I'm trying to learn why people do things like you do." She said she didn't even have any idea that she had that kind of attitude. I think she was a liar because as we go on in my book, you're going to see several of those kinds of women I've had to deal with. Believe me they're gonna get theirs this day because I'm reading and telling you about them in my book. People who have caused so much sorrow and so much hatred and so much awful negativity. So that lady ended up giving me five dollar tip. I didn't call her a name but I just put her groceries in her car and said, "if you're not gonna tip me, I'm not gonna bag your car because I'm working for tips." And let me tell you what, folks, I use to make a fortune in tips. I turned that job into the job that you're gonna want if you work at Hill's Supermarket. So that's one bad thing that I did that ended up turning out to be positive.

So I see a lot of kids today when I go to the supermarket, and they take your cart out to the car and you're not supposed to give them any tips. Actually Mrs. Rogers gives them a dollar for me. And that's all about my first job at Hill's Supermarket while I was still living with Uncle Nick and Aunt Ro.

I've moved into Goodrich Avenue which was across the street from Hill's supermarket and I lived upstairs above a guy named Salvatore Vecci. He and his young bride and his little baby son rented me a beautiful bedroom and a bathroom, and he would come up and talk to me about different things and try to be nice to me, and it seems like I lived there forever. Here I was living in my own little room. I'm sixteen now, at least, I'm going to work now at Hill's and I'm coming home.

37

Arthur Murray's and Dancing

Finally to the story about the Arthur Murray Dance Studio in Bay Shore, Long Island, New York. If you guys get any business because of my book, you better give me twenty percent. I used to call them every day after 3:00 p.m. religiously. They knew me, "Vinnie, Vinnie, Vinnie, Vinnie." Finally Mr. John Smith said to me, "Vincent, Saturday morning at 6 o'clock, meet me in the back stairs of the studio." Now I remember I went and had an interview with them a year prior to this actually at the age of fourteen and I danced with Tonya Neevas (*who I hear has a boat full of children now and lives in Puerto Rico on welfare*). I would love to see her; she was such a gorgeous girl. Anyway, we did the boogie woogie and the jitter bug, and then I dropped her, and for an encore, I fell on top of her. So there went that. "We'll call you, don't call us." I swear, it was just like in the movies, folks. At time this whole book is like in the movies. So for a year I persisted, and then here we were, it was six o'clock on Saturday morning. Mr. Smith thought he was gonna be rid of me. But at Six o'clock Saturday I was up on those back stairs, but asleep. Then at 9:30 I heard, "Oh, my God Vincent," and I knew it was 9:30a.m., because we had a Big Ben clock across the street. He said, "I forgot all about you. Please let me take you for breakfast." Listen to this guy now he takes me across the street for breakfast a place just like Mr. and Mrs. Green had except these people used to sell heroes, now folks, you never had a hero sandwich like you could have in New York. They're nothing like it here in North Carolina. You'll never eat pizza here either like you get in New York. Anyway, he got me a glass of milk and a doughnut, and I said, "Oh, crap, is this what I'm in for? Is this the kind of man I'm gonna work for?" I said, "I want bacon and eggs, thank you, right now." And I had bacon and eggs, milk, doughnut, the whole ball of wax. Then he took me up to the studio and they started to begin to train me. I have to tell you, I didn't know my butt from elbow and elbow from pipe (*laughter*).

So three or four of the boy teachers said, "What are you doing here? You can't dance. You're such a sissy. You're such a faggot. You can't dance. You won't learn anything." Once this guy named Chico asked me, "What are you doing here?" and I said, "I'm going to win a big-time dance-a-rama." We used to go to upstate New York. He was this big old Italian fellow, who use to call me a 'sissy' all the time; he was a big old Catholic boy. He was terrible. And he was supposed to be a good Catholic. Anyway they all do it, Catholics, Jews, Irish, Italians, if you get a kid that's a little whacky, all of a sudden he's queer. That's fine with me, dear reader. So here we go.

Trying to make this less painful and a long story short, three years later at the Hawaii Open with the Arthur Murray Dance Studio, Bay Shore, Long Island, New York, I kicked this guy's tail and beat him hands down, first place, ten times. (*Laughter*)

Later, he had the nerve to get up into the public and to say he had changed his name. You see in this business, you change your name so my name was Jay Marco, and I will explain to you later, just how I became Jay Marco. Anyway here we are, this is years later, I'm getting ahead of myself, I beat him, and then he tried to tell everybody he was my first teacher, and I got up on the stairs and pushed him off the stage. I am so terrible; when I have enough of you, boy I let you know it, and I'm sure most everyone is like that. Now, Christ would prefer that we don't behave in that manner, and I'm working on it, I truly am. So I said, "Folks, he is a liar. He called me a 'sissy' and a 'queer.' He dumped me, and he's a liar. Don't give him any credit for anything." And that took care of the story of Chico.

Understand, folks, this was way later in my ballroom dancing. This was while I was still at Bay Shore, boyfriend and girlfriend, Audrey and Vinnie.

38

My Second Job

Now because of my time feeling I was raised by all these religious prelates and subjects and yet here I'm this fifteen year old kid, who is acting like going on seventeen. I got another job and this time I was making swimming pools. Now at this time I had moved from Goodrich Avenue to live with a dance student lady. Someone who was big-time in Catholic charities an official who used to see me dance at the studio. They used to tell me, "Vinnie, you can go live with her. She'll rent you a room." So, it seems that God sends everybody to you; and here she comes, and we start dancing, and she starts teaching me and then Bob Boyd starts dancing. We used to sneak away to just get away like I still do, and we would go dancing somewhere where people were going to appreciate you. You know not look at you, and you have to be 'on'. When you're in the public, you always have to be 'on'. Ask Oprah, she'll tell you. Anyway, we'd go off and have a good time, and then I came to live with her and we'd cook and we'd…. Oh, God rest her soul, she was the dearest, dearest women, and if she's not a saint today, she will be by the time this book is over.

She was a good woman, she put up with me, and she would teach me. She would say "Vincent, you don't do this, you don't do that. You want all these people to like you, and you're a handsome boy, and you're this and you're that, don't be such a dip-stick".

Now we're going to as I mentioned a little while ago, talk about the religious subjects during this time I've always felt in my heart, and I think it's because I was raised by Catholic priests and raised by Catholic brothers and been influenced by Catholic nuns (*not the ones that hit you on the knuckles, by the way—God spared me that cause I'd probably have killed her*), good holy people. Deep down, you would probably feel that you may have a calling. As far as even still today, I yearn to love my God more than anything else, and what have you. So I have been contemplating joining a religious order. Now you would think why would I want to join the society of Mary, the Sons of Mary, the Marionist Brothers, but somewhere along the line through going to mass and to church, I was inspired toward a more contemporary kind of life style, the Franciscan Capuchin Order of Friars, Capuchin Franciscans. So I have put in an application, and I talked to a Father Kemen. They're a little bit like the army and navy—they have guys that recruit you.

39

The Monastery

There's been quite a long silence and a lot of devastation up to this point, and I gotta regroup and get organized. At this time I have to attempt to continue the saga, the story of my life, Vincent Nicholas Mirabella, and today is Thursday, October 9, 1997. I'm seated at my desk at the dance studio watching two silly women trying to do the step called the swivel. Aileen Massey and Jane Rogers and it's very distracting, but I am going to try.

But now, I'm going to start this chapter with me entering into the religious seminary. I feel I was very fortunate that as a youngster I had been thinking I had the call to the religious life. As all children or young people think that they are to dedicate their life to Christ, so the church gave me a chance. Very immature, very frivolous, full of a lot of baloney and never took a thing serious. Off I go on February 2nd, Audrey Benedetto's (who was at that time my girlfriend) birthday, and later I learned I had broken her heart by taking this action. Little did I know that this would have happened. I boarded the bus with my little black cabinet that you take, and six of this and six of that. They tell you what you should bring, you know. I don't think there was a whole lot of people who said good-bye, and that was Audrey's birthday, she tells me. Well, I know it was her birthday, but I didn't know it was that day, so now I know that I did leave on February 2, 1959 or 60 maybe. And it broke Audrey's heart. I had no idea.

I rode to a place called Middletown, Connecticut, to a young church called St. Pious the Tenth, and I was greeted by my to-be novice master just a fine human being. So here I am on a bus from Long Island, New York, going to Middletown, Connecticut. Sometime during the day or early evening arrived at St. Pious the 10th Holy Catholic Church and Friary of the Order of Friars Minor Capuchin Franciscan. These are the austere sect of the three Franciscan sects. Here I saw this man in a long brown robe with a white cincture with three knots on it and a wooden rosary with a wooden cross hanging from one side, bare-footed in sandals and a big old beard. He said, "Are you Vincent?" said, "Yes, Father, am."

Regarding my book, if you're going to put down the priests, and the nuns remember in every walk of life there's a bad apple. I'm a bad apple in anybody's life, but that doesn't mean God doesn't love me. So if you're going to sit here and put down my faith and the people in my faith, you're going to have to deal with God for that. But I want to tell you that as God is our judge, in the years that I was in the religious seminary, I have never once seen anything or anyone less than holy and struggling and striving to become God-like. Anyway, that's an opinion, and it's a truthful opinion. I have lived with hundreds of men in this environment, in the monastery, and I actually have seen some of these priests glow. We had a Brother Guido, and he would glow, God love him. With due respect, this is where I received my education, and I got to know my God on a personal level, and where I certainly have studied the Ten Commandments, very simple, folks, just ten requests that God asks us. And we can do it.

Anyway, let's begin by going back to Middletown, Connecticut. Father Barnabas, this was a little short gentleman; he wore the brown habit, with the sandals, and the cord around his waist with the three knots to communicate the vow of poverty, chastity, and obedience. He had a beard. St. Frances wanted his followers to be austere. Can you imagine me being austere? Quite a holy Jude, really he was a wonderful person. I didn't appreciate him until after my year and a half as a novitiate so here we were in our little black suits with black ties and white shirts and we're introduced to all the frater and one in particular was Brother Daniel B. That guy was a character an Irishman Just the greatest guy. And he'd just look everybody up and down, you know, and he'd talk to us with his Irish accent. "What kind of knot heads are these?" (*just a little Jewish in there*) He'd scrutinize us.

He said, "Well, welcome, and come in." Now this is the novitiate. A novitiate takes a year of canonical enclosure where they try to conform your will to that of the law of God, and you try to learn obedience, and you try to learn humility, and you hope to God you continue your vow of chastity which you will take in a short time. So we lived in small rooms which were really very comfortable. The austerity has really gotten a little more comfortable in the 1900's. It's a cement block room with a little closet type thing without a door and a desk, a lamp and a chair. And this would be your life. The novitiate takes a year, but there's a period called postulancy where we become postulants. That's six months, and that's why we would wear each day our dark suit and our white shirt and our black tie to mass and to the community. The novitiate was attached to the secular church, so the brothers would have their own little chapel, and we'd walk through the sacristy as it were and go into the main church, and there's where the people would see these boys, and the whole congregation knew that these were young men in training. I was a class of three.

Let me recall the characters; though you don't say the word character; although this man really was a one, he was a good character. His name was Brother Daniel B, another Irishman, and he was a cook, a chef. This guy could flat put it to you. He could make anything, everything, and it all melted in your mouth. And he really would scrutinize us. He'd look us up and down, you know, and if you did something dumb, he's swat you in the ear. He was just a good guy. These men is this particular house were four priests and Brother Daniel, and the priests were about the business of the church to raise funds to support the church, and they were each and every one of these men absolutely unique. The Father guardian who was our superior was in charge of the entire church and in charge of the brothers and the priests, and of course he had a grave responsibility. Brother Daniel B was the brother who would be our inspiration because we were going to enter his vocation either as cooks or sacristans or laborers or whatever it took. Generally the Brother's life is spent in prayer. In the capuchin order it's a lot of prayer and work rather than in the tertiary orders where they teach or minister to hospitals or whatever they do. We're sort of more the austere role of St. Francis.

By the way, in our room which we refer to as cell, there was always a crucifix. So between spiritual reading and following the schedule, they kept the brothers busy, and at the end of your postulancy, they vote on you by throwing white beans in a platter. And if there's one black bean in there, you're in trouble—you're out. And I made it. I got to become invested as a novice and oh, let me tell you, that was the proudest day of my life. You tell in front of God and everybody that you're going to serve your Lord. I'll tell ya its hard stuff. For those of you that want to believe or for those of you that are skeptics or whatever problems anybody has, when you live in the house of the Lord, and any time the presence of the blessed sacraments when you're living in the house of God, there's a strange feeling, a feeling of protection and comfort. And let me tell you folks, if you don't believe in God, you come to my house you call and make an appointment first and if you're sincere, before a day is over with me, you're going to know God is around. There's no reason for anybody not to believe in God, there really isn't. I can't get off on that—I'll get letters! I tell a story later about teaching in a college, and I'm always getting letters. I feel like David Letterman. Maybe he'll read our book.

Novitiate is a year where you really spend you time learning about the gospel and learning further about the Old Testament and the New Testament, and the part that a lot of people get to miss out on: just getting to know Christ. And you remember somewhere in the book we were talking about this little boy. Well, you're going to be surprised what happens next. No big deal. I mean don't want anybody to think God has revealed himself to me in the person of a baby boy. That's blasphemy. I'm gonna be excommunicated from my church.

But I don't care who you are I met this little boy; he was my friend and still is.

Believe it or not! So at that, I'm sorry, don't care who cares and who don't care and who don't believe it, this is it. But now the novitiate, this wonderful, holy, humble man, Father Barnabas, and I sincerely hope that I'm not insulting or hurting any of these great man's feelings cause they're all still alive today and I'd love to see them again. In fact, ladies and gentlemen, if there was a way for me to sell my riches and give it to the poor and this order would take me back, would go yesterday, and I would spend the rest of my life in humble submission to try and die in the grace of God. This is really what I would love to do at the very end of this passage. I don't care about diamonds. I don't care about all that crap that I got. I want to be in a monastery with my brothers and sisters in Christ.

This man he was a little older than we were, just the nicest man in the world, and he just couldn't be bothered with little immature people like me, you know. He would tolerate us, and you know that's what religious life is. They don't really spend their life trying to keep the Ten Commandments or trying to conquer venial sin. They work on perfection. Like the brother next to you breath smells 24 hours a day. Well, you can't do what I do, tell him, say, "Go take a bath and wash your mouth out." You have to live with it and offer it up to God. So that's the stuff they deal with. Perfection—to "b e c o m e p e r f e c t" like Christ. And they say that St. Francis of Assisi was the one and only human since, before, during or after, in between, up, down, over and out that came close to being a model of Christ's perfection. And let me tell you what, Folks, you can put me in 20 monasteries, I'm never gonna become like Christ. But I certainly am trying to be Christ-like. But one of my biggest problems is I have a mouth on me like a sailor. At times I think I'd make a sailor sick. But I'm working on it. I get angry. I'll cuss you out in a heartbeat. But I'm working on it. We are all sinners, and we all love God, and that's why we're here.

So, here I am in my very 100 per cent wool habit with a little cowl like a hair shirt type thing, and you know its 98 degrees outside in Middletown, Connecticut, and hot heat, and we're on open ground and brother I'll tell you his name later. Why can't I remember his name? Because I think he kind of put up with me, but he was always nice to me. He would never yell at me. I just remembered his name it was Brother Eugene.

We built a cross with a crown of thorns and all the brothers put rocks around it, and I said, "What are we doing this for?" But anyway, just like in the movies, right? Big old can bucket with guess what in it? Holes, very good. And what do we do with the bucket with holes? We fill it with water and take it to the trough and pour it in and come back and go back and…. well, heck, didn't get no water in that thing cause the holes were big.

So just like in the movies, I went to Father and he says "Well Vincent no, we took religious names in those days, and Vincent Nicholas Mirabella became Brother Matthew, Order of Friars Minor Capuchin, and anyway, he said, "Brother Matthew." And I said, "WHAAAT!"

He said, "Why aren't you finished yet. It's almost time for lunch." said, "I don't know, the thing's got too many holes in it. I'm sick of this mess," and I threw the bucket.

And he turned around, and he walked away. And I just stood there. Two hours later he came back and he said "What are you doing, Brother Matthew?" said, "I'm waiting for you to forgive me."

He said, "You better go eat, you missed your lunch." So I gave that man another star in his crown because for the year and a half he put up with me, he can be canonized a saint now. And Brother Daniel, he was neat. I used to sneak in the kitchen, and we'd tell little jokes, and we'd be little sillies, you know, and he had an accent on him that was incredible. And then on feast days, they would have. Now ladies and gentlemen, let me tell you one thing about religious people—thank you, Jesus—they know how to celebrate a feast day. For those of you who don't understand what that means get a book and read it. If you love your mother with your heart and soul and you celebrate her birthday, if you're not a sorry son, you're going to go out and get her a big birthday. If you're an idiot like most people are, it's not going to mean anything to you. So with us with the saints who we know have proven in their lives that they are in the hands of God, that they do help our lives Somebody told me I was too Catholic. Then somebody else says, "You're very Catholic." Don't get the wrong idea about my Catholic. I am not a good Catholic. I am not a practicing Catholic. I'm too lazy to go and get my butt out of bed and respect my Lord, but if you were in my house, you'd think it was a church. So don't ask me what's wrong. Its laziness, and surely God's not going to condemn you to hell for being lazy. However, can't think for God because God does not think like we do.

So we are now doing what … oh back to Brother Daniel. They had a little cocktail occasionally so he says, "You want a cocktail?" says, "Does a bear crap in the woods?" So he'd hide a martini, and I'd have a martini. Well, was kitchen help, see. Boy, I'd get so scrunched, but one day they played a real good one on me. They were gonna get me. They filled my martini with vinegar. (*Laughter*) had a vinegar martini, and I went blaaaa, screaming and yelling at everybody, and the friary just burst out laughing. So that was Brother Daniel, full of the baloney.

Now Father Anscar, he was a very handsome young man, very muscular man, a pretty cool dude, a good guy. You know, folks, you gotta understand something about loving God, okay? It's not boring, and it doesn't mean you gotta walk around like you got a needle up your ass. It's a celebration. Loving God is a joyous experience. It doesn't mean you gotta walk around beating your breast. It doesn't mean you gotta go around saying, "Jesus, Jesus, Jesus." It doesn't mean you gotta go screaming out all these damn Matthew 2 and verse 3, and Mary 4 and Uncle George. Please, get a grip. Loving Christ is a celebration. He will take you to eternity. You better remember that word, forever and ever and ever, we're gonna spend our eternity whether we're in the presence of God or not in the presence of God. So off the soapbox, but let you understand that religious subjects as dedicated to God as they are they gotta be very happy people. If you're not a happy person, you're boring, then go to hell with the devil. That's where the devil and the boring people are.

So anyway, it's a celebration. And Father Anscar certainly was an example of celebration. He'd get up in the morning, come down, get ready to say the mass, he'd kiss his little (?) amet, put it around his neck and say, "Oh, what a life without a wife and ten thousand kids," and knock all the altar boys awake, you know. Clean fun, you know a very nice, holy man. And he was in charge of the Boy Scouts, and he was the priest that was in the National Guard so they went away on maneuvers, you know. He was good for the brothers because it was nice to see his presence. Now during this visitation or this year we did all sorts of chores. We were taught to iron and clean all of the linens on the altar. That had to be a wonderful experience. To safeguard the appearance of the sanctuary and clean the church. Whatever it took to run a church and be a good sidekick for the people and for the priest. To cook, sew, bake, and outdoor rugged stuff. Just whatever it took to either teach in the community—we were trained to handle everything. But most of all we were trained to get solidarity with our faith and our belief in God so that when we do as we are today in this lousy world, can survive and persevere. Be in the world but not a part of the world. And I'll tell you, in my three, four years in this service of God, would give up apple pie every Sunday to go back and do it again. I was too immature as you're e gonna see. Oh, you talk about Dennis the Menace.

Let's move on out of this novitiate, and I graduated the novitiate. We took our simple vows right there at St. Pious, and my mother came to that. Let's see, think somebody else came to that, but my mother was there. Oh, boy, that was quite a thing. Got a picture of her with that. So she was just really proud, and said, "Well, Mom, good." So anyway, here we are now, we can smoke, and now we have all the privileges. You know, it's amazing how you have to work for all these privileges in life, but the simple things. You know, we didn't get to go out on dates and run motorcycles. We were religious subjects, you know. So they took us now to spend three years of our simple vows, and the Brothers went to St. Anthony's Friary, Hudson, New Hampshire. Oh, maybe two, three, four hundred priests and us little green horns. Now St. Anthony's Friary was also a college. St. Anthony's Friary sits directly across the river from West Point. You can see West Point. West Point can see St. Anthony's friary. Two great schools of discipline and except in ours there's a reward of love and in theirs, it becomes a little bit monstrous, I'm sure. But anyway, we can hear them sometimes, and they in turn can hear the friars chanting on occasion. This Gregorian chant stuff is incredible. So let's start. I met Brother Pious, of course Brother Pious was in the monastery with me and Brother Ignatius was in the monastery with me, but don't think they were in my class. I don't know if they were; everybody made it at the end except for me. Anyway, Pious, Ignatius, Bendino, and an Italian fellow, and that boy suffered with falling arches, and he never would cuss or swear. Oh, the Lord sent him a lot of sorrow. Pious was the sweetest, nicest and Ignatius, God love him, a little skinny old thing, bless his heart. He was just a little bean pole with a beard. He looked like a rabbi but he wasn't, he was Catholic. But anyway, all those guys were really nice. Brother Marion, another brother. So now they put me to begin my chores. I think they had me in the kitchen with Brother Conrad. Well, that was all right. I know how to cook, and I learned how to cook. Then from there my next one was making bread. Oh, let me tell you this Conrad could make bread. I have recipes for a hundred loaves of bread; don't have them for one loaf of bread. Conrad used to say, "Brother Mattchew, Brother Mattchew, you're too worldly, you're too worldly." So you know most of our time we would greet each other in a religious manner, and we would enter each other's room and leave each other's room with a blessing. And the brother's would spend their time saying a lot of "Our Fathers" and "Hail Mary's" and little prayers for the souls see we prayed for the souls who had no one to pray for them, and when you're in the state of sanctifying grace, these prayers, the Lord promises to sent comfort to these poor creatures who died and have to make up everybody's gotta pay their bills, you know, you gotta pay your bills. Yes, I'm sorry, well you're forgiven, but now you also gotta pay. You don't necessarily have to be punished. So I finally learned that. So then for the bread ... let me tell you, that boy could bake bread, and he could cook, and he could set up menus—little old tiny thing, just the sweetest, nicest guy. I'd love to see Brother Conrad. I'd love before I die to have a reunion. I wish somebody would arrange it—to see Brother Conrad and Brother Anthony and Brother Pious and Brother Ignatius and Brother Lawrence. When we used to have free time, Father would give us cigarettes for those that smoked like on a feast day or free day, and Brother Lawrence was on the road again before he came into the priesthood. He was quite a worldly man, and he played guitar, and he did a lot of folk songs. So he did entertain the whole entire friary on many occasions with his nice little Irish lassie tales. He's still a priest—Brother Lawrence. And then we had Brother Pascal, and he was so nice, but somebody told me he may be deceased and that's sad. Oh, no, it ain't cause you go to heaven. I mean right now if God said to me, "Vincent, you want to die? I'll take you to heaven."

I'll say, "Immediately." Go. Cause that's what it's for. What am I doing here with all this crap and I'm miserable, you know? So then from the bakery went to now, here's a guy, let me tell you, this was a sweet man. Brother Angelis, very quiet, didn't talk, had been a Brother for years. He was the tailor, and I would sit at a window looking into the courtyard where all the frater would play after school, and where was I? Sewing cowls, and everything I did was wrong. And I would just give Angelis hell. But he never threw the black bean. Brother Angelis, a good man. So what happens in a monastery? For all of you people who make up all these stupid sordid things about holy men of God. Can I tell you what, lived with as much as five hundred men and the men that were already established ordained ministers of God for years and years and years, if you walked by one, one would glow, if you walked by another, a shadow would fall. And I'm not talking a lie. These were fricking (excuse my language), these were really holy people. Our Brother Guido died suffering with a hernia from his neck to his knees, and never said a word, never complained, and that man would glow. It's true. The stories you hear about priests being this and listen, if you're in the army, I'm sure there's one general that's an alcoholic, if you're in the army, I'm sure you're gonna find one general who's a pedophile, if you're in the army, I'm sure you're gonna find one general who beats his wife, so there's one of everything everywhere. That's the devil getting in it. What can I tell you? I have never met one homosexual male in the holiness of our Lord Jesus Christ service. Never! I've never met a pedophile man while I was in the holy service of our Lord Jesus Christ. Never! Ever! These were holy men of God, men who prayed, fasted, and did penance. Does that mean we don't get tempted? I can only speak for myself. That's all I can speak for. I live in temptation. I live in torment, but there you go. So I don't want to hear this crap about people talking down holy men of God. Just be careful, Folks, cause God'll get you for this crap. There are some people today that I see are so nasty and so disgusting so I sincerely hope that my story is not going to hurt the holy church in any way because these are god-fearing men. I'm afraid of Him myself. I fear Him, and when you fear God, you're in good shape. (*All these bloody clocks and bells*). Now to answer Becca and her little questions: This little time at the monastery went on for about two and a half years. We had a lot of wonderful brotherhood, but I started swaying. I was restless and so I left, and I am so sorry did. But I tell you what, rather than go to hell, I hada get outta there because at least I was man enough to know, this is my vocation, but not at this time. You know, it's sad Folks, being raised the way I was raised that I couldn't stick to anything for many, many, many, many years. Only later in my life have I done the same thing for thirty years. Only now. So we're going to go to a little thing of questions and answers and this will conclude the chapter on Vincent at the monastery.

To Clarify: When I went to St. Pious the 10th, if you will read clearly, it says that I went to St. Pious as a postulant for six months, remained at St. Pious for a year as a novice, then we were put in simple vows to the monastery. So a year and a half at St. Pious and two and a half years at the monastery. If I would have stayed three years, would have fulfilled my simple vows so I had to get a special dispensation at the end of two and a half years, and I cried all the way home.

As a novice, you are inducted into the order; you receive your habit in the novitiate which is a year and a half. Then after you graduate there you take the simple vows there at your novitiate and you're transferred to your monastery for duties. Then after three years the final vows. So it's like this, six months as a postulant at St. Pious Church and then receive our habit at a ceremony, then at the end of that year at St. Pious, we lay on the floor and get prostrated like a priest—but not quite like a priest—and give our simply vows. I take the vow of poverty, chastity, and obedience. My problem was obedience. Now my problem is probably obedience and chastity. Poverty I have no problem. I'm living off of everybody and their grandmother. (*Laughter*) Then your simple vows are for three years, and at the end of that time, you become a full member, they can't do nothing to you. You're in, good or bad, see? And I just could not live a lie. If didn't do anything decent in my entire life, that's the first and only thing I've ever done.

Brother Matthew

Brother Matthew & Mother

40

Marijuana Use

Let me talk to you about the cannabis days. This time was a very interesting, eventful and enjoyable time for me. I remember there were a couple of friends of mine, and we would all get together on Friday and the weekend nights just to go over what we did during the week. One friend I had was a government agent and the other one was a youth counselor. I was working for a merchandising sales department store, and I would always be the last one home. Coming home at five o'clock, and everyone would be there waiting on me.

We would come into the house take the phone off the hook, then put it back on the hook, we didn't want to miss a call in case. First we would start by having some cocktails, which was enjoyable, and after having a couple of cocktails we would all start giggling, and having a good time. And one day I asked these friends, "you know I want to ask you something, you are always giggling, I mean you laugh at everything I do, everything I say" I said "what is this, am I really that funny?" Now let me tell you in those days, my dream was and is still to be a comedian (laughing). So that's the way it was, and it's always been that way, anyway so I thought boy if they are really laughing at me, and my material you know, then I ought to go on stage.

So anyhow, they said, "Yes were laughing with you, and you are funny, but we are also under the influence of the cannabis and we've got some ready for you because we think your ready to try this, so come on and smoke it". They continued, "but this time you hold in the smoke, it's not like a cigarette, you hold it in and get your fill". So I did that and within a very short time, they used the term 'high', I was 'high', oh boy was I high. And it was quite a high, quite enjoyable, if I said a prayer it was intense, if I cleaned the house it was perfect, if I sang a song, I was Mario Alonzo, or if I listened to music, I was the conductor, so you see you just become many things, only super personified. It seemed as if I could drive perfectly. I know there was nothing I ever did under the influence of this marijuana business that ever caused me any problems.

To this day I don't know where they are getting this crap about how bad it is for you. I think alcohol which is still on the shelf, it's killing our loved ones every single day of the week. And yet, we still keep that crap on the shelf as we still keep cigarettes on the shelves. Which we all know both are killing us. These things are killing everyone who uses them, with lung cancer and cigarette companies just won't stop making the shit. Saying they got employees to feed, feed my ass. They are killing people, and that's what their doing.

Now the cannabis as far as I am concerned, I believe I would be an advocate to legalize it any day if everybody could get along on the cannabis the way I did, it would be a happier life to live, cause I am a manic depressive, and it made me happy. Anyway, not that you are asking my opinion, but all throughout this book all I have done is give you an opinion.

So we all had a great time when we were under the cannabis. I could be a comedian during those times, and I was very funny. We had a room we would sit in and we use to call it the 'Marijuana Room'. The marijuana room with Vinnie and I would do a show a total comic show done in different dialects, as I would imitate all kinds of different people. It was like I would say it was President Nixon it would be Richard Nixon. If I said it was George Bush then it would be George Bush. If I said it, then what came out was what I intended, and my friends would just fall over laughing I mean I have had them off the couch, on the floor, back to the couch, back to the floor, giggling, snorting and laughing, and praise be to thee O Lord, that was a wonderful time.

Also during this time, I ended up friends with George and Carolyn, who were painters. We met, when they were to come in and paint my apartment. They came in and asked what color I wanted the apartment painted, and I told them a 'bright white'. Well, they must have been stoned, because they brought back this off white color, more like ivory. To make a long story short, we all ended up getting high for the next few weeks, while they were painting my apartment, and what I remembered about this was we just giggled our asses off the whole time.

Now that I have become very ill and have all these problems I kind of stay away from cannabis, but I'll tell you what, if you come over and ring my doorbell and offer me to get high, I don't think I would turn you down. Of course I won't let you smoke in my house anyway, because were not allowed to smoke. But I'm just saying ladies and gentlemen, take a different look at this marijuana business, I know most of you really won't care about what I have to say, so I am going to say it anyway. It has been a great thing for me, and I will probably smoke it when I get a chance, until I die. I am going to try and will hope and pray to God, that one day they legalize it, because I don't want to go to jail. However, I know that it helps with my neuropathy, and takes away some of the pain which I endure everyday now.

There are some stereotypical people reading this who will say 'Oh my' and beat their breast and talk about how bad marijuana is and then say I am a bad example to be around children, and then here they are smoking it themselves. So there you go, I have seen people straight as an arrow, daily communicants, absolute perfectly, breast-beating Catholics, and Protestants, smoking marijuana. Now I don't think it's a sin to smoke marijuana, but I know it's against the law.

Those were my grand old days with the cannabis and I'll tell you what, if it's for you go ahead and smoke it, but don't get caught.

I started smoking cigarettes when I was eleven years old, and was up to four packs a day when I quit smoking in 1990, so it was a great thing when I quit, because that crap will kill you. I underwent bypasses on my legs and I almost died, but it is a hard habit to break. You can't just tell a smoker not to smoke.

I guess you can say this is an extension of the hippie movement in 1970's, and I suppose this particular herb, brought about a lot of brotherhood. There were people that were at concerts, turning everybody on, no one messing with one another's girlfriends, people showing respect to one another. It was an unbelievable time of life you just had to be there. It was really true, there was very little crime, and when we would go to concerts there would be hundreds, sometime thousands of people, and not one incident. It seemed as though kindness prevailed throughout the land, because of this herb. So I can't condone or condemn I just know what worked for me, and I hope it will continue to work for me and that you will endeavor to choose what you do. However, don't put me down for what I have done, or may do in the future.

I hope that you have enjoyed this small story, there are so many things I can say I have done, under this influence, and they were just incredible. But that is neither here nor there. Once again I don't want to hurt any ones feeling by saying I am a firm believer in this particular herb. But I am, always have been, and always will be. I have not seen this herb deter anyone in anyway whatsoever, at any given time. So those of you who may have approached it and it did not work for you, and then stay away from it.

I quit smoking it because it is illegal, but if and when it ever becomes legal I will certainly have a good time. So remember cannabis is not legal, and you cannot smoke it. If you smoke it, you may get put away. Again I will recommend cannabis, and God bless America and good old cannabis. Thank You.

41

Shamus and Valentino
Faithful Friends

Shamus, a Tibetan terrier, came into Vincent Mirabella's life in 1978 and was Vincent's faithful and steadfast friend for a little over 12 years. He was a middle size all white ball of fluff, who was friendly to all. Shamus was the 'dancing' dog of the Mirabella studios, you can ask any of the students who went there. He would gently let you know if you missed a step by letting out a bark.

Over the course of his lifetime, Shamus probably aided three to four thousand dancers who passed through the studio. He would always go to the door and greet a newcomer. But most of his time was spent lying in front of Vincent's desk, patiently waiting until a student repeatedly messed up a dance step.

Shamus was also a faithful watchdog of his master. If Vincent became ill during the night, he would awaken him. Or if the trunk was open on the car and he was about to pull off, Shamus would give a gentle tug on his arm and show him his error.

Shamus's life came to an end and the clock even stopped, when he developed a weakening heart, and Vincent had to make one of the most heartbreaking decisions, and that was to put to rest his companion of over 12 years, so he would not suffer. Shamus was a faithful friend, a pal, a teacher and so much more. He has been greatly missed.

After Shamus came another Tibetan terrier, to Vincent's life. Valentino was the total opposite of Shamus. He really didn't want to be bothered by anyone, and he would let you know it. He would go to the dance studio also, but unlike Shamus, he would lie in a corner and just watch the dancers. There were times when he was mean even to the master, who he was so much like when it came to being stubborn or having an attitude. When Tino, which is what everyone called him for short, would be mean to Vincent, he would have to tell him he was going to smack him in the snoot if he didn't behave. Tino was in Vincent's life for around ten years, when Vincent found out Tino had leukemia. So once again Vincent had to make another heart breaking decision to have Tino put to rest. Both of his faithful companions, who were with him for a good portion of his life, have been cremated and now they both reside within a ceramic urn which Vincent keeps in his living room.

Vincent's faithful friends Shamus on top and Tino on bottom

In memory of Shamus

To our dance students near and far,

Shamus, Vincent Mirabella's pedigree "dancing" dog, went to his final rest on Friday, May 24, 1991, at 3:35 p.m. A strange truth indeed is that Mirabella's home clock stopped at the same moment!

Over the last thirteen years, three to four thousand dancers in the environs of Winston-Salem, from Wilkesboro to Raleigh, have known and been aided by Shamus, our "cha-cha" dog.

Past and present friends, I wanted to share with you the news that Shamus is now with God. Thanks for the memories and love of Shamus.

the folks an extra class. We can only concentrate on you!"

Private lessons and group classes at the studio were even more eventful. Vincent need not go to the door and greet a newcomer. Shamus always did that. Though the most frightening move for the new student is always entering that large room, Shamus immediately put the student at ease and in his inimitable way bridged the gap twixt teacher and student. Secretly, the teacher is just as wary of that first hour. As progress toward

learning the patterns and mastering the musical beat stagnated about the fourth hour, who but Shamus entered center stage and again broke the ice?

The love from our dog surely taught us the lesson that God is in every creature, great and small. Shamus was a long-haired whose white glowing face attempted to hide huge black and all-knowing eyes. No matter what kind of day we were having, that magnificent face would always share a smile with us. Regardless of his ancestry, he was our pedigree.

SHAMUS

Here comes the round, jolly man. What? With a little white puppy? Is he going to be one of those dance teachers with "the dog act"? You know, the teachers who put on a show with the "sit-bark-roll over" stuff. Seems like that, and then, alas, not at all.

The dog was teaching the teacher how to teach the students. Can you believe that when we would do a step in error, about the third time, one could hear a "woff, woff" sound, and eyes gazed not far across the room.

Shamus! Stretched out like a white blanket with his paws crossed, he would cause the whole group to laugh, some even to tears.

"Now Shamus, we have to give

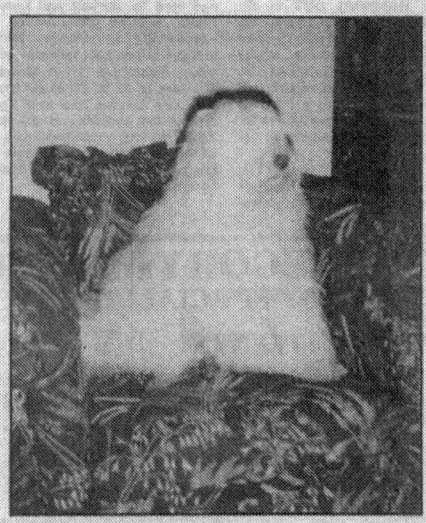

Article in Winston Salem Paper when Shamus passed away

NOTICE TO THE READER

Within the past chapters of this book, I have had my editor's to try and change every cuss word which I had actually said. After talking with my editors however, I have come to realize this was part of my diseases, so in the chapters here out, I will not have them do this, as this is how I was. This is how Nick was prior to coming back to Vincent and my conversion back to Christ. Within these coming chapters are depicted some of my youth, and the periods of my obsessive compulsive and manic depressive states. Within this period, I was a sinner, who thought nothing of swearing and cursing. But I do no justice to you the reader or to my novel, in changing every cuss word, to something else as this was a part of me. This was during a part of my life when I had not converted back to my faith. All I can and will ask of the reader is to understand the context in which certain language is used within the interviews within the next chapters of my book. I believe you will come to understand more about me, my life, and how I lived through it all.

Here starts the section of Vincent's Mortal Sins ...

42

The Interviewing

I must preface the following and let the readers know that I finally had someone come in and I had all of the tapes that were done transcribed. What follows, are questions by an interviewer in order to clarify some of what I have been talking about.

After this, will come the year or so in which two of my very dear friends will be interviewing me in order for you the reader to know the 'rest of the story' …

Interviewer: *You said on the first tape that your grandmother destroyed your future by spoiling and coddling you. Talk some about that.*
Nick: She really did not do any of this intentionally. Let me explain. The Italian women are very heartfelt. Because I was so-called a "bastard" child, her heart went out to me because no one would take care of this orphan. Like when a mother leaves a little animal, some other mother takes up for it. So with that she gave me a lot of care and protection. She really did not ruin anything. Nobody ruins anything for anybody.

Interviewer: *In what way was all the protection bad for you?*

Nick: Because that's an Italian saying that you spoil them so much you ruin them. In a lot of this there is some truth, and in a lot of it there is not. This lady did nothing in the world at all to hurt me in any way. I didn't grow up as much of a sissy as everybody thought I was because she taught me how to kick ass herself, so there you go. I believe I was with my grandmother from birth, from a very little baby. She raised me as a little boy. In that picture in the sailor suit, couldn't of been three years old.

Interviewer: *So you were never with your mother.*

Nick: Never. They took me away from my mother, you see. My family said, "That lady," meaning my mother, "was a witch." was scared of her, but yet was attracted to her because she was extremely beautiful. That's why I say in my book, "Don't tell a little sissy boy his momma's a witch. He's gonna believe you."

Interviewer: *Talk about why you were afraid to go outside when you were really little, when you wouldn't go to school.*

Nick: In that case, it was just the fear of not knowing what was beyond the door because I was so protected. When you go though the book you see I started going places by myself throughout the neighborhood, it tells you I wasn't as easy or as much of a sissy as everybody thought I was. I ended up beating kids up, but I always did it in front of an audience. I didn't do it in the back streets.

Interviewer: *Do you know how old you were when you started going to school?*

Nick: School—I never remember really going to school.

Interviewer: *You said you did when you were older.*

Nick: I remember they put me in kindergarten, but I don't remember being in kindergarten; I don't remember first grade.

Interviewer: *What's the first grade you remember?*

Nick: Gads, I don't remember any grade specifically, the only time I really remember being tied down to school was when I went to St. John's Home, and when I was in Mrs. Post's class. I guess it is because I liked her class. Maybe as I have gotten older I'm exaggerating the fact some, but I remember they were always coming to take me to school every morning. The truant officer would come and take me to school.
Every morning they would come and take me to school.

Interviewer: *So if you didn't have much schooling before you went to St. John's, it would have been really hard to catch up when you went there?*

Nick: Actually, I don't think I ever caught up, but I think I sort of by-passed. I know I told you the story about Brother Matthew. How the only subject I was failing was mathematics. This man told me, "Against all odds, Vincent, you will never learn mathematics, and I have spent two summers of my time teaching you mathematics." I remember they wouldn't let me go in the yard and play, all because I couldn't learn mathematics or geography. You ask me where Connecticut is, and I'll tell you, "I don't know"

Interviewer: *Talk about the animosity you caused between your grandmother and her children. I know you've already talked about that, but how did that affect you.*

Nick: Let's assume you've got two or three brothers and a couple of sisters and you're the baby of the family. They're all struggling just to make it with their own lives because they're all young kids and just married. This one and that one is pregnant; she would turn to them and say "look, I have no money. The boy's got holes in his shoes. Give me five dollars to buy him a pair of shoes." They would tell her, "Ma, I don't have it, I just don't have it. We love Vinnie, but we just don't have it."
So she would say back to them," Find it, and if you don't find it, I'll busta you ass." That's the way my grandmother was. She was very severe with her children. Didn't make no difference what their problems were. Her problem was, she was raising this child after raising eleven of her own children, because the father of this child was a sorry ass and didn't support and take care of his kid, and never came around. He was too busy getting laid, or going out and making the moon with the man, he was the ladies man. There are pictures of my father with nothing but women around. He would never take care of his son and they wouldn't give me to my mother where I should have went in the first place. So the animosity was not like, "I hate you, Mother." They would just tell her, "When you die, we're gonna cuss ya, because you're gonna leave back a real spoiled brat, who is uncontrollable, for us to take care of." I was uncontrollable anyway, from the word go. (Pause)

Interviewer: *Were your aunts and uncles mean to you?*

Nick: It seemed as if everybody was mean to me, that they resented me. They didn't know how not to be mean to me. Although some of my aunts weren't mean. My godmother was all right until the end of her life.

Interviewer: *You mentioned being locked in the cellar, but you never really said who locked you down there.*

Nick: There were several cellars, but it was never grandma's cellar I was locked in, although we did spend a lot of time in grandma's cellar, the lights would always be on. She'd say to me, "Vinnie, help me find this." I remember she had a lot of things down there; all the things I had as a little boy, but they're all gone. I had things then that would be worth money today. My cousins and other people stole them, robbed them, and took them.

It's funny because all those tenements had cellars, and I can't remember exactly who it was that would lock me down in them, but I remember they would go up the stairs and turn out the light, and I would start screaming and yelling and crying.

Interviewer: *Did they let you out?*

Nick: No, not all the time and that's when I started to see the little boy that I would want to say was Jesus.

Interviewer: *Do you remember the first time you saw the little boy.*

Nick: Yeah, I'll never forget it. It was rainy stormy night just like in the movies, and I had gone down to get coal, and I wasn't going to be locked up. I was at Seia Maria's house and as I went down to get the coal, I was really brave because I had all the lights on. And I was carrying the coal pail, and I was determined I was going to do this. I was just not going to be freaked out anymore. But, just as I got to the coal bin and opened it, all of the coal pushed forward, and I fell onto the top of it, and then the lights went out and it just terrified me. I didn't know how to find the way to turn the light on downstairs; I only knew how to find the way to turn the light on upstairs. So, I was just carrying on and then I saw something moving around.

In trying to let the reader know how the bins were set up, they are all to the right, and they are slotted. You have to walk down this big long hallway into the middle because this is where you shovel it. Then on the same side, there are long bins which are for each person's apartment, which is one, two, three, four, five, six and sometimes twice that, many for them to shovel the coal into. Anyway, I saw this movement and I turned around and said, "Who are you?" And I swear to God, he turned around and then the whole room lit up. But I bet people won't believe that. I went on and said, "Wow. My name is Vincent." And you know, for the first time, I was not scared at all, and then I said, "What's your name?" and he just smiled. So I said, "What's the matter, has the cat got your tongue, you won't tell me your name?" He looked at me and he laughed like a little boy. So I asked him, "Well, did you fix the lights?" And he still didn't say a word. So then I asked him, "Can you please help me get upstairs, I'm sort of nervous?"

Then he said, "You're not to ever be scared when I'm around." And I said, "Well, tell me your name." Then this is what I learned, when I turned around away from him he made sure I got all the way to the top of the stairs. And when I turned around it was all dark again and he was gone. I was going to tell, "Seia Maria, I have a friend that lives in the cellar" But I didn't. Seia Maria was always nice to me, even if I was scared to death of her because she jumped all the time because of the St. Vitus' dance. But after my grandmother died and my father and his wife didn't want me, I used to sleep at her house on chairs a lot.

Interviewer: *Go back—how old were you when this happened in the basement?*

Nick: I believe I was six or seven because this is the same period of time when from the Catholic Church this big black veil went flying. I think we need to elaborate on that. When I lived at grandmas, next door there was this lady, Donna, and her husband, Mr. Joe. Mr. Joe would sit at the window, and he'd tell me, "Vincent, don't go in the parlor tonight." There was a black veil which went flying around the room, and all the ladies came running to the kitchen and one woman even fainted. And I thought, wow, these Italians are witchy people.

Anyway, back to the little blonde boy in the basement he was gone, I came up the stairs and I turned around and it was dark and then I got scared again. I yelled out, "Hey, kid where are you?" I remember he had on this beautiful white robe like on my card, with gold. I remember I thought it was a dress because I said, "What are you wearing a dress for?" However you could see underneath it wasn't a dress. He was my size, curly blonde hair, and looked like a little Italian girl.

Interviewer: *The other times you saw him, was it always in your aunt's basement?*

Nick: No, I saw him in the cellar at grandma's house, and I saw him in my Aunt Mae's cellar. It was always in the cellar.

Interviewer: *Did you ever go to the cellar just to look for him?"*

Nick: Yeah, only he wouldn't be there. He only came around when I was being traumatized in some way. He did come in my bedroom one time after grandma had just whooped me, and he said to me sort of in baby talk; the reason she was upset and whooped me was because she couldn't sleep. He told me "when she starts to fall asleep, you interrupt her sleep."

Interviewer: *So after that did you stop calling her in the night?*

Nick: No, I didn't stop. But I only saw him three, four, five times in my childhood.

Interviewer: *You said before that he used to go places with you and you'd argue with him.*

Nick: Yeah, like when I would go to the park or anytime I was in danger, he would be there. And it is like I'd be distracted by him and I would say, "Hey, wait for me," and I'd run to get him, and then he would just disappear, and then the damn building would fall in or something! That's a joke. But he saved me from being hurt by distracting me, by my running after him. Like when I'd be walking through the park, and there'd be a gang of kids that beat people up, I'd see this little boy and say, "Hey, wait for me," and I'd cut across, and they would bypass me. The little blonde boy would play marbles with me and beat me every time. That's what made me think he was normal because everybody else beat me at everything every time. We played on the street at my stoop, and people would say to my grandmother, "Who is Vincent talking to?" and my grandmother would tell them, "Forget about him, he talks to everybody; he talks to the ants; he talks to the cracks." So it wasn't anything unusual. Another time he was there was when I got run over by the car. What actually happened was the car went right over me didn't touch me. I think he just pulled me out, and I turned around and everybody was going, "Oh, look at the miracle." He hasn't disappeared; he's just not there anymore. (*Laughter*)

Interviewer: *Anything else mystical ever happen?*

Nick: I'm not going to tell you the girl's name, and I'm not going to mention the boy, but there was a little tragedy for one of my neighbors who lived here. In fact, the poor man blew his brains out, God love him. He was a beautiful fellow, and his brother was just as beautiful as he was. Well, the girl he was marrying was just gorgeous, and it was the week just before her wedding, and they were all coming in and out, you know. Every time they had time they would come and sit with me and take a sip or whatever. They were really nice neighbors. Anyway, one day

I said to the boy's baby brother who adored his older brother I think they were roofers or carpenters; anyway I said, "I'm very concerned about your brother, he's acting rather strange." Then his girlfriend said, "You're not going to ruin my wedding. You're always starting that old lady shit and getting me upset. I said, "I swear to you I won't say anything anymore." But then the boy came into parking lot and took off all his clothes, and there he was standing in all his glory, what a beautiful man this was, and he changed clothes. So I said to him, "Come on over here I don't like your behavior. Come sit in the house with me for a bit." He didn't want to hear it. To make a long story short, I knew there was something wrong, and I tried to tell that family, and they didn't want to hear it. Anyway, that night he killed himself, he literally blew his head off his shoulders I suppose. As sad enough as that was, you know, there was a girlfriend of the boy I told you about on the motorcycle, and I told him, "You're gonna kill yourself," and he did. His girlfriend used to come and say to me, "Read my tarot cards." I'd tell her, "No, you're not 21, I can't read your tarot cards, plus I'm not a diviner." But the lady upstairs who is a certified tarot card reader gave me the cards so I am actually a diviner if you believe in such a thing. When I read the cards, I take those cards and use God in it so I get people off their baloney and try to sneak God in it, see? So we were sitting right there in that corner of that couch. Now let me tell you, at that time I had my dog, Shamus, my white dog. And we started reading the cards, and all of a sudden a cold beyond, it was so cold the fan stopped. I swear to God, the fan stopped, and Kathy said to me, "What is wrong?" so I said, "Don't get scared, but I think his spirit is here." So I went to the back room and my dog came flying out the front and my bedroom was i-c-e cold. I said, "Kathy, come here." She couldn't get up. She couldn't move. She was mesmerized. I said, "Let's tell Ronnie to go. So I said, "Ronnie, go rest in peace. You're okay. Go." Fine, he went. We didn't actually see anything; we just sort of felt it. It really scared the crap outta her. But that night, you know when you sleep and you don't know if you're really asleep, he came to me and I said, "Oh, Ronnie, oh look at you." He was all dressed up and he was happy. I said, "Are you in a good spot?" He said, "Yeah, you know I think I am. Do you think Kathy would get mad if I came and took my dog?" I said, "Oh, Ronnie, please don't do that, you'll devastate the girl." He said, "Oh, I gotta have my dog." He had given her a big, gorgeous dog. Then I said, "Well come on in, I'll make you something to eat." Never turn your back on these spirits or whatever the hell they are. You see, I turned around, and then I turned back and said "Damn you, you shit, you got away" So I told her the next day that he came and I saw him but I didn't tell her what he said. The next weekend, I was talking to Kathy, and I asked, "Kathy how's your dog?"

She says, "He's fine" and I said, "Just sort of keep an eye on him." She says, "Oh no," and she started crying. She said, "What are you doing to me, Nick?" And I told her, "I ain't doin' it." So Saturday night 2:00 in the morning, I got a phone call, and it was Kathy, I said "Your dog is dead isn't he?" And she said "It was just hit by a truck and the guy in the truck looked just like Ronnie." So then I said, "Let me tell you what, I know it was Ronnie. He wanted his dog, and I didn't have the heart to tell you." Kathy was the prettiest, nicest girl. I wish she would please still be my friend. I miss her friendship she was so sweet. I have not seen that girl since; she will not talk to me.

Interviewer: *Tell me about Miracles*

Nick: I went up for bypass surgery in my legs, okay, and the doctor couldn't find anything. They said the man came out of the operation sweating bullets. This was my dear friend, Buddy, Dr. Goko, who's going to become a Catholic again. Now he will that he hears it. I'm haunting him. Anyway, God bless him, he washed, scrubbed up again, went in, and they saved my legs. God gave me the miracle by giving me this man to take care of that.

But the real miracle—which I can't say there's such a thing as a fake miracle or a real miracle—was that he had done some work on my anal gland, outside the anus. This is as a result of something they call a condoloma. Now a condoloma is supposed to be the wrath of God from having anal sex on a regular basis. However I will now tell you the story of how this happened to me.

When I was a younger boy (*now here's a sad part of my life that will make you cry*) one of my heroes who was my older dance buddies; everybody liked him and I won't say his name because he's dead now and the other two are dead. He says, "Come on Vinnie, get dressed up. We're gonna take you to 42nd Street and let you see all the beautiful women you like." Now in those days, the X-rated ladies or to put it more frankly, the whores were gorgeous women, gorgeous! They were perfectly groomed. They were perfectly tailored. They were the most beautiful women in the world. Today, garbage; but back then they were gorgeous. Now what happened was they got me a little bit drunk. I didn't even know I was getting drunk. They were letting me drink out of a bottle in a bag. Somewhere along 42nd Street, it's all windows; well, let's just get it over with and say it; I was raped by three men with instruments no smaller than nine inches, three of them. They screwed me in the buttocks, and then I was left there bleeding. And I will never forget them saying, "if you say anything Monday, we're gonna kill you." And I thought this guy was my hero. A little old lady who was panhandling didn't believe me that I was bleeding and had been hurt until she saw the blood and then she called the police. And as a result of that rape, I came out of it with, all kinds of sexual diseases like gonorrhea, but the doctors took care of me, and made me better. There was one doctor who told me, as a sixteen year old boy he said Vincent, when you grow older, be very careful, you don't develop this little lesion, he said, "You may end up with anal condoloma, it's a disease." that's what they gave me, a sixteen year old boy.

I wanted to get up and start therapy walking moving after the surgery on my legs, and it was a Friday and the doctor walked in to me and he says I got some good news and I got some bad news. You have cancer of the anus gland. Anal condoloma. Now anal condoloma is attributed to people who have rectal sex, from what I understand. Well I don't have sex, let alone rectal sex. And so the surgeon, I says now you gotta get that, ya know. So he did, he operated once on it, then he operated twice on it, and now they came into my room, and they said now you have this and we have to put you on chemotherapy, were gonna radiate you and for thirteen days you will stand with your butt spread out, getting air, and I said "Your full of crap, man and get out of my room or I'm gonna kill you!" Now I was seven days on morphine, you don't do this to somebody after seven days of morphine; they will kill you, and tear you to pieces. I threw the phone at the guy and everything. So anyway they took me downstairs and I cried like a baby. And as I'm going downstairs, the priest from my church came, and this big boy named Sampson. Oh he was like my savior, I could of just laid in his arms and he'd have taken care of me. And the priest gave me holy communion and I said Lord, if you will take this away from me, this will be a miracle, because who is going to take care of me, through all of this, who no one but you. And if you don't take it away, I'm afraid the devil will get me to rebuke you and then I'll really have a bad time, with you. So do me a favor, please, ya know I'll tell you something, all of you people who may be reading this book, there isn't anything you can't ask of God that he won't give you. But it's when he wants to give it to you. And he took it away. The lady downstairs, she said "Come on Mr. Mirabella, lets take another X-ray", and I said "I got my miracle, I felt it. I felt it go away, I felt it go away! It's like you know you got a thing on ya and all of a sudden pfst it's gone." So anyway, she took the x-ray, and she said "Were not gonna operate on you." Four o'clock that afternoon she calls me on the telephone, she says "Your friend Jesus gave you a miracle Vincent, I'm gonna show you." And she came up to my room, and showed me. Black negatives and white negative, she says "Now may I look."

I said "Go right ahead", she said, "Hallelujah!" She was the only doctor that praised God and thanked him for a miracle. All the other guys, the Jewish guy, said "that must be a mistake" and I told him "Aw your full of shit get outta here. God gives you this gift and you don't even thank him for being a good servant," ya know it pisses me off, excuse me, but God gave these damn fools these things, and they wouldn't admit that it was a work of God, so who cares. And now later in my life, this thing we're talking about, this condoloma, we're talking about which happened twenty, thirty years ago, has come to take its place, its toll. And this is where the Lord gave me my miracle. So, for three years, it's been perfect. It came back a little bit, and the doctor operated again, and it's better. This condoloma going away was my miracle.

Interviewer: *In what ways were you disobedient?*

Nick: I just don't listen to anybody. You can't tell me to do something, I just won't do it. I think it's just because I'm stubborn, but now anybody can tell me anything they want, and because I know who I am and what I can do, I'll say, "Okay." don't play argue. I didn't argue with the Brothers; I just would not do what I was told. If I had stayed … they're pretty smart. I probably would have gotten a couple of black beans. (*Laughter*) You know it's really not funny because if they would take me back tomorrow, I would go. I would go! I'd give up my diamond rings, I'd give it all up and I would go.

Interviewer: *Have you asked to return?*

Nick: No, I'm afraid to. I don't have anything to offer. You can't just be a liability. You know the church has enough liability on her ass, she doesn't need any more. But it's got to be God's will. But of all the time of my life period even up till now, that was the only time that I felt close to God, that I felt satisfied. Now there was a lot of dry spells, that's spiritual life. In fact, let me tell you something. The more you love God, the more he wants, and you don't think well, love God, and then you're gonna be walking around doing the hula, hula. Uh, uh, honey. He's a jealous God, he's a possessive God. I don't care what anybody tells you. Because the more you give him after he takes everything he wants which I will never know because I haven't talk to Job. Read the story of Job. He said, "God I want to know all this stuff you're doing and appear to me now and let me know it." And he did. So I can't do that or I'm a nothing, I'm just a pssst. We're just snot's blast away. But I just couldn't love Him I was tormented. I think the reason why the Lord let me go there, I got my religious training, I got my education, and I got myself together in a way. I have a better self-esteem so that was a necessary thing.

And it was a wonderful life. I couldn't get out of bed and go to mass. I have a hard time in the mornings even till today. Today more for my pains and aches.

Interviewer: *Talk about how you made the decision to leave.*

Nick: There were lots of thoughts, lots of distractions. I couldn't focus. I was seeing the other side of the grass. I was seeing the frater playing, having fun. See the school was also a college so everything was catered to the frater, frater meaning father junior, becoming priests. We were called brothers, they were called fraters. "Friar" is all of us, then the guys that were studying to become priests who had the academics were just a bunch of young kids, nice boys, and to see these boys being boys and being men and loving God was the most incredible thing. Today it's all who's gonna get laid and how they're gonna get laid and who's gonna go to bed with who and who is gonna conquer who. And none of that (stuff) happens in the house of God. These are special people, and I've seen some guys come and say, "Brother Matthew, I just can not do this."

And I say, "Well, I can't either, but I'm trying." And there were a few that got in and fooled the man. You don't fool nobody. You don't fool God. Who the hell do you think you are that you can fool God? So I knew that I was being so distracted, don't ask me by what. I knew that I was tired of everything I was doing. I just didn't want to go to chapel and pray to God. Now that's what the devil does to you. When he knows he's going to lose a soul, the devil works very hard to trick you. I mean temptations against the flesh were incredible. But so did St. Francis of Assisi have those temptations, but he's him and I'm me, and he's a saint, and I'm going to hell so there's the difference. But what I'm saying really got me was that these boys right at their peak of erections and sex and what is it called? You know nineteen, twenty, at their peak of hormones were giving their lives to Christ, sitting there with their arms in the air and praying.

After a year I saw the bunch of guys I came in with.... they all changed, they all just had cleanliness about them. You know what I'm saying? And they're all priests and brothers now. "Many are called and few are chosen. I had to go. I just knew if I'm having these temptations and if I'm looking at people in different directions and if I'm starting to see my superiors and these men of God as bad, you know 1 think I can go in anybody's house and cause Wit, but in God's house, 1 just don't think he's gonna let me. You gotta know when to get off, and

God is very powerful. And then that morning when I left, Father Maurice said to me, "Well, good luck and you'll find a place, and you're very brave to do what you did." And I just cried all the way on the bus, and I ended up going to Woodridge, New Jersey, to see my mother and just cried and cried and cried. And I hada leave my mother and that's when I returned to Uncle Nicholas.

It was hard for me to do that; now that I'm older it probably would be harder because you have all the security you'll ever want. You have your bed, you have your food, you have your chapel, you have your brotherhood, and if you're sick, they take care of you. I had an ingrown toenail during the time I was in Connecticut and it took forever to heal and they paid for everything. If you're looking for materialism, even though you own nothing, you own everything, you see. Today, I'm 56 years, and I have no idea where my next meal is gonna come from. I could be next month in the street panhandling. People laugh at me, but it can happen. That's why I want to get this book done.

43

Interviews by the Editors

In the following section I am being interviewed by two of my very dear friends. It is now 1999. Interviewer1 is Laura and Interviewer2 is Roberta

Interviewer1: So you had just finished the section in the book where you had gone back from the monastery back up to your uncles.

Nick: In Bayshore Long Island New York and while I was there I had several different little jobs, one job I had was helping to make swimming pools. I hated it. Then I worked at a supermarket to become a butcher and cut the heck outta my wrist, and I did all these little jobs, worked for Sears and Roebuck in maintenance and met a very nice person who kinda Mr. Joe him and his son were very kind to me. During that time of working I also went to Arthur Murray to continue my dance education and established a wonderful friendship with John and Doris Smith who are still very, very close to me. And from Bayshore, in New York a couple of years later I graduated to a place called Tallahassee Florida. You know what ball team is there. And I did some quadrille work at the University of Florida State University and I also taught dancing at the Arthur Murray Dance Studio. My career started to kick in place during contests and what have you. And that went on for a couple of years, and I was transferred to a place called Cincinnati Ohio on Main Street, South Main Street. Now South Main Street in Cincinnati Ohio, with no offense to Cincinnati, is the pits. I mean it was the roughest, meanest, dirtiest place I have ever lived. And this is what it is and if you become offended Cincinnati, that's your problem, clean up that dump.

Interviewer1: Was this the seventies?

Nick: This was the seventies it was a real nasty and there was these black guys laughing at me because we were learning how to do certain thing called the 'spin turn' in ballroom dancing. And these guys, that were doing these spin turns were incredible. And I just wasn't gonna have less than incredible. So coming from the dance studio, down to the main street I would do spin turns. And these two black guys on that particular main street, it was all buildings that had glass, I've been surrounded by glass buildings all of my life. Ah and the guy laughed at me, and started to call me names so I said "Hey why don't you call me a fairy?" So of course he says "Hey you fairy" and then I said "'Poof' you're a pile of shit," and let me tell you I spin turned and brought up my foot and I kicked him in his damn neck, I got him right in the neck, and then he fell into a plate glass window. And I just said laughed and said "Make fun at me again." So the police came, the whole bit and I thank god, these two guys didn't even get one piece of glass on them. But the whole window was shattered, so that's my remembrance of that wonderful nasty place. I'll never go there again. And no offense to the people that are good people but that place was nasty to me. It was a traumatic experience it was the first nasty place I had to live in.

Interviewer1: How did you get out?

Nick: I left, I just quit and packed my bags and left. This guy that was running that dance studio, was really hustling all these women, it was nothing like a dance studio I knew of, where it as nice. You didn't take the ladies money, you were kind. He had all these guys walking around with things popping outta their pants, and little tight cute butts. These women were just goin for it, ya know and I can understand that. I would too. Now that I'm old, I just might, and anyway … *laughing*

Interviewer1: That's another story …

Nick: That's another story right?

Interviewer1: So you got out of Cincinnati?

Nick: Got out of Cincinnati and where did I go? (*Pause*) Jesus God, where did I go? I think from there from Cincinnati I think I went to …

Interviewer1: Atlanta?

Nick: You're absolutely correct. Atlanta Georgia. Absolutely and worked for a couple that were from England, very lovely people. Now I was the new kid on the block there in Atlanta, and the dance studio was at a triangle across from the library, which was across from the grand theatre where they redone this movie about Gone With The Wind. That's another story but anyway, I'm making a lot of success in this school. They gave me all the people nobody else wanted to dance with and I came upon a little old lady, God bless her. She was one of the nicest sweetest women. Mrs. Williams, if you're still alive, I love you. And this gal loved to do the tango. We became very good friends,

Interviewer1: You did a tango huh?

Nick: We did a tango and she would always say, "Come and dance at my church". She lived, in Carrolton Georgia. And happen to be a neighbor of a very famous celebrity. Now as I got to know Mrs. Williams she says, "you gotta come to my home" in Carrolton, and see. She had a big, big beautiful home in a big field. And at that time I was in charge of a youth group, it wasn't necessarily boy scouts, but it was juvenile court kids. Now let's explain this. Not only was I a dance teacher, at the Arthur Murray dance studio, in Atlanta Georgia, but I was also a juvenile court probation officer for the Jonesboro county of Georgia, under a couple of different judges and anyway I took my kids there one weekend and let me tell you we ate and oh it was just a godsend. Even made them go to Catholic Church. (*Laughing*) Mary was catholic, and now in her home I would notice pictures of a movie star by the name of Susan Haywood. And I said to her "Mary, what are all these pictures of Susan Haywood?" She said "Oh she's a friend of mine," And I said to Mary, "Well dap a do do do" and she said "Yes she is" and so I said "Well when does she come and see you?" And she told me she came by all the time. She said to me "You saw her at church when you went in fact you sat right next to her." I was flabbergasted. She told me "'She's my neighbor," meaning a half a mile down the road, you know. Susan Haywood married a man named Floyd Eaton Chalkley, who was a lawyer, and a book writer, and when he died, she converted to Catholicism because of him and when he died she built the Catholic church and the whole thing to go with it for him, and anyway she would come to church in a little scarf not tell anybody anything. I said "Well come on Mary I wanna meet her." She says "ok." So finally I was it was just a thrill you know for me to meet a movie star. But she was just a little thing you know and just as sweet, kind and wonderful. Now we all sat and we drank Hurricanes, for all you teetotalers, Hurricanes are wonderful, there even good for teetotalers, (*laughing*) and ya know in moderation everything is blessed by God, so in those days I would drink a little bit, just a little bit, just a drink. And so I got to meet her and the few things she told me that have stuck to me was that "Don't ever look back" "And don't ever be concerned of what people say about you, she says you're very sensitive. She says let them say everything and spell it right. Get upset if they don't spell your name right." So with that she sent us a card. She developed a horrific, horrifying cancer, where everybody thought she was a drug addict. It affected her brain I think. And she did the Joey Bishop show it took them twelve hours to prepare her for that show. And she did another show before she passed away, the Academy Awards, she was one of the readers or something. She looked incredibly beautiful then she passed away from a seizure and it was standing room only at her funeral. And it was the saddest thing because she was a very sweet lady, she surely was one of them little Scarlet O'Hara's. She really was a Scarlet O'Hara. Two very nice sons, Timothy, he became I think a veterinarian, and then her other son he was Mr. Slick, Mr. Broadway.

So this is my experience of that time, and then I came back and continued to teach dancing and I think at this part of my life, I'm trying to remember when I came here, to North Carolina, Atlanta Georgia, oh and then I know one time I met Mary Williams on the bus. And there's a club called the Millionaires Club, and you bring a certain amount of money and ya know they decorate you forever. Now ya understand something about these boys, they were all slap ass beautiful boys. They have wonderful bodies, their breath smells good, their bodies smell good, they keep themselves clean, their handsome, but they have that heart that comes out of their mouth, they seem to say everything it takes to make somebody spend their money and wiggle their toes. That's a great gift. Ah it's a subtle way of being a hustler, ya know. And so here she comes she had a sack with money in it. I said Mary T, I got on the wrong bus, what are you doing? I'm gonna join the Millionaires Club tonight. She had a bag with a hundred thousand dollars, fifty thousand dollars, I said "lets get off the bus darlin, I'm gonna call a cab. I said you got money Mary, she said yes, I says well were going to Carrolton and I took her back got into the bank and cussed out the bank for giving her all the money and decided that ya know we were not gonna do this and I told her she would thank me latter and she wasn't gonna live long enough, ya know which I hope she did live long enough but your not gonna live twenty five more years. She was already up in age, but really energetic. Now I don't wanna get away from you folks without telling the story about the court. What, during my time as a probation officer, there was a lot of resentment cause I was young I went for my test and then, then family services said they lost the answers to my test. That I flunked so the judge says, "Well he might have flunked, but he's hired". So he superseded everything, I was done dirty it's a rough business ya know this, but I know that while I was working with these boys, I really noticed for the first time in my life this is when I fell in love with young people is these are people that are pushed down, because "I'm your father you do what I say". Whether you like it or not, ya can't go. Ya never tell a kid "NO". Ya never tell a young boy you can't be his friend or you can't because their gonna go out while your doing your crap and their gonna party and their gonna be with these people. Their gonna do the things you tell them they cannot do.

So if parents would understand, I've learned this Rose, over the years of working with young people don't put them down. Show them the same respect and earn the same respect, just because you're a parent don't mean crap. Don't mean a hill of crap. Ya gotta respect your siblings. But here are the stories that I want to tell you. As a probation officer, I had a little bit of authority and ya know when you were my age you wanted to play with that authority. And I'll always tell the story of this boy 'Junior'. Junior was six feet tall and eight feet wide, and he was thirteen years old. *Laughing* ...

His father was a little short ya know nasty little Irishman, walked into my office and slapped this boy up side the head and hit his head against the cement cubicle, and then he threw him down on the chair and then he took his finger and stuck it between my eyes and said "You make him get a hair cut". So I says well Mr. J ... for the sake of saying your name, I says sit down and calm down. I says give me your probation paper, and he said "I don't have it" I said well Junior give me your probation papers, because it was required that parents carry a copy the boy carry a copy and me I had to carry a copy. I said "All right now, here's a page one for you and one for you now follow me, read all of those things he has to do. He has to go to church, and he has to try to make passing grades. He has to use his curfew. All of these things. And your boy has not broken any of these rules for six months." I said "But ya know Mr. J.I have a hard time finding anywhere in here that he has to get a hair cut. It doesn't say a thing about getting a haircut." I said "Now I'm gonna tell you something. I'm gonna give you an opportunity to think about what you just did, as this is called child abuse" I said "And I can put you away right now for about seven to ten years, for hitting your son like that." I said "But I'm not gonna do that, but I'm gonna tell you when Junior starts to realize he's mister haw, haw, haw and he can sit on you and squash you, you better be careful, cause that boy can tear you up with one hand, and if you don't continue to watch it, I'm gonna encourage him to kick your butt." I said "You just don't do that to young people." And then I told him "Now it's Thursday" and I pushed my little button, "Your gonna go in the jailhouse until Monday, and think about how you treat your son." And he stood there and said "You can't do this to me" I said "Yes I can. And by the way Mr. J. you're the first."

OK, I set that aside now and I talked to the kid and he was afraid of his father. If you have to be afraid of your father, you don't have a father what I mean is he's not worth being a father. Period. When you gotta be afraid of the people that shit you out you should be able to leave them. This is what is going on with one of my kid friends now.

Now if the judge was to call you to his chambers, it means he's gonna fire you. Terminate. (*Laughing*) So the following Monday I was told to be at the judges office at seven thirty. I said "awww nooo, what am I gonna get fired?" They told me "We don't know." So I went up there and he said "Vincent" I said "Yes your honor" He asked me, "What do you want in your coffee" and I said "Well cream and sugar" then I asked, "Am I getting fired?" He told me to sit down. I said "Yes your honor" The judge asked me "What are you trying to do to me, you know I'm up for election and your putting all the parents in jail" I said "Well your honor you hired me to protect children and if their bad they get punished and if the parents are bad they get arrested. This little boy had the biggest black eyes and I went into their home and here the kid is hiding in a loft because his father is sitting there drinking and cussing and swearing and peeing on the floor. Am I supposed to put the kid in jail?" He said "OK" Then he says "Let me ask you another question. Everybody that's in lockup; meaning when you get locked up on the weekend, you go to the court, they all ask for Vincent". I said "Well your honor you'll have to ask the kids that, I don't know why they asking for me." I said "But I'm trying to do what you hired me to do. To respect the system, to love the children and to see who is right and who is wrong." He said "Well you have a lot of tenacity, and I'm very proud that your on my staff" and that thrilled me to death. And that's the story there are many more stories about this relationship that I have with young kids, but this is enough for this chapter because we gotta hurry up and get on to my present time. Which is now 58?

Interviewer1: No

Nick: Yeah I'm 58,

Interviewer1: Well your 58 but you don't just want to take the book to just 58; you want to take it back to what age?

Nick: Well this is 27

Interviewer1: Let's get you out of Atlanta,

Nick: Yeah all right lets get out of Atlanta,

Interviewer1: How did you get out of Atlanta?

Nick: How did I get out of Atlanta, bear with me, we may have to change. I got out of Atlanta and came here.

Interviewer1: Why would you choose here?

Nick: Well I came here to go to Wake Forest University to obtain a degree in law.

Interviewer1: No!

Nick: I did, (*laughing*) isn't that funny? You know its news to me, so that did not work out. Simply because of the culture and I was a Brooklyn Italian from New York.

Interviewer1: In the 60's.

Nick: In the 60's yeah and in the bible belt. So these guys accepted me, but then they rejected me, and that's fine. I decided that I would stay here, I couldn't go, couldn't go to college at Wake Forest and I, I gotta job with Joseph Schlitz brewing company. Working on a production line. Met a lot of wonderful men there, they were really good friends, some good guys, I still know a lot of them and they have a lot of respect for each other. And I just could not just watch bottles go by all night long, It was just not my mentality, not that it, it takes a very special mentality to do that (*laughing*), so I'm not trying to put it down, but I could not do that. Plus that was a time in my life when I was doing a lot of partying, in the nighttime partying, oh we never did, well maybe we didn't have to talk about those bars and stuff that I went to.

Interviewer1: So you did a lot of partying?

Nick: Yeah I did a lot of partying, heavy duty. But always was nice, I didn't do anything stupid or dumb, or hateful or I never hurt anyone, I never took anything from anyone and I never abused anyone. But anyway so then I would just not go to work. I worked there five, six, seven years. And one day they said look were gonna take you to Georgia for a hearing but your not gonna get your job back. And you know I couldn't blame them the union, got tired of my crap. I mean ya can't ya gotta do something right ya know ya can't just blame the company. I just didn't want to work nighttime. So I got fired.

I think from there I went to the Children's Home and became a cook for the boys. I redone the whole entire kitchen, repainted everything and at Christmas I would put Magnolia leaves all over the tables and give them a beautiful Christmas, and buy them all Christmas presents. I remember I worked with a lady who was very jealous of me and very, very evil she would put garbage pails in front of my door and not let me in. These are people that were supplementing their income, and were trying to act as if they really liked the kids. I saw one of the old ones hit a little black boy, and knock him down the stairs. I said to her "Ya know, ya know you could get your ass kicked for doing that" and you know they didn't like little black children, but anyway. For the boys in my house, I put Jesus lives here too with lightning going into my kitchen, ya know. I use to make them Hoagies right off the grill man, chopped hoagies, they loved me, they loved my cooking but ya can't give boys turnips mixed with mashed potatoes, it won't work. (*Laughing*)

Interviewer1: Why?

Nick: Why? Oh they'll know its turnips. They don't like that crap. So anyway that was a nice experience and from there I went to the Ramada Inn Airport, here in Winston Salem,

Interviewer1: Cooking?

Nick: Oh Yea, actually I took that whole entire dining room and destroyed it, and rebuilt it. And this is when we come across Rose. I saw this girl come in one day and I said this girl was just a scrawny looking thing and she says, "I need a job". I says what makes you think you could work here? She said "Well I got two kids to raise", and that got me right here (pointing to his heart). I said to her, leaning across the desk, I want you to know that I am a SOB to work for, and she said "I don't care I have two kids I have to feed". Ya know so I couldn't act like my heart went out to her and I liked her automatically. I said well be here at five o'clock in the morning, smell like a woman, and look like a woman and be all dressed up and she did.

Then that's how we became very good friend's ladies and gentleman, she was really a wonderful person and we did some really extraordinary things in this hotel. One Thanksgiving we made a cake, to look like a Turkey, twenty tiers high and all the employees had to walk by for a week and squirt it with wine. But when I had Walter the kid I was training cook this cake with my supervision for about five hours at three hundred degrees it came out as hard as a brick and Walter said 'Hey NICK' I said what Walter? He says smacking something on the cake, I said "Yea it's as hard as a rock, ain't it" he "says were gonna eat this?" I said "In twenty-one days we are" *(Laughing)*

Interviewer2: "Make a cake twenty one days before its ready to eat"

Nick: And it was a cake boy I want to tell you all these little old ladies came from the church across the street, and you could hear the cackling.

Interviewer2: "By the time we were through we sprayed it with water or something to start with then we sprayed it with rum or" …

Nick: Oh yeah, all kinds of rum, and wine and, every day you would walk by it and sprayed it, walk by it you sprayed it, walk by it you sprayed it. When we were done, it was just full of fruit and full of cherries, it was good really and the menu, the food was great we had homemade breads, and we did all these wonderful and this boy Walter, he was and still is the love of my life, Walter if you ever happen to read this story, call me. He was the sweetest nicest kid I don't care what his problems were to me he was a godsend. He did everything I told him He was never late to work, and I put his ass to work every morning. Every morning and he stayed there until six or seven at night. Yes but let me tell you what, he was a master salad maker when I got done with him. I couldn't make a salad to match his after I taught him, remember the macaroni salads and stuff? Anyway we touched a lot of lives I think at that time and now they're all gone. The Ramada Inn Airport is many, many stories about this airport this, this, this hotel. We went from cockroaches, with ladies with nasty looking legs and smelly bodies to first class women I mean a touch of god came into that hotel after I got rid of all the trash. You get rid of the trash in you life ladies and gentleman, and god comes in. He's right there—boom. He's right there anyway. And I firmly believe that

that god loves us unconditionally so that's the Ramada Inn, what else, what else, what else ...

Interviewer1: You went to Hardee's after that?

Nick: Oh Yeah, No did I go there after that? Yeah then after that, I went from the sublime to the ridiculous. (*Laughing*) Hardee's, I got a job at the Hardee's and I ended up being a troubleshooter for five stores.

Interviewer2: "He did the same thing at Hardee's putting flowers on the tables".

Nick: I had flowers on the tables at Hardee's, all the kids couldn't work unless their eyes were clear, anybody ever had a red eye, and I wouldn't let them work. Cause you know you can't get high and they were getting high, and deal with 800-degree fire. And I had a parent that got very upset about that he said, "You sent my son home, are you implying that he's smoking marijuana"? I says No, I'm not implying he's smoking marijuana, but I says his eyes are red and I don't know that he's got allergies. But I know that he was gonna be on the fryer tonight and the fryer is 800 degrees, I says come over here and let me show you, let me show you how that crap is and I showed him. I said now just in case he would have been impaired, he could kill himself and I'm not gonna have it. If you don't like my decision, go anywhere you want to and I'll join you. Just like when that girl was taking money out of my cash register, $20.00 damn dollars a day, sticking it in her crotch in the bathroom. I told her I said girl I'm gonna catch you, and I'm gonna eat for breakfast. And finally I caught her, in the ladies room, putting it up her dress, and pulled her out and fired her and they started all kinds of crap like I was invading her privacy, bla bla bla and I said I wanna tell you right now, you give me back my 20 dollars a day and I won't invade nothing, What are you invading on me when your cutting me short $20.00/day. I said this girl is beyond white, black or anything else, she's just scum. And she's robbing my store and I'm not gonna have it. And they tried to get me fired, and they didn't fire me I got commended. I saved a little girls life. A little girl liked hot dogs, she was a paraplegic, and it was a busy afternoon, and she came in and she wanted a hot dog, she loved my Hardee's hotdogs, and I made her the hot dog. And she started to eat my hot dog and she got choked, and I helped her and her mother came the next day and kissed me, so that was rewarding. And then the girl died, a few years later.

Interviewer: How did your dancing experiences get infused with the Ramada Inn and Hardee's?

Nick: Oh well now the Ramada Inn I wasn't really dancing, I was just doing the restaurant. Same with Hardee's. Now, the owner's son, who went to college, got a graduated college business education. Now this was the time when they introduced the biscuit for breakfast, A BIG DEAL the biscuits for breakfast. Now what ya gotta understand is the Hardee's on Akron Drive was for Piedmont Airlines. That's how those guys got their breakfast. At six o'clock in the morning they all hit that room and I knew everybody who wanted what when and we just had it ready, we just fed them. So I ran that with two cashiers and a cook and a boy to clean up. Nothing but cleanup. Change garbage, cleanup, keep the bathrooms clean. So this little fat boy and I don't mean to call him a fat boy but he was a fat boy, and he was not very nice. He said to me "Well you know I'm what's his names son," and so I says "Congratulations, please to meet ya," he says "Well I been watchin you" and I said "Yeah, I don't like that, you don't watch me, if your gonna work here, you get your ass back here and put an apron on and work. But you don't watch me. See" Then he proceeded to say "Well I'm gonna show you" then he says "you come in tomorrow at ten o'clock. And I'll come and do the breakfast, and show you how to run it with just myself, and a cashier." I looked at him and said "well now let me explain something to you young man, look at the register receipts here were doing a seven hundred to a thousand dollar a morning breakfast. Nobody else does that and it's all because of this biscuit. People were buying two and three and four sausage and biscuit, two and three and four sausage and eggs two and three and four gravy and biscuit." I had a girl back there making the, oh yeah then I had a black girl in the back, making biscuits, and gravy. And we were the talk of the town. Round the corner from your house Rose. So this little fat ass comes in and when I walked in at ten o'clock there was a hell of a mess, everywhere. He says "I been trying to call you, but I couldn't get to the phone." I said "See you screwed up, everybody at Piedmont called me all day saying 'What happened, what happened?'" I said "Well ya screwed up the business, man. You made forty breakfasts and everybody walked out of this place because it is a disaster, so now you can take these keys; and stick them up your ass I'm gonna go back to dancing.

The night before I saw the disco, on TV ya know I said to myself 'I'm getting outta this crap.' And I started my disco classes and worked for the Casa Blanca nightclub for several years all I could drink, and a hundred dollars a night.

Interviewer1: So what did you do for them?

Nick: I taught dancing, disco. And yeah I had to end up suing Hardee's because they were so totally indifferent, ya know I hope none of these kids get moved by the fact that when they tell you hey Johnny your gonna be manager, were gonna give you thirty dollars more a paycheck and then your gonna work your ass off till you die. Doesn't work see? Now I had eleven kids on Akron Drive. All black kids, sweet wonderful kids, Audrey, oh I wish I could find Audrey, anyway and I would feed them, and they could have their drinks so the office said "No you can't do that," and I said "I'm doing it". I said "Number one, these kids are coming in out of school, they don't make a whole lot of money, they come from poor under privileged families and their trying to look cool their and their gonna eat, cause I'm gonna feed them. And your gonna pay for it." So I told the kids to eat what you want, but eat it. Don't come in here and throw a half a hamburger away or I'll really give you hell. So they liked me, I was fair to them I treated them with respect. Ya gotta treat young people with respect whether ya like it or not. And if you're an asshole, then your not gonna know how to treat, figure a better word than that ya know, but I don't think there's a better word to describe some of these parents. Ya know and if you want to put it down just like I said it then that's fine to. Because ya know these kids, well I'm prejudiced; I've never found a kid I didn't like.

Interviewer1: Their children of God you know.

Nick: Oh they really are children of God. So anyway that's the story of Akron Drive and Peter's Creek Parkway,

Interviewer1: Did you successfully sue Hardee's?

Nick: Successfully? Yes.

Interviewer1: How?

Nick: How? Well ya know this guy had five franchises and I worked from eight in the morning, till eight in the morning, and they never paid me overtime, they never gave me anything, or paid for my vacations they never gave me anything. So I went to the labor board and they wouldn't do anything either, I think they wrote them off, paid them off you know, ya got a lot of money you can do a lot of things. So my lawyer sued for an undisclosed amount.

Interviewer1: So it worked?

Nick: Well you know you can't really mess with someone's dignity, see people are afraid, like the period that I'm going through right now, I am down under, under the down under. I am so oppressed, so depressed, that the only thing that's gonna happen is an explosion to bring me back up. Or I'm going to wither away and die. So I'm trying very hard to keep it together.... But will get that part later. Were done now with Hardee's were done now with Akron Drive.

Interviewer1: You were working at the discos, getting all you could drink

Nick: Well yeah, but that wasn't the only thing I was getting, I was getting a lot of business, I was starting to teach in peoples yards, in the summer ya know, the garages and I was doing dancing from door to door. And then F. Baylan, who is a very wonderful lady who is still here with us, would go away in the summer and give me her dance studio all I had to do was pay the light bill. I mean how incredibly wonderful was that, she never asked for any money. I did a lot of that and then from there I went to the D ... studio, these are two legendary names here in the dance business, and she's a mess but I love her

Interviewer1: Did you keep up with Rose during those years?

Nick: Yeah, Certainly

Interviewer1: So you were still in North Carolina?

Nick: And I rented some space from her remember, and then at the Casablanca I started teaching in nightclubs, as well see.

Interviewer1: So you were out of the food business all together then?

Nick: Yeah, Oh Yes. And then from there I opened my own school.

Interviewer1: What town was that in?

Nick: Here

Interviewer1: What year was the first ball held in?

Nick: Oh I don't remember, but I have all of the tapes.
Yeah and then I would have a ball every year, this was like a graduation ceremony where people come up and dance and they get a medal and ah Roberta and Ron would handle all of the music, I mean all I had to do was walk in and go why isn't the speaker working (*laughing*)

Interviewer2: "And after your coffee was given to you, then the speaker would get fixed".

Nick: And she Rose was absolutely superb, she really was everything went so smoothly this was a gift that we could do this, and it would go perfectly. Perfectly, perfectly it could not have been better.

Interviewer2: We had fun, it was professional

Nick: Well I mean the music was right, the food was right, the attitude was right, the atmosphere was right,

Interviewer2: 'The last one that we did Shawn danced at'.

Nick: Shawn danced with Mrs. Feldman
He was a cute little baby; he was a little sweet puff. So were that far huh, ok and I think its very important for me to state that there was a period of time in my life that I experimented like everybody else does with drugs. I spoke about marijuana, just prior to these interviews, but now I will tell a little more about it. Hallucinogenic, all kind of drugs, be it the grace of God, I'm still here. But I remember that I've done some drugs where I would stop my car, on Reynolda Road, and allow the leaves to cross pass me (*laughing*)
I actually had a conversation with the leaves that day I was so spaced out. That's gotta be the pits ya know. And then there was a time I live in a house in Lake Hills where I had two little frogs that would come and sit next to me, I kid you not, a frog would come and sit next to me, now I got three people that will attest to this. So Rosie O'Donnell if you have me on your show, I want you to know this story and I'll get my friends Wayne and CL to attest to this. This frog sat

next to us every night we would party, he was the sweetest little frog I swear to God. One night I came out cross-eyed and I said "What are ya doing here, go get yourself a girlfriend". The next year we returned to the same place partying, again outside and here he comes the same frog only this time with a girlfriend. Now some of these things are outrageous unbelievable and I really don't care if you believe it or not folks but this is it. Now I said to him "And so when are you getting married?" Off he went, latter that summer he pop's up with two little baby frogs and a girl frog and boy frog. And I swear it to the lord himself this is not a lie, and it's not the drugs. But if anybody's having any intentions of dealing with these psychedelic drugs, be smart kids and don't do that to yourself, your all beautiful kids, stay away from that crap, it'll kill you. It liked to have killed me but I'm still alive (*laughing*)

Interviewer1: Mutated maybe
(*Laughing*)

Nick: So you know I don't do drugs now, I go to God because he'll handle that. But I had to tell you the story about these drugs. Oh, and one other time I was working on the bottle line, I don't remember what drug it was I did, but I will tell you the bottles in a beer factory come straight down in groups. And if there's a piece of glass out there you have to stop the line, and that's lots of money, like a million dollars a minute to stop the line ya know. Well this night I saw a little piece of glass screaming at me saying "Take me out, take me out, take me out" (*laughing*)
And I pushed the button and stopped the line, and then I heard Mr. Shim, who was a wonderful guy God Bless him, he comes flying down on his little cart, Mirabella, Mirabella, Mirabella what are you doing? I said look, look, look, look so the mechanic came in and he saw that piece of glass and he took it out and he says I ought to get raise. I saved the day, you know but you know drugs don't always work that way. So God spared me and I think maybe I did all that stuff so I could tell you now. You know not tell you but suggest to you, you know, don't do it but if ya gotta then that's up to you and God, but take it from me an old man whose done it all, it's not worth it.

Interviewer1: Where you at the peak of your career when you were doing the balls would you say?

Nick: Yeah because I think we went all over the country, and we were like first place champions, constantly cruises, the whole thing ya know I worked on cruise ships,

Interviewer1: And all this time you had this apartment and Shamus

Nick: I think so

Interviewer1: Tell us a little bit about Shamus

Nick: Shamus, he was the love of my life; he was the sweetest little puppy. He was given to me by a girl who was at that time my neighbor upstairs, little, little ball of fur and I said oh is that my birthday present? She says you don't like dogs you won't like him. I said Wanda give him to me I want him. So she went out played with him a lot, she had a cat as big as a mountain lion and the cat did not like Shamus. So she says I'll give him to you, I said the only way I'll take him is you don't come down here and mess with him for about eight weeks, and you don't come over here and screw everything up because he's gotta get use to me. And then he became my little dog; I didn't name him for several months. And then one day I looked at him and I said I'm gonna call you Shamus. Shamus, now there are two things attributed to the word Shamus. One I think a Jewish chanter, but the Shamus I related his name to is, is a Scottish protector, those police people, Shamus's police. And let me tell you he protected me, and he went everywhere with me.

Interviewer1: Describe him to us.

Nick: He was white and fluffy, and just a sweet as he could be

Interviewer1: What breed of dog was he?

Nick: He was a Tibetan terrier. I use to tell people, if you don't do it (your dance steps) right, he'll bark at you. So he would sit like this and there was this one girl (*with a laugh*), she did it wrong every time, I said Margaret, if you don't get it right he's gonna bark at you. And she did it wrong and he went 'rrrough'. She started laughing and peed in her pants. She couldn't make it to the bathroom, but this is how he was, and he had a knack of loving people, when he died was probably one of the biggest tragedies of my life.

Interviewer1: How many years did you share with him?

Nick: Oh, thirteen I think. Yeah he was a sweet, just as this one here is a sweetheart too. (*Talking about Tino*)
So I have a lot of blessings, the fact that God still loves me as bad as I am but we all need love, I don't care who you are, we all need someone to hug us we all need someone to love us, and misfortunately I have to buy my love, that's the saddest thing of all. But it's better than no love.

Interviewer2: But you're not buying love though, your buying temporary satisfaction

Nick: Yeah, temporary companionship, I suppose and if you really are into God, you don't need that. And as much as I've learned about God, as much as I've learned about how wonderful and kind he is, even though I said he was jealous and possessive, how giving and forgiving he is. I for some reason have to have the love of a human being more than the love of God. And that's pretty bad. That's, also pretty sad. But maybe someday I'll make it you know. Now were here we go into the next group.

Interviewer1: What happened in 1990?

Nick: Well in 1990, they discovered there was something wrong with me

Interviewer1: Were you having any symptoms?

Nick: I was very, very syonotic and very yellow, very sick very tired, I really couldn't understand where the pain was coming from. Finally after this doctor decided to do all these tests he said "I want to test you for aids" I said 'Nooo Way'

Interviewer1: Were you still overweight at this time, or had you quit smoking?

Nick: Oh yeah I was way overweight, no I hadn't quit yet.

Interviewer1: But it could have been a bad life style, you know smoking, drinking, cussing, cavorting that was making you sick

Nick: I wasn't really cavorting I wasn't a whore

Interviewer1: But you weren't partying the way you use to?

Nick: Oh no,

Interviewer1: Ok so you had calmed down.

Nick: But they found out I was diabetic, but they didn't find that out until they saw; here is what they saw, four packs of red Marlboro's a day, because of that they found, my blood would not circulate, because of the poison. Now the next big poison I have to encounter is the poison from cholesterol, triglycerides. They were always high 5,000—7,000 unbelievable, people would not believe this, you see. One doctor said "Your dead what are you doing talking to me?" Should we do all this now?

Interviewer1: Yes

Nick: I ended up with Dr. G god bless him he was a sweet, sweet man. A brilliant man. Like Dr. F. who saved my life. He's the only general practitioner I ever met that can find out what your problem is, in a heartbeat almost by the first time. They decided lets operate and see what the blood does, and the way the story went, the way I understand it through Mrs. Feldman who has passed away, the doctor was in there about six hours. And couldn't find a way to make a new avenue and he came out and he says listen, there are so many of you people over here helping me, I'm going to go take a shower and smoke a cigarette and have a cup of coffee, and then I'll come back, and see what I can do.

Interviewer1: What were they operating on you for?

Nick: My legs for blood circulation to find a new way to route the blood. What they said to me was, the poison not necessarily the nicotine but the poison that it creates, there's a poison that can become so hard that nothing (tapping on the table) can get through it. So what happened was he told me I had to quit smoking. So let me give you the story I was in that hospital for four days, before they put me under and I said I will go and have this operation, if you give me unconditional promise that I can smoke anytime of day I want to, till I get this operation. He said "I will give you that permission but you will have to do it outside." So I said "roll my bed outside then," it was July, and it was a long day. I sat out there, puffin eaten hamburgers, for some reason I had to have a hamburger. So when the time came which was a Wednesday night at 7:00 pm, first of all that morning the nurse was very rude to me she said you're not going out no where today and you're not going to smoke. I said "Don't let me knock you off that chair, ya know for God sake don't do this to me." There's always somebody doing something like that ya know? Well the guy gave me permission, and this nurse thinks she's gonna be my mother. So I knocked her off the damn chair, I did. Yes, I ain't going to take this shit and I took off the damn plug and went out on my own. This little old black lady, you know, the black people are wonderful people they are wonderful people. Mr. Mirabella, Mr. Mirabella, Mr. Mirabella, wait now I gotta use saline, I'll take you downstairs, don't worry. So we went downstairs and I said well I didn't hurt her did I? She said No you didn't hurt her but … ya know that wasn't nice. I said I guess so, and I'm sorry. So I went down there, and I smoked and I smoked the last cigarette till it was red. This nurse came and got me; she says "The doctor's are waiting for you in the waiting room" (in a high shrill voice). I said ok, just go away, and I had that thing on glow. You know glow, and I flicked it and I said "I rebuke you in the name of Jesus, I rebuke you". I said today I'm gonna be protestant, cause if it works for them, it's gonna work for me. And I said in the name of Jesus, I rebuke you, you will never be monkey on my back again. It controlled me. Four packs of red box Marlboros a day. So off we go and let me tell you, Jesus gave me … I have not smoked a cigarette since 1990. Not one. Do I want one? Occasionally I want one Yeah, I would love to start up again, but I promised God I would never smoke again.

So anyway we got that done and then the operation starts and I started getting better. But anyway, so I got that miracle, however they decided that I had very, very bad diabetes, my sugar was up to 500 and then my cholesterol, was 7,000 tri-glycerides. I'm not exaggerating, folks, 7,000 to 9,000 were my tri-glycerides. And they put me on all kinds of pills, but the most devastating illness of all and I hope that I could live long enough to find a cure for this. Is the incredible sadness, that I have experienced, with the days of curling up in fetal position, crying like a damn fool, not knowing why your crying, being oppressed and like I told my friend Roberta its like an elephant is sitting on you, well I don't know what an elephant sitting on you feels like (*laughing a little*) but and he won't get off.

Interviewer2: Large weight on your chest.

Nick: Very, very, very and it's in your soul and you cry and your just so sad and you want to die. So I'm at the mercy of the psychiatrists, and psychologists and nothing is taking place at this time. But you know that happened during that time from 1990 till now, I've had all these experiences and I can't walk because of the pain in the legs, excruciating pain. And you know you tell people and they look at you, I don't know what I would do if somebody came and told me. I sometimes think we need a hug. I don't know what the hell it is, but it's bad. And it hurts.

I think that most people go through what I'm going through, I have no idea, I don't understand this part of life, and I feel like I am the only one in the world that has this thing you see. If your having it that's fine, that's your problem, but not to be callous but

Interviewer2: You have your version of it.

Nick: Yeah,

Interviewer2: But you have also been diagnosed with Bi-Polar right?

Nick: I was also diagnosed as a manic-depressive, oh yes, two years, three years ago, I went to the bank, no I went to the store and I spent every credit card I have, every single one. For, it was at Christmas time, the first Christmas I new I was going to be alone; I suppose I said the heck with it, I went to the store, and I bought all this stuff. I came home and I was thrilled to death, things were coming in the mail everyday you know, and that got me I sat and cried, I said "Holy mackerel, what have I done?" you know so I went to one doctor, he said to me "Vincent you're a manic depressive" and I said what do you mean? He says "Well you come to my office at 8:00 in the morning, at 10:00 they call me to see how much money you got" "You spent $10,000.00 in one day". (*Small chuckle*). It's not funny, but now that I look back I bought things that I'm not even interested in having. Well that is all gone now anyway, so that put me in a state of depression for bankruptcy. I went completely bankrupt. I lost everything I have so is it a case of immaturity or is it a case of sickness, I think it's a sickness. I'm smart enough to know not to do anything that irresponsible. Of course I am. But folks when this sadness or this depression or this oppression gets into your body, it takes up your soul. And just like I have company now, which I haven't had company in six weeks, when they leave I'm gonna be very depressed. So why I don't know. I went to mass and communion yesterday, told God how much I love him asked God to do several little things for me, since yesterday and he's done them, why should I be depressed? What is this madness? What is this sickness? We have to find out. Cause a lot of young people, are dying because of this. A lot of beautiful young people.

Interviewer2: This is an epidemic of depression, bi-polar disorder?

Nick: Yes, I read the life story of Daniel Steele's son, (His Bright Light) precious beautiful child, killed himself because of this crap, ya know and I've come close a couple of times

Interviewer1: You get consumed by the way you feel?

Nick: Yes it's devastating.

Interviewer1: And it leads to physical sickness, which then consumes the way you feel more?

Nick: Well it also does your mind, nothing

Interviewer1: You don't have energy?

Nick: You don't want to do nothing don't want to go no where, now the fact that I had to forcibly retire and I'm at the mercy of the state of North Carolina which everybody says how horrible they are they have been the most wonderful kind people to me. You know there helping me with a little bit of food, their helping me with a little bit of medicine, you know even with a little bit of housing, they haven't quite clicked on that but I'm sure they will by the time you write this story, and it's the grace of God, and God bless them for helping me. Somebody wrote an editorial, how horrible they are, there not horrible. And you know me, if your horrible I'm gonna tell you you're horrible. I never let it slip by any, so it's all very depressing but then again its still the grace of God, I don't got any money or anything.

Interviewer2: How did you get involved with doing figurines?

Nick: Oh how did I learn to do ceramics, figurines? I'll tell you how I did that.

Interviewer2: When did you start doing them?

Nick: Well I did that when I lived on Summit St. here in Winston, with a room-mate. And my roommate was, the first time you know we were three buddies, he would do ceramics, and he would also eat sweets, honey buns, and I use to say, "What are you eating that stuff for"? and he's the one, (*with a snicker in his voice*) I'm gonna blame him for my diabetes, yeah (*laughing*)

Interviewer2: The honey bun ...

Nick: The honey bun, I started dunking that crap every morning for breakfast with him you know, Woo was that delicious. And then one day he gave me a lit-tle thing, he said, "here paint this" why I couldn't paint that thing, I was just as restless, and sloppy. And then one day I decided, well let me just sit down and he taught me how you do it. Now I'm not that good, but I give them as gifts some-times and people are very happy, but there are some really incredible ... now I'd like to go sit in Mocksville at the ceramic class but this girl is way out of the way, you know. And she's really a great teacher.

Interviewer2: Why not do ceramics right here, just a little bit?

Nick: I do them right here look

Interviewer2: No I mean, with a student

Nick: I don't have a student

Interviewer2: Well advertise for a student. Say I'll teach you how to do ceramics ...

Nick: Then I'll get some 90 year old, (*laughing just a little*)

Interviewer2: Well so what if it's a 90 year old?

Interviewer1: But you could say "Looking for a young aspiring artist, to teach ceramics to"

Interviewer2: But does that give you any peace?

Nick: No, No, No see when you're in this condition, there is no peace.
And what I want to talk about is my other good buddy, there was a period of time that my other friend, came, this always happened at Easter. And this place was called Union Grove North Carolina, and they would have a fiddler's convention there during Easter. Now when we went there, there was nothing but dirt, no building, no house, no nothing. They have a building there now. And my friend says "Come on Vincent, I'll take you". I said no I don't want to go I don't camp out. He says "come on," I said no I gotta have to have a bed and a carpet and sheets and the whole bit, hot and cold running water, or I ain't gonna go. "He says OK I'll get you hot and cold running water and I'll get you a bed and get you a carpet and you can have some pillows and sheets, now get in the car and go". Well I wasn't gonna go. So this is when people use to get mad at me, they would ask me to do something, and I wouldn't do it because of fear. So he got in the car and I came screaming out of the apartment door, "I'm gonna come with ya, I'm gonna come with ya, I'm gonna come with ya". So off we went, and we ended up there with a million people in sight. Now he was a Red Cross worker, so we had the Red Cross flag, and we pulled right in to anywhere we wanted and we ended up in a big circle with people. And I sat there and I played Sonny and Cher and it drove everybody crazy. That's all I did was play Sonny and Cher, Sonny and Cher. All of a sudden up goes this big tent, looked like a darn house, and there was a bed and sheets and a carpet, so I said "Cool" and he said "Come here" he said see that, that's your hot and cold running water, when you want to take a shower. I said I gotta take a shower in front of all these people? He said no, I'll show you what to do. So this guy was brilliant at outside, outdoors stuff. Now here we are doing these drugs and I don't know what the heck it was that I was doing, but we all ended up with blankets around us. And I recall everyone in our little troop following me around this campground.

Interviewer2: Must have been good psychedelics

Nick: And we went up this hill and there they were ladies and gentleman, everybody thinks they are the worst people in the world. There are no greater people then motorcycle bikers. These guys Harley Davidson, what are they called?

Interviewer2: Hell's Angels

Nick: Hell's Angels, yes sireeee and a guy, I walked up to the guy and I started talking He said, "You know what, you're either absolutely screwed up out of your mind or you're crazy." I said I am both. He said "what do you want" I said I want to talk to you. So I went, I started preaching to them, and they got me higher than I was, asked me if I wanted his old lady, ya know and I said no that's cool and anyway they became my friends for the whole three days that we were there. Came down the mountain, walked around again, so what ever it was people were just having a good time, it was calm and cool and collected. But it was an experience. That's the experience of Union Grove. I went twice. After that I got out of it. So just to think that I was there with all these Hell's Angels, who were nice to me, is an incredible story. And I don't think there's anything else I can say. I don't recall but you hadda be there to witness this kinda action.

Now after three days of these so called festivities, when the blimp came over the thing was over, so it was Easter Sunday and the blimp big old blimp came out with girls with their boobs hanging out, the whole bit was just rah, rah, rah, you know well everybody was high you know there were either smoking pot or doing psychedelics, but anyway that's what they were doing, and I think we should be honest about it. So now I'm driving home, driving home in my car, after the other guy took off in his van, and all of a sudden I have a little Karmin Ghia, little old yellow bug and I see this thing in the horizon and there they was three guys stopped me. And they were the Hell's Angels. And they had a camp, right off the expressway. It was amazing how these people lived

Interviewer2: Weren't they broke down?

Nick: They were broke down and they said can you take us to Winston? I said to my self "Oh my God there gonna kill me". So this guy was a tall thin, very handsome young man long black hair, big black eyes, and I said "Well I'll take you, if you promise not to hurt me" (*laughing*) So he got in and off we went, and he didn't hurt me (*laughing again*) So we had to get something for his bike, some kind of thing, so I had to take him all the way downtown Winston get him that thing, now at that time, I was living at the Children's Home. And I took him to my house, my apartment and we partied, and we left. So two days later here comes a squad fourteen bikers "Vroom, Vroom, Vroom" driving into the Children's home. I went oh no there gonna get me fired. So I come out an he talked to me and he said "Well were just on our way to somewhere, and we thought we'd come and see you" So these were nice people to me, and he brought me $50.00 for all the trouble I went through, I told him keep it, ya know it's cool. So off they went. That was an experience with the bad boys, I'll tell you what folks, if there bad, there probably better then any other people I've met in long, long time. None of these 'bad people' were people who were supposed to be undesirables, have ever hurt me, in anyway. They showed me more respect, and more love and attention than most so called normal adjusted people, who are rather boring anyway. So that's my story sorry.

Ladies and gentleman, these ladies are giving me no chance to do anything, so here I am with not even a glass of soda. Shoot. (*laughing*) What do you want to ask me, my dear?

Interviewer1: Well when we last left the heroine, he or she was talking about three personalities, and that we had been talking about one of them throughout most of this book.

Nick: This is the life story of Vincent Nicholas Mirabella. When I was under the name, when I'm under the name of Nicholas I behaved in a sort of Gestapo, regimenting, perfectly, everything has to be done just so. When I behave as Vincent, this is a warm kind loving, trying to be kind of Christ like person and wants to be holy and pleasing and is just a real nice personality. And there's another personality that we won't talk about till the end of the book though.

Interviewer1: The one deep down inside?

Nick: Oh no, it's not buried that far down,

Interviewer1: Is it the dish queen?

Nick: It could come out real quick, yeah, (*laughing*) yes it can come out quite quickly, but you know we don't want to ruin this book, by....

Interviewer1: Maybe you can dedicate the book to this one …

Nick: Oh no, not at all, she's a very vicious person, a very … this other character is a, a kind of person that if you hurt someone this character gets you back, makes no difference who someone is.

Interviewer1: Why is that different than the drill sergeant?

Nick: Oh the drill sergeant, as a matter of fact, this is how it is,

Interviewer1: Ah huh

Nick: There's no choice, ask Roberta she'll tell ya. But the dish queen here over here is like a faggot that's a dish queen, worse than her. (*Crow like sound*) that kind of thing ya know,

Interviewer1: And we will leave her for the end of the story?

Nick: Oh we'll do another book for her (*laughing*)
She's in Venezuela right now. Well have to get a hold of her. (*Laughing again*)

Interviewer1: Well she's welcome to show up at anytime, during this interview. What we will do is say we left off with you a year ago, 12-9-99 to be exact, and we got Vincent to one of the sadder stages in his life which was in 1996, being diagnosed as a manic depressive, and he ended that interview talking about how his depression and manic behavior had led into an uncontrollable buying spree, which sort of tumbled him into bankruptcy. But that social services, was very helpful, and that there were other stories that you wanted to continue on that really pertain to some of the sadness you were going through, and that you found no peace.

Nick: Actually what's happened in that case was I didn't have too many friends, but a friend of mine brought a friend of his to visit me and who had an interest in modeling, of course the boy was as ugly as homemade crap, there's no modeling stuff and he started becoming a friend, hanging out, playing Nintendo you know and it was company, and for the first couple of weeks it was very nice company. Until I found out that this person was just nothing but pothead. All he wanted to do was smoke pot, do drugs, lay around, you know. Until four, five o'clock in the morning so I says, look forget it. Well I got into a real rut with the depression and I honestly don't know why people, you know people are too fast to sit and judge or say to you, "oh well you shouldn't be depressed." Well who the frick, what do they think we say 'Well today I'm gonna be depressed?' Um but it when it hits ya, I've learned now there are stages of it, and the stage that I went through, and if those of you that have known me all of my life, you would never think I would even think of the word 'suicide', let alone attempt it, ya know. That's not my character, that's not me. Or any of my other personalities for that matter, you know, so what I'm saying is, it got to the point where I had the sleeping pills, I took 25 sleeping pills out. High power stuff now. And 5 high power sleeping pills. And this is the thing, this is the most damnable part, I was gonna take my dog with me. I was gonna kill him too. So I didn't know who to give the sleeping pills to first, me or him. So they were laid out on the dresser ready for me to go to bed, and this friend came by and said look, he says I know how much you miss being with your teenage friends, but he says I want you to meet my brother, you will love my brother. And so he brought his brother, and the kid was really nice to me, and everybody made something dirty of it from the minute it started, till the minute it ended, but you know me, kiss my fat Italian butt, because I know better. And so he became my friend. So I didn't kill myself, Tino was my hero that day it's like the sun came out don't ask me why. Then you develop and this is the next thing I really want to work with is this compulsive obsession that you develop over things and people, and I don't know why that happens. Well anyway, everything went fine, and the kid he says I want you to meet my mother. So he took me to his church right away, Holiness Church ayaya, I said Holy mackerel, so here's this big lady, and she says are you Vincent are you? I said yes, and she said well look you can't be friends with my son, you're too old. You can see him in church. Well that was all I needed to hear you know, to make me really rejected. So it became a dirty battle, but the kid kept coming over and everybody kept saying your gonna get in trouble and there gonna do this and their gonna do that and then …

To make a long story short, they brought me up on charges, and these are the charges: Contributing to the delinquency of a minor or giving the child marijuana and liquor. Well they may as well have said I sucked him off to them, while they were at it but they didn't do that, yet. And then they told they told the police department at that time that I was a drug dealer. Now let me explain to you that after we go to court and the judge throws it out of court, six months later, the undercover police come to my home and tell me that how many enemies you got, somebody don't like you, we gotta ask you if you have marijuana, and I said well do I look like a dealer? Even the two girl cops that were with them didn't even want to be bothered with it but this asshole had to sit on my ass you see, so I surrendered two marijuana cigarettes and a little bit, about a half a dime.

Interviewer1: Why did you have that?

Nick: Ok now the reason why I had the marijuana, and the reason that I smoke the marijuana and everybody knows that, at one time, I smoked it for pleasure, now that I have this neuropathy, which is this horrible pain, which no damn doctor listens to you when you tell him, it takes away the bloody pain. HELLO, doesn't anybody understand that it takes away this fucking pain. NOPE, they don't want to hear it.

So this guy, I will tell you one nice thing about the guy, he didn't arrest me. Thank God, I would have had a heart attack, ok. So I went to court and the judge was very, very, very upset with the people that pushed the charges, but the second time, this was the second time I had to go to court, the judge told me, that as a matter of fact, the story was related by this lady judge, to me that I'm sitting in front of the judges desk and I guess that from the audience you can see my rings were dazzling, and she says "Well I hear you're a drug addict now Vincent. I mean a drug dealer" I said "no ma'am, I'm not a drug dealer". I said I don't even do illegal drugs." She says "Well, she says, do you know who I am" and I says "You're my judge, your honor". She told me "In 1971 you called my mother up and told her to tell her little skinny ass daughter to put on her red shoes and skirt were going dancing at the Casablanca night club until three and four in the morning." And she says "What a memorable night that was," she says "don't you know who I am." I said "no, I don't know who you are." Of course she told me who she was I said you are her? I said "you became a judge", she was so sweet, she says "let me tell you something Mr. Mirabella, just personally between you and me, and we won't say it out loud. The man that arrested you is an asshole. He would arrest his own mother. She says but there's nothing I can do about it, I have to hear it. But it's gonna be held in prayer for judgment, so you won't be going to jail, but it's still on your paperwork, when you go to get your paperwork, you know it's still on there. Even though no crime's committed nothing. So it makes you look bad. And she says the next time your gonna smoke marijuana, do it in your bathroom, and don't answer the door." (*laughing*) and I said "well your honor, I was nice enough to the man, to let him in and even those two girl cops that went through the house they would like open the drawer then just close it, you know open a cabinet and then just close it. And didn't even make a mess to try and look for anything you know. They were so sweet. But this hard on, had to get me." So here I am now, trying to do work with youth again, you see in the seventies and eighties, all right ladies and gentlemen, a man working with young boys and girls was called a 'mentor' not a pedophile not a pervert, but a mentor. Now all of these sick jealous parents, that have problems, are calling people like me—pedophiles. And if any kid that wants to be my friend, there gonna be my friend, I don't give a damn, what parents got to say about it. Now that's how pissed I am about them. Because I'm not a pedophile. So, I told this kid's mother that if I had wanted to be sexual with her son, I would have done it already. Now but what I'm saying is the brother that was suppose to be my friend, knew when the parents caught him here, you know there was nothing going down, nothing wrong. The two other brothers, blackmailed me, that night, they said "you know I'm gonna go home and tell momma that I saw you and James (a fictitious name) making love" and I said "that would be a nice thing to put James through? Well you know, we sat there and before you knew it, it was three thousand dollars that he took from me, in cash. But let this be a lesson to anybody that's sick and has these compulsive behavioral problems, just sit there and mind your business and don't get involved, you know but how do you don't get involved? How do you not get attached? The loneliness is so incredible, that you'll become attached to the first thing that comes by and smiles at you. I am so hard up for love and so what ever it is called to have a one on one relationship, that I use to have with your son, when he was little, and 'M', that was another mistake, that 'M', so I've always made mistakes because I think its because I give too much, give them too much, I smother them. You know. This kid for Christmas I bought him a five hundred dollar ring, a thousand dollar necklace, a five hundred dollar bracelet, brand name clothes and shirts, totaling approximately five thousand dollars on him.

Interviewer1: Christmas of '99 right?

Nick: Yes ma'am, indeed. Yes I did. And before that and after it. And they'd walk in my house and go into my pocketbook and steal a hundred dollars every time they came here. And my friends Roberta and Laura told me, don't do this, it's not worth it. I was even told, the same thing that Christmas by Jane, and she doesn't get mad, but I was no good to no body that Christmas. All I had was this kid James up my ass twenty-four seven, that's all I wanted, that's all I did. And you really don't realize that you're that way. Now this is the thing, we gotta find a way to realize that you're doing this so you can stop it. Now can someone tell me how? I went to the psychiatrist, he said leave that boy alone, stay away from that boy. And the psychiatrist says not because you're not a good person, but because those people are trash. And their gonna try to use you and there gonna exploit you and their gonna take your money. And nine times out of ten their people that are … what is it called … they see you coming and grab you.

Interviewer2: Want to hustle you?

Nick: Yeah, yeah, now I think seriously the mother was very sincere. Now let me say this, I did a lot of praying, a lot of begging, a lot of candle lighting, a lot of holy communion, asking God for me to not to hate the mother. Not to have any hostile thing against the parents. And she came and rang my doorbell, one day with her son and apologized, for putting me through all this crap. But it still is on the record. And I forgave her. And then I lent her two thousand dollars.

Interviewer1: How much time had passed since you first met the young boy, did that apology take place?

Nick: Well I met the boy at thanksgiving and then the court was in February then she came in March or April.

Interviewer1: that's of 2000, this year?

Nick: Yeah
But now I want to say also, now I got no money all of my life savings is gone.

Interviewer1: And it comes down to loneliness and wanting to give love and be loved.

Nick: May as well stay home and mind your business, jerk off, what can I tell you, screw it.
(*some laughing among all*)

Nick: Well that's what it comes down to. And I know there's a lot of kids out there, like I have children that come up to me in church and hug my neck.

Interviewer1: And they don't even know you.

Nick: And they don't even know me. Well they know me; they see me around, you know. But they like me. I was always loved by children. I don't know about her kids, I wasn't very nice to her kids. I was very strict with her kids. (*Talking about Roberta's children*)
Vickie and I had big problems, yeah because Vickie had a mind of her own, but I loved Vickie. I don't know how to deal with girls, you know what I mean. Now Shawn, do you think that I may have done something to him in his youth that he doesn't call me anymore?

Interviewer2: Shawn told me to be sure to say hello to you.

Nick: That's nice, but do you think that I did something to him in his youth that he's being so hostile to me now.

Interviewer1: Tell me about Wayne.

Nick: Wayne was my roommate remember?

Interviewer1: Where?

Nick: When I was talking about the three guys that were living together. He taught me ceramics remember. He was really a great teacher. I haven't done ceramics this year because of the computer.

Interviewer1: Tell me about that. When did you get the computer?

Nick: The computer I got in May and my friend Roberta and Laura came, and set it up, plugged it up, put it all together, and then said here this is what you do. And I'll tell you what.

Interviewer2: And you gave them a world of grief and said I'll never be able to learn this crap. And you asked us to sell it two months later if I recall.

Nick: I will never, I know and then all of a sudden it kicked in.

Interviewer1: What have you gotten from the computer?

Nick: What have I gotten from it?

Interviewer1: Or out of it?

Nick: Oh it fills a lot of lonely nights,

Interviewer1: Does Margo come out in the chat rooms?

Nick: Oh she did last night, bad stuff. (*laughing*)

Interviewer1: Back to Danny for a minute, he worked for your uncle Nick

Nick: Yeah, and I worked with him, he wanted me to mix cement, and I said to Danny "I will just do the pushing and pulling of the board that makes the cement smooth.

Interviewer1: When do you think the obsessive-compulsive disorder sort of kicked in?

Nick: I think it probably started with that little boy that went away on me and I got mad at him, because he never came back. That little boy, were saying now at this age, I keep thinking that that could have been a delusion, because of being afraid and scared, but until today it's as real to me today as it was as a little boy. And I got very upset when he went away, and never came back. The little baby Jesus, and got very angry. I would see him in a crowd, after a while, so evidently as I was growing up taking care of myself, he kind of let me go, as I got older, I was learning to take care of myself. I could see all that reasoning now. But other people can't. People that read this book are gonna be absolutely spooked, because it is going to be hard to believe any of it. You know, and I could give a cat's ass or not, it's what happened. You know what I'm saying? And it's gonna happen till the day I die. So in a way, I've had a very exciting and interesting life. But it's in phases of sorrow. There's no like I know it's Christmas and the whole bit, so I says now your not just gonna be a little mope, so I went and put Jesus out, and I put the tree up and that's enough. I use to decorate this whole entire apartment, didn't I?

Interviewer2: Yes, use to have a big tree and would decorate it with red bows, and white lights.

Interviewer1: So you would invite Roberta and her family. Would anyone else come at the same time?

Nick: No, just them

Interviewer1: Like family, what years were those?

Nick: Somewhere in the 80's because we were doing a lot of the balls then.

Interviewer1: You met Roberta in '76.

Interviewer2: When you say about the little boy ...

Nick: Back to her question about the obsessive-compulsive behavior, I guess I had it all my life.
Why, what causes a person to be obsessed, do you know that? I looked it up on the computer, and they got all these big fancy words there not talking to you in lay terms.

Interviewer2: You can find some areas where they will, I mean some areas, they will talk in doctor's terms, and other areas, and they talk in lay terms.

Nick: But umm in my case it's because, well first of all, every time I have something, I'd smother it, because I didn't want to loose it. So I'd loose it by smothering it. 'M' was the apple of my eye, I thought this was gonna be my son, you know this was gonna be my boy.

Interviewer1: Something I wanted to say about the smothering thing just so you know as an aside from the book is that there is a theory that says you spend a lot of the rest of you life making up for what you didn't get in your first four years of life. Now you talked about the first four years of your life as being very lonesome, and that what little you got, you clung to.

Nick: With grandma, grandma's what I had.

Interviewer1: Right and that sort of underlying fear, that things can't be counted on, always pervades with what can you trust in and what's really true,

Nick: But you know, now were grown up, and don't have to deal with that so put it away, I'm trying to put all that crap away, and it's like this, if you don't like me for what I am, then don't like me, well then nobody likes you. (*laughing*). See so you gotta change what you are, look at me I'm 59 years old, ain't nobody gonna want me, not now. Now when I was young, I could say, listen when Margo comes out your gonna love those stories, about Margo, see there's a hitch hiking scene, that I've been through, I'd go up to somebody and say 'hey, I want you, come with me now' and they would come with me. Yeah, Margo was a character, there was a gay bar in Atlanta GA, it may still be there, it's probably world famous, and well from dancing, I would go to this bar, all the gay teachers would be there, and there's grab ass, cock pulling, blowjobs, it's amazing the things that go on there. Well remember that the guys that go to gay bars are just looking for a one-night stand. And they go to bed with you, but to really be serious, oh honey then they don't mess with you the next day, they perform fellatio, they don't want to talk to you tomorrow. This is why I got in, 'oh what's a matter you had the 12 inches last night you don't want the other six?' (*laughing*) and they'd look at me and the whole bar would look up ya know, and I'd say 'Bitch, say hello queen',

Interviewer1: That's Margo coming out huh?

Nick: Yeah, Margo, Margo's coming out boy. But anyway we were five room-mates, five of us, and now you gotta understand some gay guys, are really, really pussy. Mushy, mushy, pussy, can't do nothing break my fingernails, makes you want to slap them upside the head, and there's other gay guys, that are cool, you know their nice and they take care of their bodies and they talk all queery but their really cool guys and they kinda makes that lifestyle nicer, cause I don't like faggots, I have …

Interviewer1: The nellies you mean?

Nick: Well the real sissy acting little faggot dishy mouth, nasty crotch sniffin bitches. I don't like them and I put them down every time and I will do it till I die, I don't care where you're from.

Nick: Well it really its what happens, you do each other in the bathrooms, in the hallways,
You know you gotta see that the gay lifestyle is a very sad life. Very sad life, and their very unhappy, but you know sometimes, it's the gay person himself, he meets somebody really nice, but you see they can't be faithful to each other. Cause they gotta have that dick. Honey you gotta have a different dick every day. They gotta give those blowjobs.

Interviewer1: Would you say that the majority of gay males are that way?

Nick: Oh yeah

Interviewer1: Overwhelming majority?

Nick: 99%

Interviewer1: Really?

Nick: Oh honestly.

Interviewer1: What about the ones that settle with one guy for a lifetime.

Nick: There about 1% there's only 1%, look at my friend 'W' he's been married to the same guy now for 15—20 years now, their lovers and have been faithful to each other, they got a house together, you know 'W' and 'T'. But in my lifetime, that's the second couple that I've met out of all the men that I've met, and most of the men I've met are dead of aids cause they take it up the ass, and they were promiscuous.

Interviewer1: Not careful.

Nick: And you know; its well; looking for the love, its you want the love to come out of the sex, and there's no such thing as love and sex. Not unless it's a sex promoted by love (*laughing*). You know what I'm saying, if it comes from love, then the sex is good, but if its just from lust, well its good too, but it doesn't last long.

Interviewer1: There's a shelf life, you know; you can get a blowjob and it's pretty good for about ten minutes.

Nick: But this is true this is true. And so; but as a dancer, I've seen all of these gay guys, you know the fact of when I use to judge a contest. I had one boy come up to me, and he says 'you know what, Mr. Mirabella, he says for ten years I've been coming to your contests, and you don't give me anything past a four. And he says 'could I ask you why'? I says well you'd think after ten years you could ask me why, I said your not suppose to ask me why I says but, I will tell you why, Ricky. I says now we have videotapes and you can see yourself and I want you to see yourself on your videotape. And you tell me what kinda faggot that is, that's dancing there. I said first of all you walk in with a cucumber between your pants; you got no damn dick that big, it's impossible. You're too skinny. Then his butt is so damn tight you could see his little crack. I says that's not a man, you gotta dance with the girl. The man and the girl not the girl and the faggot you can't do that. Well he says I'm gonna report you. I said "I don't give a fuck what you do. Because I'm still gonna judge your contest, and until you start acting like a male in your dancing, your not gonna be on the cover of dance magazine, I promise you." And I said "why don't you just go home and consider cleaning up your act a little bit, and everybody knows you're a queer in this room. Any guy that wants a blowjob, could get one from you, we already know that. You don't have to advertise it anymore." Well you know, he got pissed, but then I said now listen to me 'Ricky' listen to what I'm telling you. I'm your friend. You look like an asshole, when your out in public, I says you're a beauty; he was really a beautiful boy, he really was, but he was such a fucking sicky you know with all the makeup and all the pussy, pushy, (*laughing*) crap. (*laughing again*) So the next year or six months later he came to the second contest, this was gonna be in Atlanta GA, and everybody noticed, he had on a suit, wore a coat and everything and there was no more cucumbers, he wore the tuxedo, cause he was doing international dancing, he walked like a man, acted like a man, he presented his women, and he won several first places. The guy was incredible, he could have been a world champion, could have been a world champion but he needed some coaching and he had to get this faggotry shit outta his way, I mean the industry is 98% queer, ok but they don't make the money. They entertain everybody else, that's all they do, and we put up with it you know. So he comes back, (*laughing*) I said 'Ricky' you're a beautiful man. He says I know, your in a closet, you want me, I said yeah I want you, I'll screw your little butt you little bitch. I said now listen to me. Tell me something, how did you feel, everybody coming up and shaking your hand and hugging your neck? He said it's wonderful, Mr. Mirabella, I said now you owe me you bitch. You owe me. He says, but I still only got a forty, (*laughing*) I says well it's gonna take a while; you know cause it can't happen overnight. So anyway, he went home, that contest was in January, I got a phone call, and they said this is Mrs. 'E"R', I said oh I'm sorry you have the wrong number, they said "No, no, we want Vincent Mirabella, I said I'm Vincent Mirabella, she said Mr. Mirabella she says you know my son 'Ricky', I said yes, she says "I'm his mother" she said and "he's done nothing but talk about you for a whole year, you're his hero", made me cry. "She said my son died last night of aides, and I wanted you to know that." So I went to the funeral in Ohio. You know and it's sad about all these gay kids that do this, their pretty, their nice, and they have to act like that.

Interviewer1: What timeframe was that in Nick? What year?

Nick: What was that? 1978 that was when our anniversary ball was. When was our anniversary ball? 1984, I think that was in 1984, it was one of the contests in 1984. And he lived in Ohio, but the contest was in Atlanta Ga., and then it went from Ga. to NY. But it's a way of life that these kids don't understand. They don't know how to be nice; they don't know how to show respect they don't have no honor. And that's why I don't like faggotry. You know just, it's not all fuck, give blowjobs, but that's what it is for 80% of those people. No wonder why God doesn't condone it, and condemns it. And everybody else that goes with it. But there, people are not here to condemn homosexuals. The Pope said there's no sin in being a homosexual. But there could be a problem with the sex part. That's all he said. But anyway, so in the days that I went to all these exclusive joints and they were exclusive gay bars we went to, cause we went to New York City, we went to 54, oh honey

Interviewer1: Tell me a 54 story. I bet Margo come lived it up there.

Nick: Now Margo, I want to tell you, those ah we saw what's his name the little skinny guy that turned white.

Interviewer2: M J

Nick: M J there, now honey if he wasn't a faggot, nobody was. I don't care what anybody says, he has to be gay. He has to be. There were some nights, but you know what was sad about that, the guys that weren't queer, should have been queer, but they were too stoned. Big time cocaine those days. You know you'd go into 54 and every table had lines. You know, nobody got busted for nothing; you smoke pot and blow it all over the place. It was not a problem.

Interviewer1: Did you have any sex in 54?

Nick: Oh did I have sex ... in that club.... Inside it. No I went home, no I don't even go to public bathrooms, but those bathrooms were wild honey. You finish peeing and they grab your dick, it's too much. The devil is alive and well in our nightclubs, its evil. Gonna destroy everybody's souls that's what it's gonna do.
So anyway and then we'd go on different cruises. Now we had some gay people in the shows, maybe you know and they are all over I mean maybe I should find me a nice gay that I could be a sugar daddy to.

Interviewer1: That's kind of what has been happening.

Nick: Well it was happening but I wasn't getting anything for it.

Interviewer1: Right.

Nick: They could call me a sugar daddy, I'll buy them a diamond ring, I mean you know.

Interviewer2: Honey if were that easy, everyone would do that.

Nick: And gay people don't want old men, unless their gonna make money off them, you know.
Margo was a dish queen, she would absolutely sit and pontificate, in the middle of the bar, and everybody would come up and I would say, kiss my hand. (*Laughing*) I was the queen mother honey. And there were people that tried to out dish me and they would be destroyed.

Interviewer2: What's a dish queen?

Nick: A dish queen is a queen that dishes you.

Interviewer2: Oh dis queen?

Nick: Disk no I call them a dish queen. There was one faggot, come up to me in front of everybody and she stopped the whole crowd. She went you're a faggot. And everybody looked and I went ooooh, (*laughing*), she says you're a fairy, and I said "poof" well you're a pile of shit; it freaked everybody, I mean the whole place caved in. You know, that was Margo. Boy I use to couldn't stand … and they are mean and nasty little mothers. They got me; a few of them; got me good now they put me in my place. They were good. But to see all of that, it's sad, its really sad, to see all that. People doing things like that to themselves in these gay bars.

Interviewer1: Do you think it's self-degrading, or what's the sad part about it?

Nick: I think it's very degrading.

Interviewer1: Did these people have fun though?

Nick: I don't know, I think they are drunk.

Interviewer1: They think they are having fun maybe?

Nick: Yeah and they want that

Interviewer1: Nooky at the end of the night

Nick: Whatever, yeah but you know, I thought a bar was to meet someone, and go home and enjoy the evening. But not in there. They all just want to get off. Right then and there.
And that's not sex, that's not making love; I don't know what it is.

Interviewer1: That's our society, always wanting instant gratification.

Nick: It's animalistic.

Interviewer1: Very much so.

Nick: Even the gorillas have more ...

Interviewer1: Communal social

Nick: Respect than we do. Were worse than monkey's. Monkey's are nasty, but were worse than monkey's. I mean a guy is giving you a blowjob and beatin two guys off at the same time and trying to get another guy off with his feet. Give me a break.

Interviewer1: Oh you saw that one to huh? (*laughing*)

Nick: It's a movie, oh was that a movie? What movie is that? But it's true, its reality, and it's sad. And the thing that hurts is that people that are acting like that are gorgeous. Absolutely beautiful.

Interviewer1: Some anyway, many are not so gorgeous. Life has been cruel.

Nick: Well that's why they do that. Nothing better to do.

Interviewer1: That's why you have to see this Showtime show, because these are handsome and not so handsome people, but a lot of very handsome, dynamic,

Nick: And it all takes place in a bar, is that what?

Interviewer1: It's actually filmed in Pittsburgh Pa, in the city.

Nick: And it's a live real show?

Interviewer1: It's a drama, like a Dynasty

Interviewer1: Tell me about this rejection

Nick: I would not do good in this lifestyle, because of the rejection. I would kill myself, especially at this age, when everybody's looking for young new clean meat, you know. And they see a 59 year old,

Interviewer1: But wouldn't that be the time to go for a more lasting relationship?

Nick: With who?

Interviewer1: Someone like you

Nick: I got one with my dog. Yeah like me where?

Interviewer1: Out there.

Nick: I can't get excited about people my age.

Interviewer1: So your admitting, your own bias, by saying "I only want a young person" or that a young person only wants a young person.

Nick: Oh yeah, not only do I want a young person, it's the only thing I know is young people, and people don't understand that.

Interviewer1: So when you grew up, you can't have young people anymore, and that's the conflict.

Nick: Well now in the 90's, for some reason, I don't have my young people anymore, because now it's taboo

Interviewer1: There's more rules,

Nick: All of a sudden your pervert because you have young friends so, there are no young friends, the attraction has always been. Well aren't we all like that?

Interviewer1: Yeah, we go for that level of immortality, you know.

Nick: We go for that young stuff; you know you want something delicious, of course.
Oh bag boys are wonderful; you know I gotta tell you about that in my book you know, all the bag boys I use to take home.

Interviewer2: Bag Boys

Nick: No, BAD boys, (*laughing*). Oh off to prison we go tra la tra la.
But anyway what was it; the rejection itself would cause me to commit suicide. Because …

Interviewer1: But yet the loneliness also is horrifying?

Nick: Well you'll be more lonely, going in an environment like that and being put down by somebody for the rest of the night, you would be in absolute, you know, now they say that there are just like there are people who like fat, fat women, and there are people who like old men. But wherever they are, I don't know.

Interviewer1: Yeah all soft, cuddly and teddy bear like and will sugar daddy them, their out there, and that's why your vulnerable to them.

Nick: Yes sir, yeah well let's go. (*laughing*) but …

Interviewer1: Well here's the question, how do you deal with the conflict, the basic conflict spirituality, sexuality

Nick: Well good question. Now here's what, now this is where the torment is, you understand, first of all, there was a part of my life, in the 70's, or 80's you know that we did a lot of hitch hiking, you remember that? Now let me tell you something, it was a religious ceremony for me. In the morning to get up take a shower, have breakfast, my day off, and ten o'clock, hit the highway and pick up hitchhikers. Now let me tell you about hitch hikers. They come home with you, they will party with you, they've got pot, booze, anything you want they'll make friends with you, you give them a shower, clean them up and it's a way of life for some of these guys, I had three hitch hikers every year would come and see me. At a certain time of year, cause that was their life they go to different people they met and all the love you could handle honey. Their legs would go up in the air and they'd do anything in the world to make love to you. Why, they don't know you, you don't know them, their not threatened. Their inhibitions are down. And that's why we as community living people have all these inhibitions, because its "what's she gonna say about me doing this" and "what is he gonna say about it" and I'm the one that says Fuck it, stick it up your butt, and I've been like that all my life, it's in my book. I'm still gonna do what I want, because I know I'm not doing anything wrong. So and I'm telling you what, I picked up hitchhikers, that will knock your socks off. You know and a certain member of the armed forces, are the wildest. Everyone of those boys honey, pushed them legs up in the air, they want it up the butt. And that just freaked me out. I've had bikers; I've had gangsters,

Interviewer1: Would you use condoms?

Nick: Then, I didn't get no, I'm still a virgin nobody touches my butt.

Interviewer1: But you had your penis in different people's butts

Nick: No, not too many people, no. No, I'm not a butt person. I'm a head giver (*loud laughing by all*)

Interviewer1: And no one ever hurt you, all these strange people

Nick: None of these guys ever hurt me, none of them

Interviewer1: But now you have supposed friends come in your house and steal from you.

Nick: Yeah, yeah and you know these were people just trying to find themselves, going across country, I've had guys that never made love to a man, and went wild. I've have, and every man I ever picked up, and these were men, their not gay, their men, and they give you blowjobs, so talk to me. You know, what this thing is. You know this is why I keep saying

Interviewer2: It proves your theory, about …

Interviewer1: Men are just sexual beings.

Nick: Well so are women,

Interviewer1: Oh I understand that but men more so. The testosterone levels in men drive them to want to have a lot more sex than women. Women are driven to have sex, based on estrogen cycles.

Nick: But I'm also, I also think there are very few men that could get their women off, and that turns the female down, cause it takes so long, to get a woman off

Interviewer1: It's up to the female to teach her man if she wants to stay with him.

Nick: Men don't want to be bothered, they just want to poke and go.

Interviewer1: Many men are like that

Nick: So what I'm saying is that during these 20 years 70's and 80's, I have and it started dying down around 87 I think, the hitch hiking, there's no more now you can't pick up a hitch hiker, they'll kill ya. But in those days, there was always 8:00 pm, there's different spots I could pick them up you know, and they'd let you know right away if they are into being with you, or not into being with you.
I had one guy I picked up once, you know when the cars became electric, and you could 'click' and the doors would lock, he got in the car (*laughing*) and I went

'click' "gotcha" and he panicked, he got so, I said I was only kidding, look 'click' (*laughing still*) I locked the door and it Fuck him up. But I had some ... they were all ... and every one of them were party, party, party Fuck, Fuck, Fuck.

Interviewer1: You knew how to pick them, apparently. There was a look, or a gaydar or what ever you want to call it.

Nick: Well, I ... I only picked up the pretty ones; they had to be pretty, nothing fat and clumsy looking. I think that's terrible but ... I've had some pretty boys. I did it while we worked at Ramada Inn. I picked up some young men.

Interviewer2: But most of them were of legal age.

Nick: All the people I picked up were hitchhikers, I had no idea how old they were. They weren't 40 and 50,

Interviewer1: But they weren't 14 either,

Nick: I think I might have had one or two that might have been 17 or 18.

Interviewer1: It's a tough borderline isn't it?

Nick: 18 you're ok.

Interviewer2: Yes but it's hard to discern whether they are.

Nick: But in those days, it didn't make a damn hill of crap. Now their making a big thing out of it you see. They try to do this crap with this kid James. See and that's called statutory rape, however, because you don't have anything against you it's dismissed, the first time.

Interviewer1: you were trying to answer the question about the conflict.

Nick: There's really no conflict, sexuality you remember is normal, and it's been given to us by God, as a tool for attraction, so that we can propagate the faith. Correct?

Interviewer2: Procreate

Nick: Procreate, they didn't make it to recreate. Ok so he didn't. So what happens now is the person like me who wants to really love God, with his heart and soul, and be a good holy man, 'mouth'. That's all it is. Then the devil knows this lust that I have will work, you know I mean it'll be somebody will ring my doorbell, and it'll be a hunk. Now were the fuck did it come from, do you know how I get to Peter's Creek Parkway. I say come on in and I'll show you. (*laughing*) You know what I mean? You know what I mean, this is how the devil will do you, (*laughing*) so the conflict is really no conflict, you have to choose, do you want to love God, or do you want to be a pig all your life? See so, I wanted to be a pig all my life, and still love God, and it doesn't work, it's not that I want to be a pig, I just love to fuck. I love sex. And I can't have sex any more anyway; because of my diabetes, I can't get a hard-on. Takes four Viagra's and that doesn't do nothing. Or a good blowjob that'll get it hard. (*laughing*) Yeah that way …

Interviewer1: I see you've got this Hoover Steam Cleaner here, but it doesn't squirt either right (*everyone laughing*).

Nick: So what happens is you get tied up with offending God, and trying to be pure and chaste, and you pray and you do sacraments, there's a lot of things, sometimes I'm really close to God and I really behave, but once you masturbate, you blow it, boom. So

Interviewer1: And you really believe that right?

Nick: Well I'm fighting with the priests over that. And it is a self … self-indulgence. And we can get into it for days, so according to the Catholic faith, I have to understand

Interviewer1: But tell me what it's been like living here.

Nick: Here, well I came to live here … in 1973, 74, 71, I came here when I was working at the Ramada Inn, the girl upstairs, she got me this apartment first I lived upstairs with her for about six months, (Roberta, it's just a little tight, talking about a small light for a Christmas tree) (Nick: laughing, I God I haven't that in a long time, you mean there's something tight, show me) well you know what I'm saying is that I moved down here and I've been here since 1971. And it's gone through … there was a time here were we would all keep our doors open and we'd sit outside, and party and get high, and the whole bit, no problem. Didn't have any problems and it sort of…. I'll tell you why I'm here, it's because they give me special rent.

Interviewer1: Because you went bankrupt after the spending spree, right?

Nick: Absolutely, and I'm on disability now. I try to live off of my little bit of money. So there's been a lot of changes, I wish it would change again, I don't care for the Hispanic influence, and I don't like it that; well nobody's nice anymore, you sort of stay to yourself. But about the spiritual conflict, it's an incredible thing because I would like to do a whole chapter on that. You study the life of Christ, you study the law of God, you talk to God for the inspiration and the direction and at one time I always thought that God is really not there, that he's hard nosed but I have found out, let me tell you the miracles the lord gave me over this James business, I stayed in my bedroom and cried, for thirty, forty, fifty fucking days over this kid, praying to God, asking him "Lord please let him call me" the minute I would say that the phone would ring and he'd call me, and tell me what's going on. Boom I feel better, so God is here, he's right here for us, he really doesn't give a damn what kinds of sins we commit, I don't think, I don't think he gives a shack's ass, he's God, he don't care about that, he knows you'll love him. He knows you love him. He knows I love him, he's gonna send me to hell because I masturbate? Well, fuck it then. I'll wind up going to hell. But he's more than that you know I think? I hope? But it's a conflict for me, this is why I have all these 'boogie mans'. Delusion, no more voices, I told the voices to fuck off. So they don't bother me any more (*laughing*). I told that to my doctor, and he didn't believe me. Psychiatrist believes me. (*laughing*)

Interviewer1: What ever happened as a result of visiting the psychiatrist's and psychologists?

Nick: I still go. I still go. After the first of the year, but the one guy he wanted to read my book, and I sent him some pages of our book, I didn't give him the whole book. I got the book, if your taking it back. No you won't need that I need it. But the spirituality you know, if your gonna commit your life to being a good Christian and a good catholic there are certain things that God asks of you (Nick: *he's snoring talking about Tino the dog*) and one of the few things he asks of you is that you keep the Ten Commandments. Now everybody and his grandmother has an interpretation of the Ten Commandments, that's where we get in a lot of trouble. All right you look at the interpretation that's the hard nose and the hardest and that's the interpretation, not the one where we use a lot and make excuses. So, for the first time in your life you gotta be really, really, really be honest with yourself, that when he says 'thou shalt not steal' he means don't steal, you don't take paper, you don't take pencils, you don't take candy, you don't steal. But 'thou shalt not steal' was more to it than ... Well what were we talking about?

Interviewer1: I'm just wondering after everything you've been through, all the diabetes, all the cholesterol, if you can tell me what all they have you on and for what.

Nick: Ok now let me tell you about my medications, I take a million pills a day. I take 1 aspirin a day, to prevent a heart attack; and so far I haven't had a heart attack. I also take ibuprofen this is what everybody takes. Dipiridimal, that's to keep the blood flowing. Then hydrocortisone is a painkiller. Luvox, for my depression. Acupril, I can't remember (*laughing*) Neurontin, is suppose to be for the diabetes and the depression

Interviewer1: Well and its also anti-seizure medication.

Nick: Yes, but I don't have seizures. Celebrex

Interviewer1: What's that for?

Nick: I don't know. Lucopage has to do with the sugar, and the diabetes. Lithobid is for my mental status. Hydrocortisone, I said that already didn't I? That's for pain, but it doesn't do a darn bit of good and this is Lipitor for the cholesterol. Transodine the sleeping pills, I never use them.

Interviewer1: Is it because they didn't work?

Nick: I just didn't use them. Prevocate for my burps, stomach. Avandia for diabetes as well. Lamisil and the last but not least is oxicotin that's a high, high energy pain killer,

Interviewer1: So that will knock you out?

Nick: Yeah but it doesn't take the pain away, so I don't take it. Just like this other is suppose to be that hydro-cortisone, you know that's that generic pill for the what do they call … and that's what I take every day

Interviewer1: How do you remember to take them?

Nick: I got a little box that has the each day in it, best investment I ever made. So I think by taking all these pills I'm even tempered more so then I am even tempered but what I'm working on is that I know I flare off right away and I try to think before I do anything, I walk around like a time-bomb, actually. So I'm just trying to take everything a day at a time, I'm trying to say Christmas is coming, let me tell you about Christmas for me, it was always filled with a lot of cheer, a lot of food, a lot of people, a lot of love, a lot of gifts, a lot of Christmas booty, all that good stuff, ya know and now there's nothing. So I put just what Christmas is right there you see Jesus, Mary and Joseph, it's his birthday. That little boy that came to see me, it's gonna be his birthday. Don't you really think it was God, I don't know who it was, who the heck was it?

Interviewer1: I'm pretty sure there's something special going on there.

Nick: Who could that have been? But why didn't that touch my life and make me holy and pure? Why? I wonder. Yeah I started off really innocently holy and pure and pleasing. I guess we all did, didn't we? Ha, stupid question. Dumb thing I said, all right what else do you want to ask me?

Interviewer1: Would you like to come down and to see Roberta or her family over the holidays?

Nick: When?

Interviewer1: Sometime during these holidays, the second half of December

Nick: Let me tell you something, now don't misunderstand me, your gonna have a lot on ya, you know cooking, cleaning and feeding so maybe well do something together after the holiday's, just us, I'll cook for you, in fact I'm gonna have to have a dinner for Sylvia, and Jane.

Interviewer1: Tell me how you got to meet them.

Nick: Jane became a student of mine. She walked in my studio, I noticed this little red headed walked in, very fashionably dressed, very, very beautiful, beautiful girl, and I never ever got excited about red heads, you know. And she'd take root classes, and I'd bark at her yell at her, carry on and she said to me, you know I'd like to be a good dancer. I said well I think your problem is you're too pussy. Your too soft, you get nervous, you get scared, I said this is a vicious business, people are gonna intimidate you, so you get out there and dance, and your gonna screw up. I said now I'm gonna yell at you a lot, probably make you cry. Can you handle that? Well I don't know. I said well try. And that girl became one of the top-notch senior citizens ballroom dancers. Far as I'm concerned, in the whole damn country. Great dancer, beautiful dancer, beautiful, beautiful. And God she was godsend. Laura if it weren't for that lady, I don't know what would have happened to me. When I was in the hospital, she was there every day, every single day ... every single day, for eighteen weeks that lady took care of me every single day. I didn't have a back sore or a blister on my ass, and she put up with my temperament, she gave me love and affection, all from God, no queer crap, no any of that stuff, ya know. So; and oh I still yell and scream at her, you know with this mental disease. She was the brunt of my anger. And she just couldn't understand and I had to have the psychiatrist tell her "please tell this lady I'm taking it all out on her" you know and she still hanging in there. So she understood, very strong. She's got a husband, she's got three boys, she's got several grandchildren, just if they was to give the mother of the world award, I would give it to her, she's a good mother, a good, a very much in love with her husband they have a very good relationship. And you know she just told her husband "I'm gonna take care of Vincent, cause he's go nobody" and he's never once been evil or hateful or jealous, or ugly about it. She's really a great person, and I would give anything to be able to dance just one or two more times, before I die, with her I really do want to but it won't work. The legs will not work. So you know I've had to walk away from a lot of stuff. And I think this is why I'm having all these problems.

Interviewer1: Frustrating

Nick: It's frustrating, it's but in the mean time, I see God is taking care of me. I'm not in the street. I'm not homeless, that could happen tomorrow, you know. I don't know what will happen to me if they tell me to get out of here. What is ever gonna happen to me? You know, just don't you know cause they got places you can, but I can't, I'm not gonna go that backwards, I want to die with dignity, you know so and but that's one reason why, I'm putting my affairs in her hands,

Interviewer1: Tell me next about Sylvia

Nick: Oh Sylvia, is a sweetheart, she is ah ...

Interviewer1: How did you meet her?

Nick: Now Sylvia came to take some dance classes, from me, and then took some private lessons from me, and being she is Chinese, that's very much Italian, cause she's thick headed. She never listens. She went to everybody and their grandmother and then I got mad about that, you know but in the long run, we became good friends, she's very nice to me, she goes to dinner with us, you know and helps teach dancing for me, I think that if I could have the patience and the wisdom of a Chinese person, I would be a very happy human being. She's a very wise, she's very wise person, very smart, very, very, very smart person, and she hold's her emotions she knows how to control herself and this is discipline, and I always thought that discipline makes a person. I've always thought that, to be self-disciplined makes your character. And of course I would only be self-disciplined when I had to be so I haven't got a whole lot of character. But uh yeah, she's a good friend. She really is, she doesn't often go to a gentleman's house alone, she's Chinese, there like that you know and I didn't know it. And she's very ... I make her laugh, she laughs a lot and of course I tease her you know about, I kid with her, with her accent, I did that to another friend that was Japanese, a friend of Roberta's, what was her name?

Interviewer2: 'K'

Nick: 'K' and she got totally offended one time, and just gave me hell. Made me feel like shit. Excuse my language. But I go 'hro' [haro] (*laughing*) you know and she just laughs, and I told her, now Sylvia, if I'm being rude, and showing you disrespect, you tell me, cause I would never do it. She has beautiful talent she can be a beautiful, beautiful ballroom dancer. She really could be.

Interviewer1: Do these ladies still dance?

Nick: No

Interviewer1: It would be nice to have a reunion of all the people together.

Nick: If they can't dance with me they certainly can't dance with anybody, cause no man can dance them the way I do. I'm like a sickness, I could have done you know I could have been a Mr. Rockefeller if I had just played around, with all these women. I could have women coming out my ass. But I didn't. See I was very, very well, terrified. I'm terrified of women, I've always been afraid of women. I've always …

Interviewer1: You talk about your mother having this grand stature, that maybe she kind of led the way?

Nick: No, no she was wonderful, I was afraid of her, I feared her, but I still respected her, and I loved her, but it was my stepmother that turned me against women. From all the beatings, that she gave me. And she'd look at me and just slap me, you know but that's all ok, it's forgiven and there's no hate, I hope she's in heaven, and all that good totty rot. But I've never ever could get along with women.

Interviewer1: What about Roberta?

Nick: Well, I'm lucky. But see she walked away on me for seven years, that's a long time to be mad at somebody, and not tell them you are mad at them, see she's gotta learn to tell somebody 'hey fucker, I'm mad at you and this is why", then she won't be depressed. She holds it all in, doesn't she, she can't do that. And she will a couple of more sessions with the pshyc, she'll start see in the light. Don't you think?
It's very hard Laura, it's very, very hard this sickness I just cannot, I'd rather be a junky than be manic depressed. Now the medicine is keeping me from going crazy with it. I have spent no money, I won't go to stores, I don't party, you know part of the manic depression would be, I'd say alright I'm gonna call every-body I know and tell them to come over Saturday and were gonna eat. Were gonna party. And I would do that and just spend tons of money I never had for food. So I'm not doing it, any of that. Now I'm at the low end, you know. Where you just lay on the bed, and you just try. And I mean I count my blessings, I have a very easy lifestyle, uh thank God cause I can't walk from here to the corner without breathing hard.

Interviewer1: What happened with getting one of the scooters?

Nick: Oh I got a wheelchair,

Interviewer1: You did

Nick: Yeah I got one in the back, in the playroom, finally I had to fight with my doctor, and went to another doctor, and got me a wheelchair, but I haven't used it. Now the scooter is a $3,000—$5,000 Laura honey and I'd love to have one of them, it really would give me my independence, for sure on Tuesday's, but I don't have the money. But Medicaid won't pay for even part, unless I can't walk at all. So I'm hoping Sylvia will win one, there gonna give one away, and she'll give it to me. But that will give me my independence for sure, I can't walk, I can't walk, I'm way overweight, I just sit and eat and eat. You know what are you gonna do when you haven't got nobody? That's why I just want somebody I could just make over, you know fuss over them, and just....
Someday the world will miss me, don't you think? (*laughing*)

Interviewer1: That's why were getting it all down in the book.

Nick: Now but I'm saying this is....

Interviewer1: tell me about the recent church experiences you've had, when we were last here, you talked about maybe getting in on youth, you know group situation but it didn't work out, what happened?

Nick: Ok, big brother's had an advertisement in our bulletin, for an Italian person to talk with a little Italian boy, just a little buddy kid, in school, five years old. So after I had that girl in tears and had her laughing all at the same time, two-hour interview, she decided with her superior, that perhaps maybe I should not do this. And for the same reason, that my psychiatrist told me I should not do this. And for the same reason, that I know that I should not do this, is that I would become what?

Interviewer1: Obsessed with one of the children

Nick: Obsessed and attached. And there goes that. So it never got to seeing the court order. Now catholic charities are having their meeting January 17, for hosts and if I'm really smart, I should not do that. As much as I want to have a kid for fifteen days, this would not be wise, with this illness of mine, I would become so severely attached. So against all of my intelligence I may do it. You see what I'm saying? So people will say as they read this when is he gonna learn? Well I've learned. You know but there's somebody out there that needs me, I'm sure. God's got something going I think. Sometimes I just wish he'd just call me and get it over with, I'm not afraid of dying, I just don't want to die in mortal sin, you know. It's kinda superficial. It's like the church says, when you tell God your are sorry, you are sorry because your scared that your gonna go to hell? Or you're sorry because you hurt God's feelings? Well what the hell do you think you're sorry for? They make everything such a damn project. As long as you're sorry what's the difference? God does not think like we do. Thank God for that. He's loving, he's kind, he … he love's you if your lesbians, he loves you if your gay, he loves you if your Chinese, he loves you if, I don't know if you can get in now, there talking about dog and men and dogs, girls and dogs, oh please. Now this is sick. But see to me, boys and boys ain't sick. But boys and dogs is sick, so what's sick to me, isn't sick to you, what's sick to you, isn't sick to me. I use to eat snails as a kid, now thats revolting, and I got them inside (pointing to the refrigerator) (*laughing*) yuck picking that little snail out and just chewing … ugh next question please

Interviewer1: So you mentioned the last time that some times you feel this happens to just you.

Nick: What happens to just me?

Interviewer1: This sickness

Nick: Oh I am sure that there are many people that suffer with manic-depression, I know there are. But I don't know that they have the same problems that I have. I don't think so. I don't know. Some people see some people suffer externally, more severely; I suffer more internally with this madness. Now I haven't went to ask I mean I hear people when I use to go to the meetings, "I didn't take my meds" "I wanted to kill myself last night" "I didn't see my mother" I don't want to hear all that. I mean God bless em, but hey I didn't either, so but it does help you to hear it from someone else, it really helps. To hear someone else's problem, it's like a psychiatrist cannot do a thing for you, psychologists do nothing for you, they just listen, and ask the question and let the hour go by, so that they can get paid. That's what it seems like, most of the time you know. But that, that center point that mental health place got rid of that thing with James didn't it? Didn't it? Wasn't I obsessed though? Oh and I was obsessed like that with a boy in the monastery once.

Interviewer1: Tell me a little bit about that

Nick: Oh, boy I was mad about this guy, one night I snuck up into his room and spent the night with him. (*laughing*) The night before I left the monastery. So this obsession of mine, I want to know where it came from. How I got it. Why I'm like this. I mean, what a nerve to go and sneak around, I mean you know you become very euphoric.

Interviewer1: It's a thrill?

Nick: No, I don't think it's a thrill. But I had to be with this person.

Interviewer1: Why?

Nick: I, well that's what I asked them, I don't know why but I want you, I want to be with you.

Interviewer1: Did you already know you were leaving at the time?

Nick: Yeah, I thought I was, I use to teach him piano, and I couldn't wait till I get to, everyday after dinner to go down and teach him piano. Just to be with him. Everywhere I went just to be with him, I use to do his laundry, in the laundry room. They say that isn't your department, and I'd say I'm doing his laundry. Fold it and all that stuff, so I want to know and nobody can tell me why we do this. I'm no fucking moron. You know?

Interviewer1: But you're human.

Nick: I'm not a weirdo.

Interviewer1: Is it enough of an answer just to know that you're human?

Nick: I want to be, you know I've always been loved, I've always had somebody to coddle, I've always had a Shawn, you know I've always had a 'M'.

Interviewer1: So the hole right now isn't filled with anyone.

Nick: With anyone at all yeah.

Interviewer1: Can the church; can the body of Christ fill the hole?

Nick: Oh sure it can, but you've have to be ... oh yeah, all of this, let me tell you, the fact that I believe in God, and that I pray to God, and that I'm into God, even though I'm wretched sinner that I am, that's helping my depression far more than anybody can ever see.

Interviewer1: Are the drugs?

Nick: Well the drugs, and God I mean now the girl that played superman, Lois Lane, she threw her drugs away, she went to live in the mountains, and got rid of it. I don't got no mountains to go to, you know. But as long as I can live a quite life, away from most of humanity, I think I can live well. If I gotta be in mingling with people for the rest of my life, I'm not gonna live to well. Because there's always these things that I demand from people I demand for them to be the best, I demand for them to be Christ like, well ask Roberta what did I do to that girl? And none, none of it rubbed off, not any of it. You know but she's gotta respect the fact that I cared enough about her to do that to her. But people don't care, they don't want to tell you that you did something for them, they leave you hanging, like you was little creep. So I've done this to every ... so I need to stay away, I don't need to be telling people how to be better, I need to know how, I gotta be better, not me tell you what to do, see.

Interviewer1: It is easier to focus on others problems than your own. You know kinda ... and when you're helping others, you have the satisfaction of you know.

Nick: I don't know if I've ever had any satisfaction out of helping anybody, actually

Interviewer1: Well the kids?

Nick: It didn't cost money, everything cost money. Everything. All I remember is loosing money, I spent money on everybody, and their grandmother all my life and nothing, not even a thank you sometimes. So I don't know what it is. It's that nature it's my nature. I'm a person that has to have something to fondle, or coddle. Don't ask me why, you know it's a pain in the ass to have to fondle and coddle, its hard work, to show love from your heart, you know.

Interviewer1: Have you ever thought that working like um with animals in terms of the ASPCA, or helping you know, if humans are a pain in the ass, you know what about animals?

Nick: Oh animals, Tino, he's the biggest pain in the ass in my house. Tino, he'll run away on me, he'll puke up, (*ooh we got that door open too*). But anyway I worked with children you know, when I worked at the children's home, but that was a different kind of child. Imagine working with kids that have already been rejected by their parents, so they put them in a place like that, and there certainly nobody in that place that's gonna care for or love them, so they try to survive the best they can. But I had my own little cottage, and I had Jesus lives here and there, and I painted the whole thing celery green and white and gave the boys tablecloths and magnolias, and Christmas and one of the house parents was jealous of my accomplishments with the boys, they loved me. Children love me, they come up and hug me and kiss me, and even big boys come up and hug me. Boy that is so amazing, and then everybody calls you queer because of it. Now those kind of people, need to have a slap up side their heads to think I'm like that. It's there the ones with the problem, not me.

Interviewer1: Quick to judge?

Nick: Yeah, but I'm not gonna stop. I'm not gonna stop, being me for anybody. Cause I'm gonna be a lot more careful. And the best thing for me to do is to stay away from all of it. Let it come to me. And it will.

Interviewer1: Asking God for the right kind of love in your life he knows the right kind of love for you, whether it's companionship.

Nick: Yeah but he may not have that, see you know what God wants from me, but you know what he wants from me? He wants me to love him. More than anybody else.

Interviewer1: But if you can't do that 24/7, does that mean you can't love anyone else?

Nick: No, you can still love someone else, and love him. But he wants me to get into the body of Christ, into the mystical soul of the faith, where you self deny yourself, where you do a little bit of penance, where you pray, and where your works are those of Christ. I have one of the greatest blessings that has ever happened to me in my whole entire life. And that is this, I am a, what we call a Eucharistic Minister in our church, and I'll explain what that means. On Tuesday mornings, I go to mass, and the priest gives me hosts, God in an epiphany, and I go to the hospital, and pray with the sick give them Holy Communion, and bless them. God who we received is meat in my nasty horrible hands, to deal with people. That is the greatest most wonderful day of my entire week, knowing that I have God in my pocket I call it. You know, and I don't know how long their gonna let me do that, but they'll find a reason to get rid of that. I wanted to be a sponsor for the new Catholics and they never even, they dumped me so, and one of the priests told me that I scandalized one of the new guys that wanted to be catholic, (*laughing*) I scandalized them. And the guys an ex marine but what it is, is that he's nothing but a pussy and he went and told his girlfriend. He asked me a question about fornicating. And about giving blowjobs and about being queer. And I said you can't do none of that in our church. There ain't no way your gonna be with this girl and fornicate. Your gonna be catholic, you gotta hold your dick in your pants until your married and you can't screw the dog, can't eat her pussy, even before or after. Rather graphic I know. See I gotta learn not to do that, (*laughing*) he pussed out man, and he went crying to the priest, and the priest reprimanded me, severely.

Interviewer1: So the method was ok, it was the delivery that they didn't like, cause they don't want you to have sex until after marriage?

Nick: Well, no I should have told him to go ask the priest.

Interviewer1: So it wasn't your place to give that advice?

Nick: Probably, you can give that advice, but not if your suppose to be a good catholic, your not suppose to talk like that you know. And so I don't know, I'm just staying away from it all.

We are talking about a personality called Margo, because of the name in ball-room dancing when I had made my fame was Marco, so what I want to imply here to you folks is simply this, all of these events that your going to hear about are when I was taken to these homosexual bars and homosexual environment, because of my older teachers that wanted me to learn to come out and have fun in different places. And these lashing out these people, their rudeness is just an example to tell you that is the way I have been all of my life, even with the homo-sexuals, even with the marines, even with the church, with everybody, this is ME. And I'm sorry I can't change it. So I stay away. Okay

Interviewer1: Here is a question I have, when did you realize that the person Vincent, whom the main life story is going to be reflected in this book, has two distinctive other egos if you will inside? Nick the Gestapo, matter of fact SOB, and Margo the deep inside dish queen, faggot, when did that, when did you real-ize that?

Nick: You know I think I realized that, it started with the Margo dish queen thing, my early years lets say about 16 or 17; I was becoming a dancer and going to these bars with the older guys, cause if you went off with the guys, except for the ones that raped me at that time, you went to homosexual places. If you went to places where we went with the guy that raped me, you went to places were there was a lot of women. See and a lot of sex and so is the story about my rape in there?

Interviewer1: Yes

Nick: So that was me dealing and giving orders to … I didn't understand where these loose mouth you know wrist flickin kinda people, I never saw anything like that in my life and it absolutely infatuated me but at the same time it kinda dis-gusted me. Now I'm not putting anybody down and it's not my intention to make fun of the homosexual lifestyle, I'm just saying this is my experience, I was not impressed with the kind of boys that were wrist flicking and loud mouth, their rude and nasty, and faggots, that's what we call faggots. I'm sorry but they are a disgrace to the homosexual, and I met a lot of the gay people that are won-derful, sweet, I love them with my heart and soul, I got friends that are gay, and I love them all. So any of these little faggots that want start something about it that's their problem, but I think society doesn't like it either. They have nothing against gay; I think their problem with most of us is that silly sissy shit.

So because of this influence, I want you to understand partying as a dancer I also did a lot of partying with celebrities, as we danced shows and different places, and danced with other ... but you know I think folks should know this, as well as I do, there is no one any different than any one else, we are all the same, we all have the same personalities and you go to California and there will be a man with personality just like mine. Go to Europe, there will be a person with the same shit that you got. So we are all equal in this thing and it's just everybody's trying to say look at me ... impressed, impressed, impressed. So I've seen a lot of that, I've danced with some celebrities, and partied with them, and there full of baloney, just like you and me and some of them are wonderful. One of the greatest people I ever met in my life, I told the story aboout, was Susan Haywood, right. She was the most charming, wonderful incredible human being. And I also met Alice Cooper so there you go two different kinds of people. But their all people, just like you and me except that they have some celebrity status, so we have danced in a lot of what we now call heterosexual bars, and their just as piggy as the homosexual bars. So you can't put the homosexual down, anymore than a heterosexual, their just as nasty as they can be too. I partied all over the country, and all over the world and I was just a kid, sowing my oats, trying to learn and looking and finally with a status of responsibility, when I became a good dancer, I was so spoilt rotten, with everything I did, that I didn't know how good I really was. And it went right past me, that's the story of my life; my life has been a rip-off, from day one. There I was, in major dance schools a number one dance teacher, a number one dancer, three years in a row and I was such a pompous little ass, I'm surprised nobody took me out in the woods, and whooped my ass. Then you grow up. And then I realized I gotta make a living and ended up in this restaurant business, and then I became Nick rather then Vincent. Now Nick carried the cross of being a leader and an organizer I was thrown into a hotel situation, where it was just absolutely, we had to tear the place apart. We had to shoot the roaches they were so big. And got it fixed up into a beautiful place, with lace and candle light and flowers, I want to tell you. And got rid of all the whores, that sat there and opened their legs, to nice ladies, nice girls. I had a girl come to me for an interview, told her to be at work at five o'clock in the morning she was there at five o'clock in the morning and I sent her back home and told her to get dressed. I want you in a dress and make up please. So that part of my life was I hadda be on top of everything, at all times and I had to be strict. And I made it very clear to the public and to the employees that if you mess with me your out. I'm not gonna go through no bullshit if your too sick to work then stay home, don't come back. And ladies and gentleman, I'll tell you right now I never had anybody lay outta work on me never once had anyone get sick on me, and if they were sick they came to work and they died and sneezed in the food and got everybody else sick, but they came to work. So that personality was the one like the godfather. People looked up to you, you were in charge of their needs and my employees weren't just people that worked for me, they were people who worked, for themselves, I had one boy that could have been a great chef today. You know. And Roberta was one of the finest hostesses, over there. Raised her family, when somebody comes and tells you 'I have two kids to raise, and I need a job, I don't care what I'll do' I said to myself, after I get to know this girl, she's not gonna be working like a slave, she's gonna work the good part of the job.

Interviewer1: Now she's the president of her own company

Nick: Of her own company she certainly is and an activist for the North Carolina Coalition for Adoption Reform. So Nick …

Interviewer1: Became Nick who controlled and …

Nick: Controlled and ran things and got things done, he had schedules to meet see. Now Vincent is the one that loves God, not that Margo and Nick didn't, but the Margo part was a little loose. I walked into a bar one night and one of those faggots looked at me and said "well Margo" and that's how I got my name Margo, from Marco.
And they are all rude and will hurt your feelings. But so will people in the straight life.

Interviewer1: Was Margo tough?

Nick: Oh Margo was a dog, come from hell, you couldn't mess with Margo, no sir, you hadda kiss my hand or you couldn't pass me. (*Laughing*)
I'm serious. Little faggots had to come and kiss Aunt Margo's hand.

Interviewer1: When was Margo in her prime?

Nick: Oh gosh let me see that was when I was just coming out, with the dancing, fifteen, sixteen, seventeen I wasn't allowed in those bars, yet I was in there all the time.

Interviewer1: And where's Margo now?

Nick: Oh Margo's in Europe, (*laughing*)

Interviewer1: A broad?

Nick: A broad yeah, Margo's a broad. In Europe, she wants to come in and out once in a while, it was fun but now, you know Margo's old. Something like the Valley of the Dolls, you gotta have a wig,

Interviewer1: Is Margo retired then?

Nick: Oh Margo, well actually Margo retired a long time ago, she just stays inside. Margo I think gave up the ghost about 19, Margo's days were over, but it was interesting to see that all of these dish queens would come and avoid me. If they were rude to somebody, I would just let them know, in front of the whole bar. You little faggot, I'll kick your little queer ass, you don't do that, not even with faggots. (*Laughing*)
So it was just a time, I learned a lot, I know one thing if anyone in the world wants to know what sadness is they need to look and study about the homosexual lifestyle. That is the saddest life there is no God, there is no god, there is no God. No God.
They have thrown him away. You can't do what that boy did in that bar scene, and say I love God. But you can still love God, if you do that. So this is the maddening thing about faith. People say all homosexual's are gonna die and go to hell. This is ridiculous, to even think, to even make that comment, that's a comment of judgment. What are those kinds of faith, those straight lace faiths, you know with the books … where are they going, and their snake up their ass is where their gonna go.

Interviewer1: I just found it fascinating that Vincent learned, you know how to use NICK when Nick was needed, and how to let Margo out, when Margo needed to get some air. But is it Vincent still?

Nick: Oh yeah it's a form of survival; you see there are only two kinds of people in this world. The doers and the don't doers. See the doers, were Nick, it means you gotta get the don't doers, to doer. Then you gotta put people in their place, Margo was the one with the homosexuals, putting them in their place, it wasn't just the homosexuals, you put in your place, you learned to use that with Nick too.

Interviewer1: Um hmm

Nick: I'm hiring you to do this job, I'm not hiring you to do that job, and do you understand me? Say yes, yes now if you're doing this after I hire you your out, you understand, you say yes, yes. Alright you're out. I was told that I changed employees at that Ramada Inn Airport more than her husband changed his underwear. By the time I got you going, I knew you weren't the one I wanted, so I'd fire them. But you ask Roberta, we got that place down right man. We had first class cliental, we had first class, I think so, I don't know she'll tell ya, I know.

Interviewer1: Have you ever taken a trip back there to see what happened after you left?

Nick: Oh its, now there's nothing, it's a dump, oh anytime I go somewhere, it's destroyed, it's really bad. Just like when I worked at the children's home, with those kids, ya know they started that queer crap to … not to kids, don't do that. It's the damn adults that do it. The kids never had any complaint with me, at all. But they get jealous of you and they start those vicious nasty things, yeah. One of the mothers who's son was trying to become a big time politician, was a mother, what do they call them, you know a house mother, who hated me, she was the one who would barricade my kitchen with garbage pails, so I couldn't get in, so I told her once, I said "let me tell what you damn little bitch, you come and eat my food in here and I'm gonna poison your ass, your gonna die" she never came back in my dining room again. I said I'm gonna grind glass in your food.

Interviewer1: So that was Nick?

Nick: She wouldn't give me, she wasn't gonna give me nothing; she wouldn't let me get the kids any Christmas presents, anything. I said your one fucking weird lady. I don't care who your son is. I'll kick your damn ass. Stay outta my kitchen, and my dining room. I had fifteen boys, they all loved me. Every one of them.

And my heart broke for them, because they had no one. Nobody gave a crap about them. And I bought them all these things, and everything. I know the ladies name, but there isn't any sense in putting it in here. Yeah, that was Nick.

44

Chip

I'm sorry my brother Chip for some reason didn't get involved with me. Oh, he was nice, I mean you know the guy was nice, but he lied all the time. I'm gonna send you my father's ring and then, nothing you know. Oh and then my father had all the dance trophies that he told me I could have, when he died and of course Jones got all that.

And you know this is all ok because these don't bring the father back, the mother back, the aunt back or anyone. They just hang around so you can just sit and feel sorry for yourself.

I think they were pissed off at the relationship because simply when I would come home I would buy clothes, I would go out to Robert Hall and I'd give my father three hundred bucks in cash and he'd put it on his credit card. Because sometimes it would be more you see. So when it was more, I would mail back the money. So they all think he was doing things for me that he wasn't doing for them. And that's not so. It is so stupid and immature because they are at the age where you know they should be doing for themselves.

Just like when we went to New York, she got a parking ticket. "Oh that's ok, dad knows the governor". What is this bullshit? Dad doesn't know no damn governor and he can't get no ticket fixed. But she went and gave the guy a bad time because of the little backhand you see.

So I didn't abuse my father that way and so Chip related to me. Bless his heart, his dad never told him he loved him. Well he never told me he loved me either. I made him tell me. I said "You little bitch you better tell me you love me or I'm gonna come over then and smack ya" (*laugh*).

So I respected my dad but he knew damn well what he did wrong and I made sure he was gonna walk the line for the rest of my life. I have no problems with him. He just did not want this son. From the very beginning he put me in an old eighty year old ladies hands to raise me. And he just did not want the responsibility.

He had no, no absolute reason to give any affection or any…. he didn't even play ball with me. So move over Chippy cause I been through the same crap, if not worse. At least I see you sit there and bullshit with him and eat and reek of garlic together … like two dumb Italians. Anyway you can't say Italians will come and get me (*laughter*).

45

The Hospital

On May 2 2000, I was talking with a friend who was a nurse, on the phone. I had gone in and was lying down, and so tired. She told me I should come to the hospital. I said 'Nah, I don't want to come to the hospital". I finally asked her to take me to the hospital and so she did. While I was there, they said I went through two heart attacks and four strokes and my whole body shut down. My kidneys started to shut down, my brain they say turned off for almost twenty minutes. And with my brain turning off like that it saved me from going into seizures, it saved my body from being deformed.

So the doctors worked on me. They said I looked perfectly well for a person that had died.

I saw the lord about 4:00 in the morning, sitting on my shelf, the shelf over the television. He said to me "Vincent" I said "Yes Lord" He said to me "You know who I am?" I told him "Yes I do". He said, "Listen to me," and I answered "Yes Lord" "You don't listen to me, you don't listen to anybody, you don't listen" I just started crying, and I said "Lord I'm trying to listen; I'm trying to be a good person and trying to be a good Catholic, a good Christian. I want to he holy" He said "Well you keep asking me 'How to get to heaven' and it is simple, the first two rules I gave you"

1. Love the lord thy God with the whole heart the whole soul the whole mind the whole body, the whole being.

2. Love they neighbor as thy self.

I said to him "Do I have to love my neighbor?" and he answered "Yes, you have to love your neighbor". It's that simple and I am going to try. I said "Boy I ain't gonna make it but I am going to try". Then I saw a delusion again sorta like an echo you know and he said "Vincent," I said "Yes Lord" and he told me "Listen to me, the holy apostolic church are the people who pray in the name of God and become God. That's your friends at mass who have been coming to see you every day they are wonderful people. They are the mystical body along with you and they will help you with the graces to get well. Stay close to them and you will be with me. Not at me, you have me in you so you are God, isn't that amazing? You are God."

So I am trying and struggling and I will get well. I have to go to the Whitaker Care, a three hour program, for two days, and I am not well enough to do even ten minutes. You know I am doing these little exercises on my own. [*Can you put the sheet over that?*][*His feet*] and then well see what we can do about rehabilitating and walking again.

I lost a lot of weight and I want to keep it off. I don't know if I can keep it off with drinking milkshakes, every day. But it's good, I don't care.

So here we are in the room. They say I'm a little bit better, so I go to an upgrade room. They will tell everybody where I'm at you know.

So I have been here since the second of May. It has been an ordeal. But it's by the grace of God I am alive. I don't know why I had this heart attack. A poison has come into my blood. They took a little biopsy of the muscles to see. I took the aides test and it was negative, it was clear. I told the priest "There are you happy?" He said "Yeah" Not the priest, but the doctor. He told me "Yes I am happy Vincent"

A little more tragedy before this. Was it February, or March or maybe April? What month is this Ro? Ro said, "This is May Nick" What's before March? April. In April, on the fourth, I buried my Valentino. He died of leukemia. It absolutely destroyed me. I went and had a little extra money and I told the vet to go ahead and check my dog, I want blood work and everything. Were gonna do his teeth. And my little baby had leukemia. He died and it broke my heart. So right away I tried to get another dog, like a little Collie, sweet little Border collie, she gave kisses to you all the time. Little blonde thing she just gates when she walks. I said boy this is a pedigree. Yeah I had to loose her too now. So I am sick, se le vi.

My book is continuing, and hopefully we will continue to try and bring you happier things.

When you have a tragedy as this and you're in the hospital you try to do what they tell you, try to be nice and it will go better be nice. If you're not nice, it's not so hot. I'm lucky I have got several friends that will come in and out from church. The priest comes and I get communion. I have no complaints, I am very happy I got this. I have been wanting a beer, (*laughing*) "I don't drink beer. I never drink beer. Yet I want a beer"

Close of Story

✦

January 13, 2001

With the closing of this story you the reader have heard Vincent's account of the various aspects of his life, beginning with his childhood up until the present. Now I'd like Vincent to comment on what this has all meant for him. What pearls of wisdom can he give us?

Vincent:
Oh, as my story comes to a close, I Vincent have returned once more to my faith and I am once again pursuing my life in Christ. I have been going to mass as faithfully as my diabetic neuropathy will allow, and if and when I am not able to make it to church, someone comes to give me the sacraments. However, my purpose dear reader with this book is to say simply this. My life was started completely innocent with the love of God, and learning about God, and in doing so learning about yourself. As I have grown in my life, I started realizing what rejection was and have learned to accept it. There was a lot of rejection in my life and yet I still am trying to love God. I lived a life style as a youth with many sins, and many disobediences but you know we can't blame having a mental disorder or a physical disorder on self will. God gave us 'free will'.

What I would like you to walk away with; any of you who suffer from rejection, or who suffer pain, suffer sadness, or suffer hate, is that you hear all your life God is real and God is there. I am here to tell you he is real, he is here and he will love you. You could be a monster but he will love you. When I spoke about the 'faggots' it was not to put anyone down, but to put down the lifestyle. Although these children are committing the sin, God still loves them. We said that a million times. He loves you, not the sin so then he is to determine what is to happen. I want you to know definitely whether you believe in God or not your gonna believe it one day when he comes to give us our do.

So now I want to spend the rest of my life in my third calling back to God, and to the sacraments of my church. I want to spend this time in meditation learning more about myself and learning to be quiet, learning to listen. And I'm trying very hard. This is all God wants from you the reader. Whether your Catholic, Jew, Hindu or whatever religion, you know he simply says to love him, with your whole heart your whole soul, your whole mind and your whole body. Him, first, praise him, tell him you'll love him and adore him every day. Because he's kind. Then the hard part is to love your neighbor as yourself. And that doesn't mean just the good guy's but it means also the guy that irritates you. That means the people who are evil also, you have to love your enemies, you have to pray for them, this is what he wants. Believe it or not, now at 64 years old, I am learning the validity of that so I'm going to try and spend the rest of my life loving my neighbor and trusting to seek Christ in everyone and to try and keep the virtue of purity. I want to be pure of heart and pure of soul so I can see God one day.

I want to give up sin. I want to give up lust and anger and spend the rest of my life through religious scripture; with the holy men of God to guide me so that when I do die, it's a happy death in Christ. And my reverent prayer for you dear reader is that you will love your God more than anyone or anything. And don't let anyone or anything hurt you. You know, I don't care if people compliment me anymore, it doesn't make any difference. I don't care if you love me or don't love me anymore it doesn't make any difference; all of these things no longer mean a thing. I care about God, I care about trying to imitate Christ, and I am going to try to love my neighbor as myself.

I have had six friends who have tolerated me and loved me all these years. And I am going to treasure their friendship more than I have ever done before. There are many people in my church who will embrace you so I know there is a lot of love around. I was just too blind to see that.

I realize now, my love was stemming from carnal desires, impurity and lust, and when you love like that there really is no love. So give it all up and get on with it. If I can do it so can you. And with this I give you my peace and I ask you to keep me in your prayers and I hope you have enjoyed my book.

By the way so you don't accuse me rashly I will tell you, I am celibate and have been so for many years now.

And with this we say

… Forgive us our sins, as we forgive those who sin against us.

Afterword

This chapter is being told by Roberta who with Laura saved me from possibly never being seen again. After my last stay in the hospital, and then going to a rest home for a while, I finally went back home. I must have had problems in keeping track of my medications, because I ended up back in the hospital after a couple of weeks had went by.

Here is what happened as told by Roberta:
Laura and I were headed back from the cabin on a Tuesday evening. Jane had called me and told me Nick was back in the hospital. We decided to visit with him on the way home. When we got to the room, Nick was in a wheel chair, and the nurse was trying to get him to take a pill. I could tell Nick was talking gibberish, and something was really wrong. I asked where they were taking him, and she told me he was going down to floor two. I asked what room, and she couldn't tell me. She did eventually tell me floor two was the psychiatric floor. She then told me no one except for family was allowed there. I explained to the nurse, that Laura and I were the closest thing Nick had to family in North Carolina.
The nurse was a sweetheart, because she managed to pull some strings, and made it so Laura and I were able to accompany Nick down to the second floor. When we got down there with him, they gave me a passcode to be able to call in and see how he was doing and what I would have to do to come back and visit with Nick. A day or so later, I went back down to visit with Nick, and found out they were detoxing him from the Lithobid. Apparently he had been taking double doses. Nick was on the second floor for around two to three weeks and then was released back home. I started going with him to his doctor appointments after that and met his psychiatrist. I told her, that the Nick which was sitting in front of us was not the person I knew. He was a zombie of the Nick I knew. So we started working on reducing some of the medications he was taking, and he was taken off of the Lithobid entirely.
Since then, Nicks meds have changed quite a bit. Nick has been visiting the pain clinic in Winston Salem, in order to try and get the diabetic neuropathy under some kind of control. He has been on almost every type of pain killer you can

think of from Oxycotin to a derivative of morphine which he is currently on. I don't believe anyone can know the pain he is in, unless they have a nerve type of pain. It can be excruciating. Nick has not been back into the hospital since that last time in 2002. I have tried to assist Nick in making sure he goes to his doctors, and now in 2005 we are going to look into moving Nick to the Raleigh/Durham area, so he can be closer to the "family" he has here.

Final Update—2007

As editor and best friend to Vincent, I would like for everyone to know that Vincent is now living in the Raleigh-Durham area. In early 2005, we received a call that there was an apartment available about two miles from where I live. We set the wheels in motion, and started packing up all of Vincent's belongings.

We hired a moving truck and had troubles because while in the process of loading the truck the brakes gave way on the truck. Luckily for us the people who were loading the truck had one of their moving truck behind it, as the truck was parked on a somewhat steep hill. Throughout all of the trauma he experienced in the moving progress Vincent held up well, and all we lost was one glass. Vincent managed to keep almost all of his treasures from his three bedroom apartment when he moved into a one bedroom apartment here.

Vincent has started to make some friends within the apartment complex in the past two years, and friends from his old area in Winston Salem, come to see him from time to time. He is taking communion every Sunday, from a Eucharistic Minister from the local Catholic Church, and is trying to be a good catholic and has a small bible study with a friend. He is even teaching some ballroom dance steps to those who live at the apartment complex.

Vincent has had setbacks in the past three years with his health and finances, but he continues to try and have an upbeat spirit.

As an editor and close friend of Vincent's I hope you enjoy this book.

Index

978-0-595-46976-5
0-595-46976-0